BEGINNING IOS PROGRAMMING

BEGINNING

iOS Programming

BEGINNING

iOS Programming

BUILDING AND DEPLOYING iOS APPLICATIONS

Nick Harris

wrox™
A Wiley Brand

Beginning iOS Programming: Building and Deploying iOS Applications

Published by
John Wiley & Sons, Inc.
10475 Crosspoint Boulevard
Indianapolis, IN 46256
www.wiley.com

ISBN: 978-1-118-84147-1
ISBN: 978-1-118-84160-0 (ebk)
ISBN: 978-1-118-84144-0 (ebk)

Manufactured in the United States of America

10 9 8 7 6 5 4 3 2 1

For general information on our other products and services please contact our Customer Care Department within the United States at (877) 762-2974, outside the United States at (317) 572-3993 or fax (317) 572-4002.

Wiley publishes in a variety of print and electronic formats and by print-on-demand. Some material included with standard print versions of this book may not be included in e-books or in print-on-demand. If this book refers to media such as a CD or DVD that is not included in the version you purchased, you may download this material at http://booksupport.wiley.com. For more information about Wiley products, visit www.wiley.com.

Library of Congress Control Number: 2013958293

This book is dedicated to my mom, dad, and sister for always believing in me.

ABOUT THE AUTHOR

NICK HARRIS is an independent software developer at Clifton Garage Mobile LLC. After graduating from the Russ College of Engineering at Ohio University in 2001 with a Bachelor of Science degree in computer science, he relocated to Denver, Colorado, where he began his professional career. Nick began developing for iPhone in 2008 with the release of the iPhone SDK and has created and released more than a half dozen apps using every version of iOS through iOS 7. Along with his accomplishments as a developer, Nick enjoys giving back to the developer community by speaking at conferences such as the 360iDev Developer Conference, as well as helping sponsor events including iOSDevCamp Colorado. Contact Nick at nick@cliftongarage.com.

CREDITS

Acquisitions Editor
Mary James

Project Editor
Ami Sullivan

Technical Editor
Kyle Richter

Production Editor
Daniel Scribner

Copy Editor
San Dee Phillips

Editorial Manager
Mary Beth Wakefield

Freelancer Editorial Manager
Rosemarie Graham

Associate Director of Marketing
David Mayhew

Marketing Manager
Ashley Zurcher

Business Manager
Amy Knies

Vice President and Executive Group Publisher
Richard Swadley

Associate Publisher
Jim Minatel

Project Coordinator, Cover
Todd Klemme

Proofreader
Mark Steven Long

Indexer
Robert Swanson

Cover Designer
Wiley

Cover Image
©iStockphoto.com/photka

ACKNOWLEDGMENTS

WHEN THE ORIGINAL IPHONE was first released, I thought my friends who lined up and waited hours to buy one were crazy. Who would spend that much money on a phone? It wasn't until Apple announced the iPhone SDK that my mind began to change. Finally, I decided to take the plunge and headed to the local AT&T store. I felt guilty for spending so much money until I got home and started to actually use my new iPhone. I was amazed! I had to learn how to write my own apps.

Five years later I'm still amazed at the developer community that grew up around what has become iOS development. I have met so many great people who taught me not only how to create iOS apps but also how important it is to give back to the community. This book is partially to teach the next crop of iOS developers as well as to thank and honor all those who helped me along the way. There are too many to name individually and I would hate to miss someone, but you all know who you are.

I would also like to thank my acquisition editor, Mary James. I had always wanted to write a book but didn't know where to start. Mary was instrumental in getting the ball rolling and making this book a reality. Ami Sullivan, who was my project editor, also deserves a huge thank-you. Being a first-time author, I really had no idea what to expect. Ami has been a great coach, helping me get everything done well and on time while also helping encourage me to keep going when the work seemed overwhelming. Next, I'd like to thank my copy editor, San Dee Phillips, for catching all my grammatical errors and making sure the ideas I've tried to explain make sense.

I owe a big thank you to my technical editor, Kyle Richter, for finding all my technical errors and pointing out ways to make the code for this book easy to understand for all readers. Kyle also helped me put the original book proposal together and has given me extremely valuable advice. Many thanks.

Finally, a huge thank-you to my parents and sister for all their encouragement along the way. I don't think I could ever express how much I appreciate it.

CONTENTS

INTRODUCTION

WHEN APPLE RELEASED THE ORIGINAL IPHONE IN 2007, it was instantly an iconic device. No one had created such a fluid user experience based solely on touch. Using an iPhone didn't feel like you were touching a flat piece of glass but instead felt as if you were touching and interacting with physical objects. Flipping through the albums felt like you were actually flipping through albums. Panning around a map felt like you were actually touching and moving a real map. It was truly inspiring.

At the time I was writing Windows desktop applications and had just taken over a Windows Mobile project. I was still skeptical of the iPhone and its price tag. After Apple announced the SDK and the idea of the App Store, I decided to take the plunge and teach myself how to write an iPhone app. But where would I start?

Luckily, I had friends who had been building OS X desktop applications for years. They organized and hosted the first iPhoneDevCamp Colorado, which was my first exposure to Objective-C and Xcode. I was a bit overwhelmed, and because everyone was new to the platform, there were no code examples around to help. Eventually, through asking many questions and learning alongside more experienced developers, I released my first iPhone app in January 2009. I believe in giving back to the community that helped me get started, which is why I decided to write this book.

Through high school, college, and my professional career, I've had the privilege to learn how to build software for many different platforms. In my experience I've found the best way for me to understand the big picture is not through individual lessons but instead to create something I could actually use. That's the approach this book takes. You will learn how to build iOS apps by building an iOS app. The app is called Bands. It's a fairly simple app, but it will introduce you to the key concepts of Objective-C and Cocoa Touch while implementing features that are found in many popular iOS apps. When you are done you will have a real app you can actually use. By no means does it teach you all the things you can do with the iOS SDK. Those possibilities are almost endless. But it does give you a solid foundation you can use to begin creating your own amazing iOS apps.

WHO THIS BOOK IS FOR

This book is for developers new to the iOS SDK who want to quickly learn how to build iOS apps. Although not absolutely required, you should have some programming background with decent knowledge of object-oriented programming. It's also for current iOS developers who would like to learn some of the technologies included in newer releases of iOS and Xcode such as storyboards, auto layout, and local search.

WHAT THIS BOOK COVERS

This book walks you through creating an iOS app from an idea all the way to submitting it to Apple for sale in the App Store. It's broken into 12 chapters.

Chapter 1, "Building a Real-World iOS App: Bands" introduces the app you will build throughout the book. All apps start as an idea that gets fleshed out into features and eventually into a development plan to get it built.

Chapter 2, "Introduction to Objective-C" takes a unique approach to explaining Objective-C by comparing it to Java and C#. It also details the Model-View-Controller design pattern used to build an iOS app.

Chapter 3, "Starting a New App" walks you through creating a new project in Xcode. It describes the various editors and windows in Xcode you use to manage files, edit code, and build a user interface.

Chapter 4, "Creating a User Input Form" shows you how to create a basic user interface to input data. You learn how to show and hide the software keyboard as well as how to save data to disk.

Chapter 5, "Using Table Views" explains how to build a data model and display it using tables. It also introduces the idea of segues to transition between different views in an iOS app.

Chapter 6, "Integrating the Camera and Photo Library in iOS Apps" details how to use the image picker to either take a picture using the camera on an iOS device or to choose a picture in the photo library. You also learn how to use gestures to make your user interface more interactive.

Chapter 7, "Integrating Social Media" explores how to send e-mails and text messages or post messages and updates to Twitter, Facebook, and Flickr using the same user experience found in Apple apps.

Chapter 8, "Using Web Views" builds a lightweight browser to allow users to search for bands. You learn how the iOS SDK creates and loads URLs as well as how to call C functions from Objective-C.

Chapter 9, "Exploring Maps and Local Search" explains how to use maps in an iOS app by searching for record stores around a user's current location and displaying them.

Chapter 10, "Getting Started with Web Services" looks at the new networking classes introduced with iOS 7 to connect with a web service. You learn how to use the iTunes Search web service API to find tracks and preview them as well as opening the iTunes Store to purchase them.

Chapter 11, "Creating a Universal App" walks you through transitioning an iPhone-only app to also support iPad. It details the iPad-specific user interface features as well as how to effectively use auto layout to support device rotation.

Chapter 12, "Deploying Your iOS App" explains how you can send your app to beta testers as well as how you submit an app to Apple for review and release in the App Store.

HOW THIS BOOK IS STRUCTURED

This book teaches how to build a simple iOS app in iOS 7 from concept to release. Its approach is based on my personal experience of creating my first iOS app. You start with an idea for an app called Bands that gets fleshed out into a set of features. You then learn about Objective-C and the design concepts that are the foundation of Cocoa Touch and the iOS SDK. From there you start to build the Bands app by progressively building the project from what is essentially a "Hello World" app to a final app that includes all features you can find in many popular iOS apps.

If you are new to Objective-C and Cocoa Touch, I recommend taking the time to understand the key concepts and design patterns explained in Chapter 2 before starting on the Bands app in Chapter 3. If you have used Xcode before and have created a "Hello World" app or more complicated apps but would like to learn how to use Storyboard scenes and segues, you can skip ahead to Chapter 4. The more advanced features of the Bands app begin with Chapter 7. Because this book builds on a single project, it is recommended beginners read the book from beginning to end. However, the features are tackled in single chapters and can be applied to any iOS project on which you may be working. If you're comfortable you can use the example code in those chapters to implement those features in your own project.

WHAT YOU NEED TO USE THIS BOOK

All iOS apps are built using Xcode, which is available free from the Mac App Store. You need a Mac to run Xcode, because there is no Windows version. Xcode includes the iOS simulator, which you can use to test almost all the code you write throughout the book. There are some features such as taking a picture with the camera that you need a physical iOS device to try. To run an app that is in development on a physical device, you need to be enrolled in the iOS Developer Program, which costs $99/year. Though it's not required, I would recommend enrolling as early on as possible.

The source code for the samples is available for download from the Wrox website at

www.wrox.com/go/begiosprogramming

CONVENTIONS

To help you get the most from the text and keep track of what's happening, we've used a number of conventions throughout the book.

TRY IT OUT

The *Try It Out* is an exercise you should work through, following the text in the book.

1. They usually consist of a set of steps.

2. Each step has a number.

3. Follow the steps through with your copy of the database.

How It Works

After each *Try It Out*, the code you've typed will be explained in detail.

> **WARNING** *Warnings hold important, not-to-be-forgotten information that is directly relevant to the surrounding text.*

> **NOTE** *Notes indicate notes, tips, hints, tricks, or asides to the current discussion.*

As for styles in the text:

➤ We *italicize* new terms and important words when we introduce them.

➤ We show keyboard strokes like this: Ctrl-A.

➤ We show filenames, URLs, and code within the text like so: `persistence.properties`.

➤ We present code in two different ways:

```
We use a monofont type with no highlighting for most code examples.
```

We use bold to emphasize code that is particularly important in the present context or to show changes from a previous code snippet.

SOURCE CODE

As you work through the examples in this book, you may choose either to type in all the code manually, or to use the source code files that accompany the book. All the source code used in this book is available for download at www.wrox.com. Specifically for this book, the code download is on the Download Code tab at

www.wrox.com/go/begiosprogramming

You can also search for the book at www.wrox.com by ISBN (the ISBN for this book is 978-1-118-84147-1) to find the code. And a complete list of code downloads for all current Wrox books is available at www.wrox.com/dynamic/books/download.aspx.

At the beginning of each chapter, you can find a list of the major code files for the chapter. Throughout each chapter, you'll also find references to the names of code files as needed in listing titles and text.

Most of the code on www.wrox.com is compressed in a .ZIP, .RAR archive, or similar archive format appropriate to the platform. After you download the code, just decompress it with an appropriate compression tool.

> **NOTE** *Because many books have similar titles, you may find it easiest to search by ISBN; this book's ISBN is 978-1-118-84147-1.*

After you download the code, just decompress it with your favorite compression tool. Alternatively, you can go to the main Wrox code download page at `www.wrox.com/dynamic/books/download.aspx` to see the code available for this book and all other Wrox books.

ERRATA

We make every effort to ensure that there are no errors in the text or in the code. However, no one is perfect, and mistakes do occur. If you find an error in one of our books, like a spelling mistake or faulty piece of code, we would be grateful for your feedback. By sending in errata, you may save another reader hours of frustration, and at the same time, you can help us provide even higher quality information.

To find the errata page for this book, *go to*

`www.wrox.com/go/begiosprogramming`

And click the Errata link. On this page you can view all errata that has been submitted for this book and posted by Wrox editors.

If you don't spot "your" error on the Book Errata page, go to `www.wrox.com/contact/techsupport.shtml` and complete the form there to send us the error you have found. We'll check the information and, if appropriate, post a message to the book's errata page and fix the problem in subsequent editions of the book.

P2P.WROX.COM

For author and peer discussion, join the P2P forums at `http://p2p.wrox.com`. The forums are a web-based system for you to post messages relating to Wrox books and related technologies, and interact with other readers and technology users. The forums offer a subscription feature to e-mail you topics of interest of your choosing when new posts are made to the forums. Wrox authors, editors, other industry experts, and your fellow readers are present on these forums.

At `http://p2p.wrox.com`, you can find a number of different forums that can help you, not only as you read this book, but also as you develop your own applications. To join the forums, just follow these steps:

1. Go to `http://p2p.wrox.com` and click the Register link.
2. Read the terms of use and click Agree.

3. Complete the required information to join, as well as any optional information you want to provide, and click Submit.

4. You will receive an e-mail with information describing how to verify your account and complete the joining process.

> **NOTE** *You can read messages in the forums without joining P2P, but to post your own messages, you must join.*

After you join, you can post new messages and respond to messages other users post. You can read messages at any time on the web. If you would like to have new messages from a particular forum e-mailed to you, click the Subscribe to this Forum icon by the forum name in the forum listing.

For more information about how to use the Wrox P2P, be sure to read the P2P FAQs for answers to questions about how the forum software works, as well as many common questions specific to P2P and Wrox books. To read the FAQs, click the FAQ link on any P2P page.

1

Building a Real-World iOS App: Bands

WHAT YOU WILL LEARN IN THIS CHAPTER:

➤ A brief history of the iPhone SDK

➤ An introduction to the Bands app

➤ How to scope an app and define features

The idea of mobile computing has been around since the late 1970s. The first real mobile computer was the Psion Organiser, which was released in 1984, followed by the Psion Organiser II in 1986. For the most part these early mobile computers looked like calculators. Mobile computing began to pick up speed in the 1990s. That was when the Personal Digital Assistant, or PDA, began to catch on. The phrase *Personal Digital Assistant* was first used by the CEO of Apple, but not the one you may be thinking of. John Sculley became the CEO of Apple after Steve Jobs was forced out. He made the remark while talking about the Apple Newton, Apple's first attempt at mobile computing. By most accounts it was not a success and was discontinued in 1998.

Through the rest of the 1990s and early 2000s, mobile computing continued to evolve. There were many popular PDAs such as the Palm Pilot as well as devices running Windows Mobile. They had their users, but they didn't have an excited developer base.

Smartphones were also coming into their own during this time. They combined the features of a PDA with the capability to make phone calls. Palm and Windows Mobile along with the BlackBerry dominated these early days. That changed in 2007 when Apple announced the iPhone.

The original iPhone went on sale June 2007. It was instantly an iconic device. Using an iPhone felt like you were using the future. Though touch screens had been around for more than a decade, the iPhone made you feel like you were interacting with real objects, not just touching buttons on a screen. The original release of the iPhone had one big limitation, though; there was no software SDK developers could use to write native applications for it. Steve Jobs instead recommended developers write web applications that would feel like native applications. At the time the tech world was in the middle of the Web 2.0 craze, so the idea wasn't that far-fetched, but it just didn't fly with developers.

By September 2007, the idea of "jail breaking" your iPhone began to catch on. Hackers had not only figured out how to unlock the digital security Apple had in place but had also figured out how to write and run their own applications on the device. You had to be pretty brave to do this, though, because jail breaking voided the warranty of an expensive phone, and writing bad software could easily render the device useless.

In October 2007, Apple reversed course and announced that an SDK to write native third-party applications for the iPhone was in development. In March 2008, it was released to developers along with an innovative new way to distribute these new applications called the App Store. That's when the term *app* becomes the preferred term for these third-party applications. It is also when the rush to this new development platform, now called the iPhone OS, begins.

The App Store officially launched July 10, 2008. According to Apple, since then there have been more than 1 million apps written and made available in the App Store with more than 10 billion downloads. Having an app is like having a web page in the 1990s: Everyone wants one.

The developer industry around building apps has exploded. That's probably why you are reading this book. You want to know how to build an app. The best way to learn how to build an app is to actually build an app.

INTRODUCING BANDS

The app you build throughout the course of this book is named Bands. It's a simple app that you can use to take quick notes about bands you like or want to remember. It won't win an Apple Design Award, but that's not its purpose. It is meant to be a conduit to teach you what it's like to take an idea for an app and make it into a reality, teaching you skills along the way that you can apply when building your own apps. The figures in this section show what the Bands app will look like when you're done.

Figure 1-1 shows the first screen of the Bands app. It's a list of all the bands a user adds to the app, sorted alphabetically and indexed.

When a user taps on a band, they see the details of the band, as shown in Figure 1-2. Here they can take notes, add a picture, and set a few other properties about each band.

From the band details, users have the option to do a few different things, as shown in Figure 1-3. They can tell their friends about the band in various ways, as shown in Figure 1-4, search the web for more info about the band, as shown in Figure 1-5, find local record stores, as shown in Figure 1-6, and even search and preview tracks from the band, as shown in Figure 1-7.

FIGURE 1-1

FIGURE 1-2

FIGURE 1-3

FIGURE 1-4

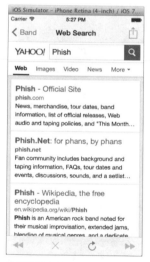

FIGURE 1-5

FIGURE 1-6

FIGURE 1-7

Now that you see what the Bands app can become, it's time to start.

GETTING STARTED

Every app starts with an idea. You may have your own idea for an app, or perhaps your boss has the idea and you are in charge of making it a reality. The Bands app also started with an idea. Say you are at a bar or concert hall, and a band is playing that you've never heard of that you want to remember. Or perhaps you are out with friends and talking about music, and someone mentions another band you would like to remember. It would be great to have a place where you could keep all these bands together so that you can go back later when you have time to learn more about them. You could use a note-taking app or send yourself an e-mail, but having a dedicated app you could pull up and have them all together would be ideal.

Naming your app may be one of the hardest parts of app development. It needs to be catchy and memorable yet adequately describe what the app does. The name has to be unique within the App Store. You can search the App Store for names you like and see if there is already an app with that name. You also need to keep in mind how the app name will look on an actual iPhone or iPad. Typically, you have about 12 characters before the app name is truncated. Figure 1-8 shows what a long name looks like. Apple apps, in contrast, are a great example of short names that describe the app well (see Figure 1-9).

FIGURE 1-8

FIGURE 1-9

> **NOTE** *Searching the available apps in the App Store does not guarantee the name is available. The only true way to know is when you attempt to submit the app through iTunes Connect, which you will learn about in Chapter 12, "Deploying Your iOS App."*

Scoping the App

You now have an idea for an app that has a name. The next step is scoping what the app will do. You want your app to be useful, but you also need to keep in mind what is realistic. Too many features can make it hard when the first-time users open your app. Too many features also mean much more development time. Too few features and your app won't be useful. Finding the balance is the key.

It helps to list all the things you would like your app to do. The following list demonstrates some of the ideas you might want to incorporate in an app like Bands.

➤   Add any number of bands.

➤   Take notes about a band.

➤   Take pictures of a band.

➤   Tell your friends about a band.

➤   Search the web for a band.

➤   Find places to buy merchandise from a band.

➤   Plot all the tour dates of a band.

➤   Have reviews from publications and critics of a band.

➤   Have a multimedia library associated with each band.

➤   Preview tracks of a band.

There are many more ideas that could be added to the list, but these will do. Now you need to look at the ideas and decide which ones are valuable and which ones are too complicated for the app. You also need to keep in mind functions and features that are used in Apple's native apps. Duplicating them can cause your app to be rejected when you submit it for approval. It's better to cut those out right away.

With that in mind, the multimedia library for all the music of a band can be tossed first, because Apple's Music app does this. Plotting all the tour dates of a band sounds great, but where would you get the information? Having a user manually enter them would be burdensome and probably seldom used, so that idea can be cut as well. Having reviews from publications and critics has the same issue of where you would get the data. There are also copyright issues. That idea can also be dismissed. The rest are all great ideas that can make a useful app.

Defining the Features

With a manageable and useful list of ideas, you can now define the features of the app. Defining the features and what it takes to create them helps you get a good idea of how much time and effort the entire app will take. It also helps you wrap your mind around the final goal, which, of course, is a fully functional app. The features you build into the Bands app in this book are chosen more for the lessons they can teach you to apply when building your own apps, so some of the features may not make the most sense. The following is the list of features you will implement in the Bands app.

Adding a band—The app needs a way to add a band. A band needs to have a name, and you need a way to take notes as well as add an optional picture. A rating would help users remember how much they enjoyed the band. A way to record if the band is on tour, off tour, or disbanded is useful as well as a way for users to mark if they have seen the band live. A simple user interface that lists all these in one place and allows the users to edit them seems like the logical choice. Having access to the camera or photo library is needed for the band picture.

Saving multiple bands—An app that saves just one band would not be useful. Saving multiple bands means you need to implement both some sort of persistent storage as well as a way to view all the bands and find them quickly.

Sharing bands—When users find a band they like, they will want to tell others. The app should be able to send e-mails and text messages preformatted with information the users add about a band. Having the ability to share a band through Facebook, Twitter, and Flickr would be useful as well.

Searching for a band on the web—Searching the web for a band a user just learned about will be helpful. This needs a lightweight browser to be included in the app so that users don't need to use Mobile Safari. It should also be user-friendly and do the initial search for the users.

Finding local record stores—If users want to buy tickets to a local show or buy a poster for a band they like, they may need to find a record store. This feature needs to show a map with pins marking all the record stores close to the user's location.

Search for tracks—Finding new tracks of a band and previewing them is a fun feature to add to the Bands app. Users can sample new tracks, and if they like them, they can purchase them through the iTunes Store.

Creating a Development Plan

The development plan for the Bands app is laid out in the rest of the chapters of this book. As a beginning developer your first task is to learn about Objective-C and Cocoa Touch, the language and frameworks used to create all iOS apps. Next, you need to learn about Xcode, the integrated development environment you will use to build the Bands app. From there you will implement each feature of the app from the easiest to the most complicated. Finally, when the app's features are complete, you learn how to get your app in the hands of beta testers before the ultimate goal of getting your app into the App Store.

SUMMARY

All apps start with an idea. The idea for the Bands app is an app that allows users to keep track of bands they hear about from a friend or at a local bar. The next step is coming up with a concrete set of features that are well defined. The Bands app will store information about multiple bands to persistent storage as well as sharing the bands with friends, searching the web for band information, finding local record stores, and previewing and purchasing tracks from the iTunes Store. To start you first need to learn about Objective-C, which you do in the next chapter.

EXERCISES

1. What do you need to keep in mind when naming an app?

2. Why is it important to scope your app before starting?

3. What can happen if your app duplicates functionality found in Apple apps?

➤ **WHAT YOU LEARNED IN THIS CHAPTER**

TOPIC	KEY CONCEPTS
iPhone SDK	The iPhone SDK was first announced October 2007, and initially introduced to developers March 2008. Since then it has been used to create more than 1 million apps.
The Bands app	The Bands app is an app that users can use to remember bands they've seen live or have been introduced to by a friend. Instead of keeping them in notes or sending an e-mail, the users can have them all in one place. You learn how to build an iOS app by building the Bands app.
Scope and Features	Scoping an app and defining its features is important before beginning development. It helps you keep the app useful without adding too many features that users may find hard to use.

Introduction to Objective-C

WHAT YOU WILL LEARN IN THIS CHAPTER:

- ➤ An overview of Objective-C
- ➤ Declaring classes and instancing objects
- ➤ Memory management in Objective-C
- ➤ The Model-View-Controller design pattern
- ➤ Delegates and protocols in Objective-C
- ➤ Overview of blocks
- ➤ Error handling patterns in Objective-C

The first step to creating the Bands app is to learn about the language it will be written in, Objective-C. Objective-C is the programming language used to develop both Mac and iOS applications. It's a compiled language, meaning that it gets compiled down to raw machine code as opposed to being interpreted at runtime. As its name implies, it's based on the C programming language. It's actually a superset of C that adds object-oriented programming methodologies. Because it's a descendant of C, its syntax and concepts are similar to other C-based languages. In this chapter you learn the basics of Objective-C by comparing it to Java and C#.

EXPLORING THE HISTORY OF OBJECTIVE-C

Objective-C was developed in the early 1980s by a company called Stepstone. It was working on a legacy system built using C but wanted to add reusability to the code base by using objects and messaging. The concept of object-oriented programming (OOP) had been around for a while. The Smalltalk language developed by Xerox was the most prominent object-oriented language in use at the time. Objective-C got its start by taking some of the concepts and syntax of Smalltalk and adding it to C. This can be seen in the syntax of message passing in Objective-C and Smalltalk.

Message passing is another way of saying method calling. In OOP languages an object can send a message to or call a method of another object. All object-oriented languages include this. Listing 2-1 shows how message passing is done in Smalltalk, Objective-C, Java, and C#.

LISTING 2-1: Message Passing in Different Languages

```
Smalltalk:   anObject aMessage: aParameter secondParameter: bParameter
Objective-C: [anObject aMessage:aParameter secondParameter:bParameter];
Java and C#: anObject.aMessage(aParameter, bParameter);
```

Objective-C got its foothold in mainstream programming when it was licensed by NeXT in the late 1980s. NeXT was a computer company founded by Steve Jobs after he was forced from Apple. It manufactured workstations for universities and big businesses. The workstations ran its proprietary operating system called NeXTSTEP, which used Objective-C as its programming language and runtime. This was different than other workstations sold at the time that ran the UNIX operating system based on the C language. NeXT was eventually acquired by Apple, bringing Steve Jobs back to the original company he founded. The acquisition also brought the NeXTSTEP operating system, which became the basis for OS X and the Cocoa API used to create Mac applications. The Cocoa API was then expanded to Cocoa Touch, which is the API, frameworks, and user interface libraries used to create iOS applications.

EXPLAINING THE BASICS

Primitive types in every programming language are the basic types used to build more complex objects and data structures. They are typically the same from language to language. The primitive types in Objective-C are the same as those in C and most C variants. Table 2-1 lists these types.

TABLE 2-1: Primitive Data Types in Objective-C

DATA TYPE	DESCRIPTION
bool	Single byte representing TRUE/FALSE or YES/NO
char	Integer value the size of 1 byte
short	Integer value the size of 2 bytes
int	Integer value the size of 4 bytes
long	Integer value the size of 8 bytes
float	Single precision floating-point type the size of 4 bytes
double	Double precision floating-point type the size of 8 bytes

As with C and C++, Objective-C includes the typedef keyword. If you are coming from C# or Java and have never programmed using C or C++, you may not be familiar with typedef. It gives you a way of creating and naming a new data type using primitive data types. You can then refer to this new data type by the name you assigned it anywhere in your code. Listing 2-2 shows a simple yet silly example of typedef that creates a new data type called myInt, which is the same as the primitive int data type that can then be used the same as int throughout the code.

LISTING 2-2: typedef Example in Objective-C

```
// Objective C
typedef int myInt;

myInt variableOne = 5;
myInt variableTwo = 10;

myInt variableThree = variableOne + variableTwo;

// variableThree == 15;
```

A typical use of typedef in Objective-C is naming a declared enumerated type. An enumerated type, or enum, is a primitive type that is made up of a set of constants. Each constant is represented by an integer. They are used in pretty much every OOP language, including Java and C#. They give you a way to declare a variable with the enumerations name and assign its value using the constant names. It helps to make your code easier to read. The four cardinal directions are often declared as an enumeration. To use an enum in C, you would need to add the enum keyword before its name. Instead of this you can typedef it, so you no longer need the enum keyword. You don't have to do this, but it's a common practice. Another common practice in Objective-C is to prepend the constants with the name of the enumeration. Again, you don't have to do, this but it helps the readability of your code. Listing 2-3 demonstrates how you declare and typedef an enum in Objective-C as well as Java and C# (their syntax is identical) and how you would use it later in code.

LISTING 2-3: Declaring Enumerations

```
// Objective C
typedef enum {
    CardinalDirectionNorth,
    CardinalDirectionSouth,
    CardinalDirectionEast,
    CardinalDirectionWest
} CardinalDirection;

CardinalDirection windDirection = CardinalDirectionNorth;
if(windDirection == CardinalDirectionNorth)
    // the wind is blowing north

// Java and C#
public enum CardinalDirection {
    NORTH,
```

continues

LISTING 2-3 *(continued)*

```
    SOUTH,
    EAST,
    WEST
}

CardinalDirection windDirection = CardinalDirectionNorth;
if(windDirection == NORTH)
    // the wind is blowing north
```

In C, C++, C#, and Objective-C, you can also create a struct. Java does not have this because everything is a class. A struct is not a class. A *struct* is a compound data type made up of primitive data types. It's a way of encapsulating similar data. Similar to enums, they often use typedef to avoid having to use the keyword structs when using them in code. There are three common structs you use in Objective-C: CGPoint, CGSize, and CGRect. Listing 2-4 shows how these structs are defined.

LISTING 2-4: Common Structs in Objective-C

```
struct CGPoint {
  CGFloat x;
  CGFloat y;
};
typedef struct CGPoint CGPoint;

struct CGSize {
  CGFloat width;
  CGFloat height;
};
typedef struct CGSize CGSize;

struct CGRect {
  CGPoint origin;
  CGSize size;
};
typedef struct CGRect CGRect;
```

Learning About Objects and Classes

Objects in Objective-C, as in any other object-oriented language, are the building blocks of the application. They have member variables that describe the object and methods that can manipulate the member variables, as well as any parameters that may be passed to them. Member variables can be public or private.

Objects are defined in a class. The class acts as the template for how an object is created and behaves. A class in Objective-C consists of two files much like classes in C++. The header file (.h) contains the interface of the class. This is where you declare the member variables and the method signatures. The implementation file (.m) is where you write the code for the actual methods. Listings 2-5 and 2-6 show how to define a class and its implementation in Java and C#, respectively. Listing 2-7 shows how you declare a header file in Objective-C, while Listing 2-8 show how you define the implementation file. If you are an expert developer of either language, forgive some of the bad practices in these examples.

LISTING 2-5: Defining a Class in Java

```java
package SamplePackage;
public class SimpleClass {
    public int firstInt;
    public int secondInt;

    public int sum() {
        return firstInt + secondInt;
    }

    public int sum(int thirdInt, int fourthInt) {
        return firstInt + secondInt + thirdInt + fourthInt;
    }

    private int sub() {
        return firstInt - secondInt;
    }
}
```

LISTING 2-6: Defining a Class in C#

```csharp
namespace SampleNameSpace
{
    public class SimpleClass
    {
        public int FirstInt;
        public int SecondInt;

        public int Sum()
        {
            return FirstInt + SecondInt;
        }

        public in Sum(int thirdInt, int fourthInt)
        {
            return FirstInt + SecondInt + thirdInt + fourthInt;
        }

        private int Sub()
        {
            return FirstInt - SecondInt;
        }
    }
}
```

LISTING 2-7: Defining a Class Interface in Objective-C

```
@interface SimpleClass : NSObject
{
    @public
    int firstInt;
    int secondInt;
}

- (int)sum;
- (int)sumWithThirdInt:(int)thirdInt fourthInt:(int)fourthInt;

@end
```

LISTING 2-8: Defining a Class Implementation in Objective-C

```
#import "SimpleClass.h"

@implementation SimpleClass

- (int)sum
{
    return firstInt + secondInt;
}

- (int)sumWithThirdInt:(int)thirdInt fourthInt:(int)fourthInt
{
    return firstInt + secondInt + thirdInt + fourthInt;
}

- (int)sub
{
    return firstInt - secondInt;
}

@end
```

> **NOTE** *The @ symbol is special in Objective-C. It has no meaning in C. Because Objective-C is a superset of C, a C compiler can be modified to also compile Objective-C. The @ symbol tells the compiler when to start and stop using the Objective-C compiler versus the straight C compiler.*

All three of these classes are conceptually the same. They all have two integer member variables that are public, a public method that adds together the member variables, a public method that adds the member variables plus an additional two integers passed in as a parameters, and a private method that subtracts Y from X. The following sections discuss the key differences between classes in Java and C# compared to Objective-C.

There Are No Namespaces in Objective-C

The first difference is the package and namespace keywords in the Java and C# code that do not correspond to anything in the Objective-C code. This is because Objective-C does not have the concept of namespaces. A *namespace* is a way of grouping related classes together. C# uses namespace as the keyword for this concept, whereas Java uses packages to accomplish the same thing.

If a class in a different namespace wants to use a class in another, it needs to link to the namespace or package the other class is in. In Java this is done using the import keyword followed by the name of the package. In C# this is done with the using keyword. The class must also be declared as public, which you should note the SampleClass in both the Java and C# examples are. In Objective-C a class is made visible to another class simply by importing the header file in which the classes interface is declared.

The public keyword is also used to declare if member variables are visible to other classes. All three examples declare their member variables to be public; however, this is not a common practice in modern Objective-C, as you will learn in the Adding Properties to a Class section of this chapter.

In Objective-C, Methods Are Visible to Other Classes

Methods in a Java or C# class can also be declared public, making them visible to other objects. This is not the case with Objective-C. In Objective-C all methods that are declared in the interface are visible to other classes. If a class needs a private method, it just adds the method to the implementation. All code within the implementation can call that method, but it will not be visible to any classes that import the header file.

In Objective-C, Most Classes Inherit from NSObject

Another key concept of object-oriented languages is the capability of one class to inherit from another. In Java all classes inherit from the Object class. C# is similar with the System.Object class. In Objective-C virtually every class inherits from NSObject. The reason all three languages have a common root class is to provide methods and behaviors that can be assumed as members. In Objective-C the code for managing the memory of an object is all defined in NSObject. The difference in the syntax is that in Java and C# classes that do not explicitly define their superclass, the root class is assumed. In Objective-C you must always declare the superclass by following the name of the class with a colon and then the name of the superclass, as shown in the example @interface SimpleClass : **NSObject**.

Objective-C Uses Long and Explicit Signatures

The last difference you notice is the signatures of the methods themselves. Java and C# both use the same type of method signatures. The return type of the method is listed first, followed by its name and then by any parameters and their type listed within parentheses. They also use method over-loading where the same method name is used but is distinguished as different by the list of param-eters. In Objective-C the signature is a bit different, which reflects its roots in Smalltalk.

Objective-C method signatures tend to be very long and explicit. Many developers coming from other languages may dislike this at first but learn to love it as it enhances the readability of the code. Instead of needing to know which method of "Sum" to use when you want to pass in two parameters, you know by just looking that the `sumWithThirdInt:fourthInt:` method is the one you want. Actually that is the full name of that method. The colons in the method name denote the number of parameters the method takes. By having the parameters listed inline with the method name, you can create signatures that are easier to understand. As you proceed through this book, you will see how this type of method signature is used throughout Objective-C and Cocoa Touch.

Instantiating Objects

Classes are only the template for creating objects. To use an object it needs to be instantiated and created in memory. In Java and C# you use the new keyword and a constructor. Both languages have a default constructor that is part of their base object class. Listing 2-9 shows how you do this in either Java or C#.

LISTING 2-9: Instantiating an Object in Java or C#

```
SimpleClass simpleClassInstance = new SimpleClass();
```

In Objective-C the NSObject class has something similar to a default constructor but slightly differ-ent. Instead of one step to instantiate an object, you do it in two steps. The first step uses the static method `alloc`, which finds enough available memory to hold the object and assign it. The second step uses the `init` method to set the memory. Listing 2-10 shows an example.

LISTING 2-10: Instantiating an Object in Objective-C

```
SimpleClass *simpleClassInstance = [[SimpleClass alloc] init];
```

If you have ever written code in C or C++, you should recognize the * operator. This is the pointer dereference operator. It acts the same in Objective-C by dereferencing the pointer and getting or set-ting the object in memory.

Pointers are part of C. The memory of a computer can be thought of as a bunch of little boxes that hold values. Each of these boxes has an address. In this example the variable `simpleClassInstance` is a pointer. The value it holds in memory is not the object but instead the address of where the object exists in memory. It "points" to the object in another part of the memory. Figure 2-1 illus-trates how this works.

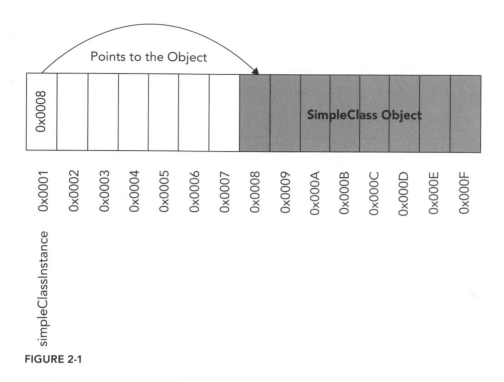

FIGURE 2-1

In Java and C# you can also declare your own constructors that can take a list of parameters and set the member variables of the object. Listings 2-11 and 2-12 add these constructors to the Java and C# example classes with sample code of how they are called.

LISTING 2-11: Defining a Constructor in Java

```java
package SamplePackage;
public class SimpleClass {
    public int firstInt;
    public int secondInt;

    public SimpleClass(int initialFirstInt, int initialSecondInt)
    {
        firstInt = initialFirstInt;
        secondInt = initialSecondInt;
    }

    // other methods discussed eariler
}

// sample code to create a new instance
SimpleClass aSimpleClassInstance = new SimpleClass(1, 2);
```

LISTING 2-12: Defining a Constructor in C#

```
namespace SampleNameSpace
{
    public class SimpleClass
    {
        public int FirstInt;
        public int SecondInt;

        public SimpleClass(int firstInt, int secondInt)
        {
            FirstInt = firstInt;
            SecondInt = secondInt;
        }

        // other methods discussed earlier
    }
}

// sample code to create a new instance
SimpleClass aSimpleClassInstance = new SimpleClass(1, 2);
```

To implement the same type of constructor in Objective-C, you would add your own init method, as shown in Listing 2-13.

LISTING 2-13: Instantiating Objects in Objective-C

```
// in the SimpleClass.h file
@interface SimpleClass : NSObject
{
    @public
    int firstInt;
    int secondInt;
}

- (id)initWithFirstInt:(int)firstIntValue secondInt:(int)secondIntValue;

// other methods discussed earlier

@end

// in the SimpleClass.m file
@implementation SimpleClass

- (id)initWithFirstInt:(int)firstIntValue secondInt:(int)secondIntValue
{
    self = [super init];
    if(!self)
        return nil;

    firstInt = firstIntValue;
    secondInt = secondIntValue;

    return self;
```

```
    }

    // other methods discussed earlier

    @end

    // sample code to create a new instance
    SimpleClass *aSimpleClassInstance =
      [[SimpleClass alloc] initWithFirstInt:1 secondInt:2];
```

There are a few things to discuss in this code sample. The first is the use of id type. Objective-C is a dynamic language, meaning that you do not have to give a specific type to an object at compile time. The id type can hold a pointer to any object. It is similar to the dynamic type in C#. Java does not have anything similar. When you use the id type, its actual type is determined at runtime. Returning id from an init method is part of a Cocoa convention, which you should always follow.

The next is the use of self. The self variable is the same in Java or this in C#. It refers to the instance of the object that is receiving the message. When you are initializing an object, you first want to call init on its parent class. This ensures that objects are created correctly through their hierarchy.

The if statement, if(!self), introduces another concept that is prevalent throughout Objective-C. If a variable does not point to anything, it has a value of nil. The nil value is essentially 0. Figure 2-2 illustrates how this works.

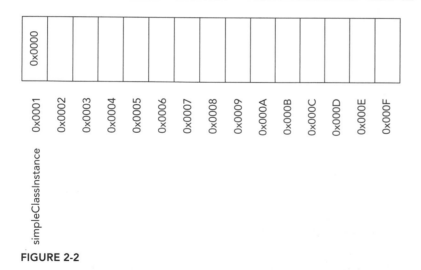

FIGURE 2-2

In C the value 0 is synonymous with FALSE, while any value greater than 0 is synonymous with TRUE. If an object has failed to initialize, then its pointer will be nil. The reason you need to check if the parent class returned nil is defensive coding. If a pointer is nil and you send it a message, it is treated as a no op, meaning nothing will happen. In Java and C# this throws an exception.

The rest of the init method works the same as the constructors in Java and C#. The member variables are set using the values passed in before returning the pointer.

> **NOTE** The NSObject class also has a new method. It performs both the alloc and init method calls and then returns the pointer. Using it means any overridden init methods that take parameters will not be called. Instead you need to set the values of the member variables after the object is instantiated.

Another approach to instantiating objects is to use a factory method. These methods are static methods. A static method does not need an instance of the class to call it. It also does not have access to any of the member variables of a class. If you have written code in Java or C#, you are familiar with static methods and factory methods. In Objective-C they are more of a convenience method than anything else, which is different from their use in Java and C#. The basic idea remains the same, though. Listings 2-14 and 2-15 show how you would implement a factory constructor in Java or C#, whereas Listing 2-16 demonstrates the same in Objective-C. These types of convenience methods are used often in many of the basic data structures of Objective-C, which are discussed in the Using Basic Data Structures section of this chapter.

LISTING 2-14: Defining a Factory Method in Java

```java
package SamplePackage;
public class SimpleClass {
    public int firstInt;
    public int secondInt;
    public static SimpleClass Create(int initialFirstInt, int initialSecondInt)
    {
        SimpleClass simpleClass = new SimpleClass();
        simpleClass.firstInt = initialFirstInt;
        simpleClass.secondInt = initialSecondInt;

        return simpleClass;
    }

    // other methods discussed eariler
}

// sample code to create a new instance
SimpleClass aSimpleClassInstance = SimpleClass.Create(1, 2);
```

LISTING 2-15: Defining a Factory Method in C#

```csharp
namespace SampleNameSpace
{
    public class SimpleClass
    {
        public int FirstInt;
```

```
        public int SecondInt;

        public static SimpleClass Create(int firstInt, int secondInt)
        {
            SimpleClass simpleClass = new SimpleClass();
            simpleClass.FirstInt = firstInt;
            simpleClass.SecondInt = secondInt;

            return simpleClass;
        }

        // other methods discussed earlier
    }
}

// sample code to create a new instance
SimpleClass aSimpleClassInstance = SimpleClass.Create(1, 2);
```

LISTING 2-16: Defining a Factory Method in Objective-C

```
// in the SimpleClass.h file
@interface SimpleClass : NSObject
{
    @public
    int firstInt;
    int secondInt;
}

+ (id)simpleClassWithFirstInt:(int)firstIntValue secondInt:(int)secondIntValue;

// other methods discussed earlier

@end

// in the SimpleClass.m file
@implementation SimpleClass

+ (id)simpleClassWithFirstInt:(int)firstIntValue secondInt:(int)secondIntValue
{
    SimpleClass *simpleClass = [[SimpleClass alloc] init];
    simpleClass->firstInt = firstIntValue;
    simpleClass->secondInt = secondIntValue;

    return simpleClass;
}

// other methods discussed earlier

@end

// sample code to create a new instance
SimpleClass *aSimpleClassInstance =
  [SimpleClass simpleClassWithFirstInt:1 secondInt:2];
```

The Java and C# implementations rely on the default constructors defined in their respective root classes to insatiate a new object. This is the same as the `init` method defined in the `NSObject` class. They next set the member variables of the new instance before returning it. Syntactically, the difference is how a method is declared as static. In Java and C# the `static` keyword is added to the method signature. In Objective-C a static method is declared by using the + (plus) symbol instead of the – (minus) symbol that would define it as an instance method.

Managing Memory

Memory management is important in Objective-C. Memory is a finite resource, meaning there is only so much of it that can be used. This is particularly true on mobile devices. When a system runs out of memory, it can no longer perform any more instructions, which is obviously a bad thing. Running low on memory will also have a dramatic impact on performance. The system has to spend a lot more time finding available memory to use, which slows down every process. Memory management is controlling what objects need to remain in memory and which ones are no longer in use, so their memory can be reused.

Memory leaks are a classic problem in computer programming. A *memory leak*, in the most basic of definitions, is when memory is allocated but never deallocated. The opposite of a leak is when memory is deallocated before it is done being used. This is what has been historically referred to as a dangling pointer. In Objective-C it's common to refer to these as zombie objects. These types of memory issues are usually easier to find because the program will most likely crash if it tries to use a deallocated object.

Languages and runtimes handle memory management in two difference ways. Java and C# use garbage collection. It was first introduced in Lisp in the late 1950s. The implementation of garbage collection is detailed and different depending on the runtime, but the idea is basically the same. As a program executes it allocates objects in memory that it needs to continue. Periodically another process runs that looks for objects that are no longer reachable, meaning they have no references left to them in any code that is executing. This type of system works very well; though contrary to popular belief your code can still leak memory by creating objects and keeping a reference to them but never using them again. This system also has a bit of overhead associated with it. The system needs to continue executing the program being used while running the garbage collection process in parallel. This can create performance problems on systems that have limited computational power.

Objective-C on iOS does not use garbage collection. Instead it uses manual reference counting. Each object that is allocated has a reference or retain count. If a piece of code requires that the object be available, it increases its retain count. When it is done and no longer needs the object, it decrements the retain count. When an object's retain count reaches 0, it can be deallocated and the memory is returned to the system.

Manual reference counting can be difficult to understand if you are not used to thinking about the life cycle of objects in use. Because languages like Java and C# use garbage collection, it can be even more difficult for developers who have used those languages for an extended time to make the transition to Objective-C. Apple recognized this and made significant improvements to the Objective-C compiler that will be discussed later in this section. Though these improvements make manual reference counting much easier, it's still important for developers to understand exactly how retain counts work and the rules around them.

The first thing to understand is how retain counts work and how they can lead to memory leaks and zombie objects. Listing 2-17 shows one way a memory leak can occur using the SimpleClass described previously in this chapter.

LISTING 2-17 Memory Leak Example in Objective-C

```objc
- (void)simpleMethod
{
    SimpleClass *simpleClassInstance = [[SimpleClass alloc] init];

    simpleClassInstance->firstInt = 5;
    simpleClassInstance->secondInt = 5;

    [simpleClassInstance sum];
}
```

A Java or C# developer would not see anything wrong with this code. To them there is a method that creates an instance of the SimpleClass. When the method is done executing, the simpleClassInstance no longer has a reference to it and is eventually deallocated by the garbage collector. This is not the case in Objective-C.

When the simpleClassInstance is instantiated using alloc, it has a retain count of one. When the method is done executing, its pointer goes out of scope but keeps a retain count of one. Because the retain count stays above zero, the object is never deallocated. With no pointer still referencing the object, there is no way to decrement its retain count so that it can be deallocated. This is a classic memory leak illustrated in Figure 2-3.

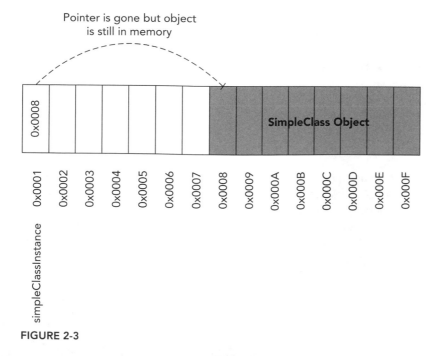

FIGURE 2-3

To fix this in Objective-C, you need to explicitly decrement the retain count before leaving the method. You do this by calling the `release` method of the `NSObject` class, as shown in Listing 2-18. Release decrements the count by one, which in this example sets the count to zero, which in turn means the object can be deallocated.

LISTING 2-18: Using Release in Objective-C

```
- (void)simpleMethod
{
    SimpleClass *simpleClassInstance = [[SimpleClass alloc] init];

    simpleClassInstance->firstInt = 5;
    simpleClassInstance->secondInt = 5;

    [simpleClass sum];

    [simpleClass release];
}
```

Another way to fix this is to use the autorelease pool. Instead of explicitly releasing the object when you are done with it, you can call autorelease on it. This puts the object into the autorelease pool, that keeps track of objects within a particular scope of the program. When the program has exited that scope, all the objects in the autorelease pool are released. This is referred to as *draining the pool*. Listing 2-19 shows how you would implement this.

LISTING 2-19: Using Autorelease in Objective-C

```
- (void)simpleMethod
{
    SimpleClass *simpleClassInstance = [[SimpleClass alloc] init];

    [simpleClassInstance autorelease];

    simpleClassInstance->firstInt = 5;
    simpleClassInstance->secondInt = 5;

    [simpleClass sum];
}
```

Using `alloc` generally means that the code creating the object is its owner, which is why it gets a retain count of one. There are other times in your code where an object was created elsewhere but the code using needs to take ownership. The most common example of this is using factory methods to create the object. Factory methods of Objective-C core classes always return an object that has autorelease called on it before it is returned. Listing 2-20 shows how the `SimpleClass` would generally be implemented now that you understand the `autorelease` method.

LISTING 2-20: Defining a Factory Method Using Autorelease

```
+ (id)simpleClassWithFirstInt:(int)firstIntValue secondInt:(int)secondIntValue
{
```

```
        SimpleClass *simpleClass = [[SimpleClass alloc] init];
        simpleClass.firstInt = firstIntValue;
        simpleClass.secondInt = secondIntValue;

        [simpleClass autorelease];
        return simpleClass;
    }
```

In a piece of code that creates a `simpleClass` using the factory method, it may want that object to stay in memory even after the autorelease pool has been drained. To increase its retain count and make sure it stays in memory, you would call `retain` on the instance. Its very important to always call `release` sometime later in your code if you explicitly retain an object, or else it will cause a memory leak. Listing 2-21 shows a simple example of this; though in a real program, you would probably call release in some other place.

LISTING 2-21: Explicitly Retaining an Object

```
    - (void)simpleMethod
    {
        SimpleClass *simpleClass =
          [SimpleClass simpleClassWithFirstInt:1 secondInt:5];

        [simpleClass retain];

        // do things with the simple class knowing it will not be deallocated

        [simpleClass release];
    }
```

The other memory management issue you can run into is referencing an object that has already been deallocated. This is called a *zombie object*. Figure 2-4 illustrates this.

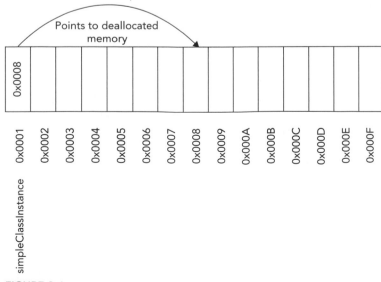

FIGURE 2-4

If this happens during runtime, the execution of your app can become unpredictable or just simply crash. It depends on if the memory address is still part of the memory allocated to your program or if it has been overwritten with a new object. Its conceivable that the memory is still there and your code would execute just fine even though the memory has been marked for reuse. Listing 2-22 demonstrates how a zombie object could occur.

LISTING 2-22: Dangling Pointer Example in Objective-C

```
- (void)simpleMethod
{
    SimpleClass *simpleClassInstance = [[SimpleClass alloc] init];
    [simpleClassInstance release];

    simpleClass.firstInt = 5;
    simpleClass.secondInt = 5;

    int sum = [simpleClass sum];
}
```

> **WARNING** *The* NSObject *class has a property called* retainCount. *You should never trust this value nor should you ever use it. It may be tempting to look at this value to try and determine when an object will be released or to find a memory leak. You should instead use the debugging instruments included in Xcode, in this case the Leaks instrument. You can learn more about the Leaks instrument at* https://developer.apple.com/library/ios/documentation/ AnalysisTools/Reference/Instruments_User_Reference/LeaksInstrument/ LeaksInstrument.html.

Introducing Automatic Reference Counting

Manual reference counting differs from garbage collection by setting when objects are allocated and deallocated at compile time instead of runtime. The compiler that Apple uses in its development tools is part of the LLVM Project (llvm.org) and is called Clang (clang.llvm.org). Developers using manual memory management can follow a strict set of rules to ensure that memory is neither leaked nor deallocated prematurely. The developers working on the Clang compiler recognized this and set out to build a tool that could analyze a code base and find where objects could potentially be leaked or be used after they have been released. The tool they released is called the Clang Static Analyzer (clang-analyzer.llvm.org).

The Clang Static Analyzer is both a standalone tool as well as integrated in Apple's Xcode development environment. As an example of how it works, Figure 2-5 shows the results of running the static analyzer on the first example of a memory leak.

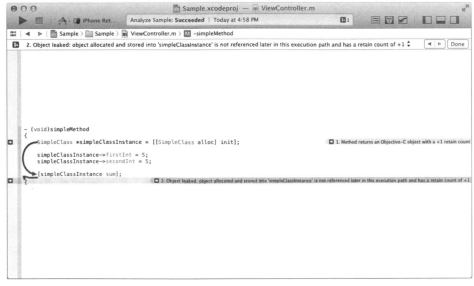

FIGURE 2-5

After building the static analyzer, the compiler developers realized that by detecting rule violations in manual reference counting they could insert the required `retain` and `release` calls at compile time. They implemented this in a compiler feature called Automatic Reference Counting (ARC). Because Xcode uses the Clang compiler, iOS developers and Mac developers could use this new feature by simply enabling it in the compiler settings and then removing all their explicit calls to `retain`, `release`, and `autorelease`.

Using ARC is becoming standard practice for Mac and iOS developers. This book uses ARC in all sample code. By using ARC you as a new developer do not need to worry about most of the details of memory management, though there are cases in which you do need to know how an object will be treated in memory.

Adding Properties to a Class

The `SimpleClass` example in this chapter has been using public instance variables for its two integer values. In all three languages this is considered bad practice. Declaring instance variables as public leaves your class vulnerable to bad data. There is no way to validate the value being assigned. Instead for all three it is common practice to keep the instance variables private and then implement getter and setter methods. By doing this you can validate the value in the setter method before actually setting the value of the instance variable. Though the concept is the same, the implementation and syntax is different.

Listing 2-23 demonstrates how the class should be defined in Java. It's the most straightforward implementation. The instance variable is declared as private, and two additional methods are added to the class to get and set their values.

LISTING 2-23: Defining Getters and Setters in Java

```java
package SamplePackage;
public class SimpleClass {
    private int firstInt;
    private int secondInt;

    public void setFirstInt(int firstIntValue) {
        firstInt = firstIntValue;
    }

    public int getFirstInt() {
        return firstInt;
    }

    public void setSecondInt(int secondIntValue) {
        secondInt = secondIntValue;
    }

    public int getSecondInt() {
        return secondInt;
    }

    // other methods discussed previously
}

// sample code of how to use these methods
SimpleClass simpleClassInstance = new SimpleClass();

simpleClassInstance.setFirstInt(1);
simpleClassInstance.setSecondInt(2);

int firstIntValue = simpleClassInstance.getFirstInt();
```

In C# this type of implementation is done using properties. A property can be referred to as if it were an instance variable but still uses getters and setters. Listing 2-24 demonstrates this in C#.

LISTING 2-24: Properties in C#

```csharp
namespace SampleNameSpace
{
    public class SimpleClass
    {
        private int firstInt;
        private int secondInt;

        public int FirstInt
        {
            get { return firstInt; }
            set { firstInt = value; }
        }

        public int SecondInt
```

```
        {
            get { return secondInt; }
            set { secondInt = value; }
        }

        // other methods discussed earlier
    }
}

// sample code of how to use these properties
SimpleClass simpleClassInstance = new SimpleClass();

simpleClassInstance.FirstInt = 1;
simpleClassInstance.SecondInt = 2;

int firstIntValue = simpleClassInstance.FirstInt
```

The Objective-C implementation is a bit of a mix of the Java and C# implementations. Like C# it has the idea of properties, but like Java the implementation of the getters and setters are actual methods in the implementation. Listing 2-25 shows how properties are declared in the interface, how they are implemented in the implementation, and a sample of how they are used.

LISTING 2-25: Properties in Objective-C

```
// in the SimpleClass.h file
@interface SimpleClass : NSObject
{
    int _firstInt;
    int _secondInt;
}

@property int firstInt;
@property int secondInt;

// other methods discussed earlier

@end

// in the SimpleClass.m file
@implementation SimpleClass

- (void)setFirstInt:(int)firstInt
{
    _firstInt = firstInt;
}

- (int)firstInt
{
    return _firstInt;
}

- (void)setSecondInt:(int)secondInt
```

continues

LISTING 2-25 *(continued)*

```
{
    _secondInt = secondInt;
}

- (int)secondInt
{
    return _secondInt;
}

@end

// sample code to create a new instance
SimpleClass *simpleClassInstance = [[SimpleClass alloc] init];

[simpleClassInstance setFirstInt:1];
[simpleClassInstance setSecondInt:2];

int firstIntValue = [simpleClassInstance firstInt];
```

Because properties in Objective-C are the preferred way of exposing data members as public, they have been made easier to use as Objective-C has evolved. The @synthesize keyword was one of those enhancements. By using it, the getter and setter methods are generated for you at compile time instead of you needing to add them into your implementation. You can still override the getter or setter if you need to. As the language progressed, @synthesize became optional as well as even declaring the private instance variables. Instead they are also generated for you. The instance variables are named the same as the property but with a leading underscore. Listing 2-26 shows what a modern Objective-C class looks like.

LISTING 2-26: Properties in Modern Objective-C

```
// in the SimpleClass.h file
@interface SimpleClass : NSObject

@property int firstInt;
@property int secondInt;

- (int)sum;

@end

// in the SimpleClass.m file
@implementation SimpleClass

- (int)sum
{
    return _firstInt + _secondInt;
}

@end
```

Another enhancement made around properties was the introduction of *dot notation*. Instead of needing to message the object using brackets, you can simply follow the instance of the class with a "." and the name of the property, as shown in Listing 2-27.

LISTING 2-27: Properties and Dot Notation in Objective-C

```
SimpleClass *simpleClassInstance = [[SimpleClass alloc] init];

simpleClassInstance.firstInt = 5;
simpleClassInstance.secondInt = 5;

int firstIntValue = simpleClassInstance.firstInt;
```

> **NOTE** *Dot notation was not a popular addition to Objective-C when it was first introduced. Since then it has become the standard way of using properties. This book uses dot notation. Some older code and longtime Objective-C developers may avoid its use altogether.*

Properties can also be pointers to other objects. These properties need a little more attention in Objective-C. In C# you declare properties to other objects the same as you do properties to primitive data types. In Objective-C you also need to tell the compiler if your object is the owner of the other object as well as how its value should be set and retrieved in a threaded environment. For example, assume there is another class called SecondClass. The SimpleClass interface in Listing 2-28 has two properties for this class.

LISTING 2-28: Strong and Weak Properties in Modern Objective-C

```
// in the SimpleClass.h file
@interface SimpleClass : NSObject

@property (atomic, strong) SecondClass *aSecondClassInstance;
@property (nonatomic, weak) SecondClass *anotherSecondClassInstance;

@end
```

In this example the first property has the atomic attribute, whereas the second is nonatomic. Properties by default are atomic. Atomic properties have synthesized getter and setter methods that guarantee that the value is fully retrieved or fully set when accessed simultaneously by different threads. Nonatomic properties do not have this guarantee. Atomic properties have extra overhead in their implementations to make this guarantee. Though it may sound like this makes them thread-safe, that is not the case. A solid threading model with proper locks also creates the same guarantee, so the use of atomic properties is limited. Most often you declare your properties as nonatomic to avoid the extra overhead.

The other attribute, strong and weak, are much more important to understand. As you learned earlier in this chapter, an object that has a retain count of zero will be deallocated. The concept of strong and weak with properties is similar. An object that does not have a strong reference to it will be deallocated. By declaring an object property as strong, it will not be deallocated as long as your object points to it. This implies that your object owns the other object. An object property that is declared weak remains in memory as long as some other object has a strong pointer to it.

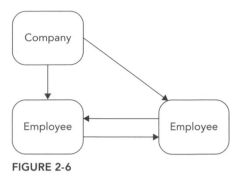

FIGURE 2-6

Weak properties are used to avoid strong reference cycles. These occur when two objects have properties that point at each other. If both objects have a strong reference to each other, they will never be deallocated, even if no other objects have a reference to either of them. Figure 2-6 illustrates the issue. The strong references between the objects are represented by the solid line arrows.

In this example there are three objects. The first is a Company object that represents some company. Every company has employees. In this example the company has two employees represented by the two Employee objects. Within a company there are bosses and workers. A boss needs a way to send messages to their worker the same as the worker needs a way to send messages to their boss. This means both need to have a reference to each other. If the Company object gets deallocated, its references to both Employee objects go with it. This should result in the Employee objects also being deallocated. But if the references between the boss Employee object and the worker Employee object are also strong references, then they will not be deallocated. If the references are weak, as illustrated in Figure 2-7, with dashed lines, then losing the strong reference to each Employee object from the Company object will mean there are no longer any strong references pointing to them so they will be properly deallocated. In this example the Company object is the owner of the Employee objects, so it would uses a strong reference to indicate this ownership.

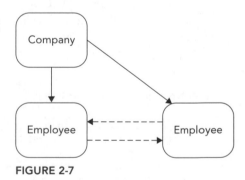

FIGURE 2-7

Explaining Strings

Java, C#, and Objective-C all have special classes for strings. Objective-C strings can be a bit confusing when you're first learning to use them, but comparing their use to Java and C# should help reduce the learning curve. This section is a light overview of strings in Objective-C just to get you started. When you understand the basics and limitations, you can easily learn how to deal with specific situations using the class documentation provided by Apple at https://developer.apple.com/library/mac/documentation/Cocoa/Reference/Foundation/Classes/NSString_Class/Reference/NSString.html.

Listing 2-29 shows how you would declare a basic string in Java, C#, and Objective-C. These examples are, of course, just one way to create a string instance. All three languages have many other methods, but the purpose here is just to show how a string would be commonly created.

LISTING 2-29: Declaring Strings in Java, C#, and Objective-C

```
// declaring a string in Java
String myString = "This is a string in Java";

// declaring a string in C#
String myString = "This is a string in C#";

// declaring a string in Objective-C
NSString *myString = @"This is a string in Objective-C";
```

In Java and C#, the class that represents a string is simply called String. In Objective-C it's called NSString. Because Objective-C is a superset of C, you cannot use only quotes to create an NSString. Quoted strings in C create a C string. By adding the @ symbol before the quoted text, you tell the compiler to treat the text as an NSString and not a C string.

The C language does not permit overloading operators, which means that you cannot do it in Objective-C, either. Overloading an operator is a way to use an operator in your code instead of calling a method to do the work. The compiler knows that when it sees that operator it uses the method instead.

Take for example the Company and Employee objects discussed in the previous section where there is a Company object that has Employee objects. Say you have two Company objects, each with their own set of employees, and you want to "merge" them into a new Company object with all the Employee objects combined. In a language like C#, you could override the + operator and then write code to do the merge, as shown in Listing 2-30.

LISTING 2-30: Overloading the + Operator Pseudo Code

```
Company firstCompany = new Company();
Company secondCompany = new Company();

// you could write a merge method as part of the Company class
// then create a new company using it
Company thirdCompany = new Company();
thirdCompany.merge(firstCompany);
thirdCompany.merge(secondCompany);

// or you could override the + operator and do the same in a single line
Company thirdCompany = firstCompany + secondCompany;
```

You cannot do this in Objective-C. This difference becomes stark when comparing the NSString class to the String classes in Java or C#. In all languages a text string is represented in memory as an array of characters. The classes you use to handle strings in code are more or less convenience classes so that you are not dealing with raw character arrays but instead a single object. The implementation of the classes hides that they are character arrays from you. In languages that allow operator overloading, you can do things like concatenating strings by using the overloaded + operator, as shown in Listing 2-31, or calling a method like concat in Java.

LISTING 2-31: Concatenating Strings in Java

```
// this code is correct in Java
String firstString = "This is a";
String secondString = "full sentence";
String combinedString = firstString + " " + secondString;

// or you could use concat
String combinedString = new String();
combinedString.concat(firstString);
combinedString.concat(secondString);
```

You cannot do either of this in Objective-C using the NSString class. First because you cannot overload the + operator, and the second because an NSString cannot be changed after it's created. It has no methods like concat. It is an immutable object. To do the same in Objective-C, you would use the NSMutableString class, a subclass of NSString. Listing 2-32 shows how you would use the NSMutableString class to append other strings.

LISTING 2-32: Concatenating Strings in Objective-C

```
// this code is correct in Objective-C
NSString *firstString = @"This is a";
NSString *secondString = @"full sentence";

NSMutableString *combinedString = [[NSMutableString alloc] init];
[combinedString appendString:firstString];
[combinedString appendString:@" "];
[combinedString appendString:secondString];
```

The idea between mutable and immutable objects is used throughout Objective-C. All data structures, which are discussed in the next section, have mutable child classes and immutable parent classes. The reasoning behind this is to guarantee that the object will not change while you are using it.

Another difference with strings in Objective-C is string formatting. In Java and C# you can create a string using text and integer values simply by using the + operator, as shown in Listing 2-33.

LISTING 2-33: Formatting Strings in Java

```
int numberOne = 1;
int numberTwo = 2;
String stringWithNumber = "The first number is " + numberOne +
" and the second is " + numberTwo;
```

This would produce the text string "The first number is 1". In Objective-C you do string formatting the way it's done in C using the IEEE printf specification (http://pubs.opengroup .org/onlinepubs/009695399/functions/printf.html). Listing 2-34 shows an example of how to create the same text string in Objective-C. It uses the stringWithFormat: static convenience method that allocates the string for you instead of needing to call alloc.

LISTING 2-34: Formatting Strings in Objective-C

```
int numberOne = 1;
NSString *stringWithNumber = [NSString stringWithFormat:
@"The first number is %d and the second is %d", numberOne, numberTwo];
```

The stringWithFormat: method looks for format specifiers in the actual text and then matches them with the list of values that follows. You get a compile error if the formatter does not match the value at the same index in the value list. For a full list of format specifiers, refer to Apples documentation found at https://developer.apple.com/library/ios/documentation/cocoa/conceptual/Strings/Articles/formatSpecifiers.html.

One last thing to be mindful of when using strings in Objective-C is string comparison. The difference again goes back to the ability to overload operators. In Java you can compare two strings using the == operator. This ensures that every char at every index is the same between the two strings. In Objective-C you need to remember that the NSString instance variable holds only a pointer to the object in memory. So using the == between two NSString instances will look to see if both are pointing to the same place in memory. Instead you would use the isEqualToString: method, as shown in Listing 2-35.

LISTING 2-35: Comparing Strings in Objective-C

```
NSString *firstString = @"text";
NSString *secondString = @"text";

if(firstString == secondString)
{
    NSLog(@"this will never be true");
}
else if ([firstString isEqualToString:secondString])
{
    NSLog(@"this will be true in this example");
}
```

> **TIP** The code in Listing 2-35 uses the NSLog() function. This is how you write debugging information to the console in Xcode. It also uses format specifiers followed by a list of values the same as stringWithFormat:. It's comparable to System.out.println() in Java or Console.WriteLine() in C#.

Using Basic Data Structures

Data structures in programming languages are ways to organize data. An object is a data structure, though you may not think of it that way. You are more likely to think of data structures like arrays, sets, or dictionaries. All languages support these types of data structures in one way or another. They typically play a major role in how software is written in various languages. Because of this it's important to understand them and how they are used. There are a handful of data structures available in Objective-C. This section covers only the ones you use while building the Bands app.

The most basic data structure is an array. The simple definition of an *array* is a list of items stored in a particular order and referenced by their index number. Arrays can be either zero-based, with the first item being at index number 0, or 1-based. C based languages use zero-based arrays, whereas languages such as Pascal use 1-based. Listing 2-36 shows how you would create an array of integers in a C-based language and set the values at each index.

LISTING 2-36: Creating an Array of Integers

```
int integerArray[5];
integerArray[0] = 101;
integerArray[1] = 102;
integerArray[2] = 103;
integerArray[3] = 104;
integerArray[4] = 105;
```

In Java or C# you can also create arrays of objects using a similar syntax. This is not possible in Objective-C. Instead you use the NSArray class and its subclass NSMutableArray.

NSArray is like NSString. It is immutable and its objects cannot be changed after it's created nor can you add or remove objects. This follows the same immutable reasoning as with NSStrings in which your code is ensured that the objects in an NSArray will not change. For arrays that need to change or be dynamic, you need to use the NSMutableArray class.

NSArray is a little different from your typical array in Java or C#. In those languages you always declare what type each object is in the array. You don't do this with NSArray. Instead it will hold any object whose root class is NSObject. Listing 2-37 shows the different ways you can create an NSArray instance in Objective-C. The syntax is a bit different with each, but they all create the same thing. Also keep in mind that you can create an NSString using @"my string" syntax and that NSString is a descendant of NSObject.

LISTING 2-37: Creating NSArrays

```
NSArray *arrayOne = [[NSArray alloc] initWithObjects:@"one", @"two", nil];
NSArray *arrayTwo = [NSArray arrayWithObjects:@"one", @"two", nil];
NSArray *arrayThree = [NSArray arrayWithObject:@"one"];
NSArray *arrayFour = @[@"one", @"two", @"three"];

NSString *firstItem = [arrayOne objectAtIndex:0];
```

The first array is created using the alloc/init pattern. The second creates the same array using the arrayWithObjects: convenience method. Both of these take a C array of objects that is basically just a list of objects followed by a nil. The third is also a convenience method but takes only one object. The last uses NSArray literal syntax, which does not need a nil at the end.

Getting an object from an NSArray is slightly different from arrays in other languages. In Listing 2-38 the items were referenced by their index number by following the name of the array with brackets and the index number. Because brackets are used in Objective-C to send messages to an object, you cannot use this approach. Instead you use the objectAtIndex: method. You can also search for objects in an NSArray using indexOfObject:, or sort them using the sortedArrayUsingSelector:. You learn how to use these later in this book.

As mentioned before, the NSArray class is immutable, so you cannot change the values or the size of the array after it has been created. Instead you use an NSMutableArray. Table 2-2 lists the additional methods in the NSMutableArray class that you use to modify the array.

TABLE 2-2: NSMutableArray Methods

METHOD	DESCRIPTION
addObject:	Adds an object to the end of the array
insertObject:atIndex:	Inserts an object into the array at a specific index
replaceObjectAtIndex:withObject:	Replaces the object at a specific index with the object passed in
removeObjectAtIndex:	Removes an object at the specific index
removeLastObject	Removes the last object in the array

> **NOTE** *Literal syntax as described in Listing 2-37 can be used only to create an* NSArray. *You cannot use literal syntax to create an* NSMutableArray. *Furthermore this book does not use literal syntax in any of the sample code; instead it uses the methods. This is for readability. When working with the sample code feel free to use the literal syntax if you wish.*

Similar to the NSArray data structure are the NSSet and NSMutableSet classes. This type of data structure holds a group of objects but not in any particular order. A *set* is used when you don't need to access individual objects but instead need to interact with the set as a whole. There are no methods in the NSSet class that return an individual object in the set; however, there are ways to get a subset of a greater set. Sets are particularly useful if you need to check only if an object is included in it. You will not use sets while building the Bands app, so there is no need to go into further detail on them in this chapter.

The last common data structure in Objective-C is a dictionary or hash table. It uses a key/value storage paradigm. The NSDictionary and NSMutableDictionary classes represent this type of data structure in Objective-C. An NSDictionary has a set of keys that are an instance of an NSObject descendant. Often you will use an NSString as the key. The value in a dictionary is also a descendant of NSObject.

As a way to illustrate how you could use a dictionary in code, think of the company example used previously in this chapter. A company has many employees. Because employees may have the same first and last name, each employee is assigned a unique ID. When employees get a new title, their information needs to be updated, but the only information you have for employees is their ID. If you were to use only arrays or sets to keep track of employees, you would need to iterate through all employees, checking their IDs until you found the correct employee. With a dictionary you could simply look up employees using their unique IDs. Listing 2-38 demonstrates how this would be done in Objective-C using an NSMutableDictionary.

LISTING 2-38: Using NSMutableDictionary

```
NSString *employeeOneID = @"E1";
NSString *employeeTwoID = @"E2";
NSString *employeeThreeID = @"E3";

Employee *employeeOne = [Employee employeeWithUniqueID:employeeOneID];
Employee *employeeTwo = [Employee employeeWithUniqueID:employeeTwoID];
Employee *employeeThree = [Employee employeeWithUniqueID:employeeThreeID];

NSMutableDictionary *employeeDictionary = [NSMutableDictionary dictionary];
[employeeDictionary setObject:employeeOne forKey:employeeOneID];
[employeeDictionary setObject:employeeTwo forKey:employeeTwoID];
[employeeDictionary setObject:employeeThree forKey:employeeThreeID];

Employee *promotedEmployee = [employeeDictionary objectForKey:@"E2"];
promotedEmployee.title = @"New Title";
```

In this example there are three Employee objects each with a unique ID. The NSMutableDictionary is created using the convenience method dictionary. The Employee objects are added to the dictionary using the setObject:forKey: method. To get the Employee object whose unique ID is "E2", the code can get it quickly using the objectForKey: method.

> **TIP** Because both NSArray and NSDictionary store NSObject instances, you cannot set primitive types such as integers or booleans as values. The NSNumber class can be used instead. It is a descendant of NSObject, so it can be used with both NSArray and NSDictionary and can hold any primitive data type.

DISCUSSING ADVANCED CONCEPTS

Objective-C is similar in syntax to other C-variant programming languages. Some of the concepts and patterns, though, are different. The rest of this chapter discusses these concepts and patterns so that you can see how they are used in practice while building the Bands app.

Explaining the Model-View-Controller Design Pattern

The Model-View-Controller design pattern is another influence of Smalltalk. It's a high-level design pattern that can be applied to almost any programming language. In Mac and iOS programming, it's the predominant pattern and is ingrained deeply in Cocoa and Cocoa Touch. To begin developing iOS applications, you need to have a good understanding of how it works so that the classes and user interface design of iOS apps makes sense.

The idea is to separate all components of a piece of software into one of three roles. This separation helps to make the components independent of one another as well as configurable and reusable. If done correctly it can greatly reduce the amount of code that needs to be written as well as make the overall architecture of the software easy to understand. This helps new developers coming to a project get up to speed quickly.

The Model

The first role is the Model. It is the knowledge or data of the application as well as the rules that define how pieces of data interact with each other. It is responsible for loading and saving data from persistent storage as well as validating that the data is valid. The Model role does not care nor does it store any information about how its data is to be displayed.

The View

The second role is the View. It is the visual representation of the model. It does not act on the model in any way nor does it save data to the model. It is strictly the user interface of the software.

The Controller

The last role is the Controller. It is the link between the model and the view. When the model changes, it gets notified and knows if there is a view that needs to update its visual display. If a view is interacted with by the user, it notifies the controller about the interaction. The controller then decides if it needs to update the model.

To get a better understanding of this, think of a software that might be used by the Company example. The software will be used by administrative assistants to keep track of employees and update their information. Figure 2-8 illustrates how the Model-View-Controller pattern could be used to build this software.

The model in this example would be the Employee on the left side of the figure and its underlying database. The employee has three properties: the employee's name, the employee's title, and a unique ID for the employee within the database. It is responsible only for loading the employee information from the database and keeping its values in memory.

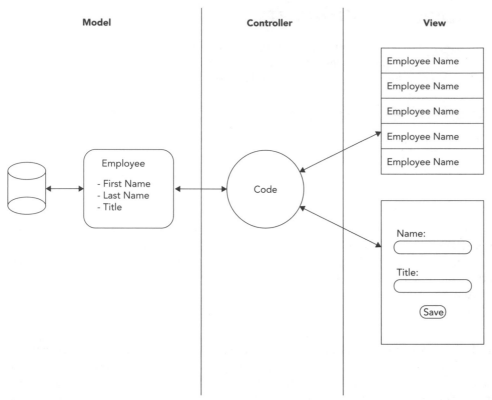

FIGURE 2-8

The views in this example are the list of employees and the employee detail view on the right of the figure. The list of employees shows the name of each employee. The administrative assistant can use this view to select an employee. The employee detail view again shows the name and title of the employee but gives the administrative assistant the ability to change the values displayed. It also has a Save button the administrative assistant can click when he is done updating the information.

The controller is the circle that connects the Employee model to the employee list screen and the employee details screen. When the employee list screen needs to be displayed to the administrative assistant, the employee list asks the controller for names of all the employees. It doesn't care about the employee's title or unique ID, because it does not display those. It acts as a filter of the model data, so the administrative assistant sees only the information he needs to select the correct employee.

When the administrative assistant selects an employee, that interaction is passed again to the controller. The controller then changes the screen to the employee details screen. When this screen is loaded, it asks the controller for the employee's name and title. The controller retrieves this information from the model and passes it back to the detail view for display.

The administrative assistant then changes the title of the employee in the detail view. At this point the change is only a visual change in the employee detail view. It has not changed the value in the model, nor has the database been updated. When the Save button is clicked, the view informs the controller about the user interaction. The controller then looks at the data in the view and determines that the model needs to be updated. It passes the new value to the model and tells it to save it to the database.

The controller can also update either of the views if another administrative assistant has made a change. Say for instance there are two administrative assistants looking at the same employee detail view. The first changes the name of the employee from "Tom" to "Ted" and then clicks the Save button, which tells the controller to update the model. Because the model changed it notifies the controller that its values have been updated. The controller gets this notification and determines that the value being displayed to the second administrative assistant is out of date, so it tells that detail view to update the visual display of the value.

This example illustrates the usefulness of this design pattern. The employee model is independent from the rest of the software yet very reusable. The same can be said with the views. They don't care what employee model object they are displaying, because they can display any of them. The controller acts as the facilitator, keeping the views and the model in line with each other. In a bigger piece of software, you could have different individuals or even different teams working on the code for each of the layers without needing to know the specifics in the code of other teams.

Learning About Protocols and Delegates

Model-View-Controller is a great high-level programming pattern, but to use it in a programming language, you need the tools to make it work. Objective-C has these tools. The model layer is implemented using classes and properties to create reusable objects. The view layer is implemented in the Cocoa and Cocoa Touch APIs, including reusable views and subviews such as buttons and text fields. The controller layer is done by using delegates and data sources to facilitate the communication.

Delegates and data sources are used heavily in Objective-C. It's a way of having one part of the software ask for work to be done by another part. This fits the MVC design pattern with the communication between views and controllers. Because views interact only with controllers and never with the model, they need a way of asking for model data from the controller. This is the role of the data source. When a user interacts with a view, the view needs to tell the controller about it. Delegates are used for this role. Typically, your controller will perform both of these roles.

A view needs to define all the questions it may ask its data source and what type of answer it expects in return. It also needs to define all the tasks it may ask the delegate to perform in response to user interaction. In Objective-C this is done through protocols. You can think of a protocol as a contract between the view and its data source or delegate.

Consider the employee list view in the company example. This is a simplistic example in this chapter to illustrate how a protocol and a delegate are coded. You implement a list similar to this in Chapter 5, "Using Table Views," when you learn about table views.

In this example the employee list is called the EmployeeListView. For the EmployeeListView to show all the employees in the company, it needs to ask its data source for them. When the administrative assistant selects an employee's details to view, the EmployeeListView needs to tell its delegate which employee was selected. This calls for two different protocols to be defined: one for the data source and one for the delegate. These protocols would be declared in an EmployeeListView.h file. For the EmployeeListView to ask its data source for employees or tell its delegate that an employee was selected, the view needs a reference to both the delegate and the data source. The references are added as properties with a type of ID, because the view doesn't care what type of class it is, just as long as it implements the protocols. Listing 2-39 shows how all this would be coded.

LISTING 2-39: Employee List Data Source and Delegate Protocol Declaration

```
@protocol EmployeeListViewDataSource

- (NSArray *)getAllEmployees;

@end

@protocol EmployeeListViewDelegate

- (void)didSelectEmployee:(Employee *)selectedEmployee;

@end

@interface EmployeeListView : NSObject

@property (nonatomic, weak) id dataSource;
@property (nonatomic, weak) id delegate;

@end
```

The controller in the example is called the `EmployeeListViewController`. In order for the `Employee ListViewController` to communicate with the `EmployeeListView`, the `EmployeeListView Controller` needs to declare that it implements the `EmployeeListViewDataSource` and `Employee ListViewDelegate` protocols. Controllers often have a reference to the view they are controlling in a property as well. In this example, the reference to the `EmployeeListView` is set through the `initWith EmployeeListView:` method. Listing 2-40 shows how to do this in code.

LISTING 2-40: Employee List Data Source Protocol Declaration

```
#import "EmployeeListView.h"

@interface EmployeeListViewController : NSObject <EmployeeListViewDataSource,
EmployeeListViewDelegate>

- (id)initWithEmployeeListView:(EmployeeListView *)employeeListView;

@property (nonatomic, weak) EmployeeListView *employeeListView;

@end
```

> **NOTE** In both the interface for the `EmployeeListView` and `EmployeeList ViewController`, all the properties have the `weak` attribute. This is to prevent the Strong Retain Cycle issue explained earlier in this chapter.

In the implementation of the EmployeeListViewController, you need to add the actual implementation of the methods listed in the protocols it declares. You also need to set it as both the data source and the delegate of the EmployeeListView. There are a few ways to do this in Xcode, but as a simple example, it is done in the initWithEmployeeListView: method. Listing 2-41 shows what the EmployeeListViewController.m file would look like.

LISTING 2-41: Employee Controller Implementation

```objc
#import "EmployeeListViewController.h"

@implementation EmployeeListViewController
- (id)initWithEmployeeListView:(EmployeeListView *)employeeListView
{
    self.employeeListView = employeeListView;
    self.employeeListView.dataSource = self;
    self.employeeListView.delegate = self;
}

- (NSArray *)getAllEmployees;
{
    // ask the model for all the employees
    // create an NSArray of all the employees
    // return the array

    return allEmployeesArray;
}

- (void)didSelectEmployee:(Employee *)selectedEmployee;
{
    // display the employee detail view with the selected employee
}

@end
```

Now when the EmployeeListView needs to get the employees it needs to show or when an employee is selected, it can simply call the methods of the protocols using its references, as shown in Listing 2-42.

LISTING 2-42: Calling Methods of Delegates and Data Sources

```objc
// in the implementation of the EmployeeListView it would
// get the array of employees using this code

NSArray *allEmployees = [self.dataSource getAllEmployees];

// to tell its delegate that an employee was selected
// it would use this code

[self.delegate didSelectEmployee:selectedEmployee];
```

LISTING 2-45 *(continued)*

```
        {
            // uh-oh, something happened. Alert the user!
        }
    }
```

In this example the code first creates an NSError pointer with a nil value. It then passes the error instance to the method *by reference* instead of by value. The idea of passing a parameter by reference or by value is in both C# and Java. For typical method calls the object is passed by value, which means the method gets a copy of the object and not the object itself. If the method modifies the object, it modifies only its own copy of the object and not the original. When the method returns, your object is the same and does not reflect those changes.

In this example you use the & (ampersand) symbol to pass the address of the object and not the object itself. If an error occurs while reading the file, the method creates a new NSError object and assigns it to that address. When the method returns you check to see if your error points to an actual error object now or if it still points to nil. You know when to pass a parameter by reference when you see ** in the method signature. The full signature in this example is

```
+ (instancetype)stringWithContentsOfFile:(NSString *)path
encoding:(NSStringEncoding)enc error:(NSError **)error
```

Though using try/catch is not recommended, it is possible. There are base classes that throw exceptions. Using the NSString class again, you could get an exception if you try to get the character at an index that is out of bounds for the underlying character array. Listing 2-46 shows what this looks like.

LISTING 2-46: Catching Exceptions in Objective-C

```
- (void)someMethod
{
    NSString *myString = @"012";
    @try
    {
        [myString characterAtIndex:3];
    }
    @catch(NSException *ex)
    {
        // do something with the exception
    }
    @finally
    {
        // do any cleanup
    }
}
```

The Objective-C way to handle this situation would be to add a check to the code making sure the method will not fail before calling it. Listing 2-47 shows how you would use this approach instead of a try/catch.

LISTING 2-47: Catching Exceptions in Objective-C

```
- (void)someMethod
{
    NSString *myString = @"012";

    if([myString length] >= 3)
    {
        [myString characterAtIndex:3];
    }
    else
    {
        // nope, can't make that method call!
    }
}
```

SUMMARY

Objective-C can look strange if you are coming to it from other object-oriented languages such as C# and Java. The syntax is kind of funny, but the basic concepts and programming constructs are all similar. There are fundamental differences; the biggest being memory management. Objective-C and its tools and compilers have come a long way, however, in recent years, making it less of a burden to developers. If you are comfortable with other object-oriented programming languages, the learning curve of Objective-C is smaller than you may think.

The more advanced topics covered in this chapter may seem difficult to understand at this point, but as you move through the book, they will become clearer. The easiest way to understand new concepts and patterns is to use them in practice to build something. In the next chapter that is exactly what you do as you begin writing the Bands app.

EXERCISES

1. What language is the messaging syntax of Objective-C based on?

2. What are the two files used to define a class in Objective-C and what are their extensions?

3. What is the base class almost all Objective-C classes are derived from?

4. Define the Objective-C interface for a class named `ChapterExercise` with one method named `writeAnswer`, which takes no arguments and returns nothing.

5. What code would you write to instantiate the `ChapterExercise` class?

6. What are the keywords in Objective-C that increment and decrement the reference count of an object?

7. What does ARC stand for?

8. What does the `strong` attribute mean on a class property?

9. Why can't you concatenate two `NSString` instances using the + operator as you can in Java or C#?

10. How do you compare the value of two `NSString` instances?

11. What is the difference between the `NSArray` and `NSMutableArray` classes?

12. What does MVC stand for?

13. How would you declare that the `ChapterExercise` class implements a theoretical `Chapter ExerciseDelegate` protocol?

14. What class is recommended in Objective-C in place of using `NSException`?

➤ WHAT YOU LEARNED IN THIS CHAPTER

TOPIC	KEY CONCEPTS
Objective-C	The language used to develop both Mac and iOS applications is Objective-C. First developed in the early 1980s, it has evolved into an incredibly powered object-oriented programming language with many similarities to Java and C#.
Classes and Objects	The basic building block of all object-oriented programming languages are objects and the classes that define them.
Manual Reference Counting	There are two mainstream approaches to memory management. Languages like Java and C# use Garbage Collection, whereas Objective-C uses Manual Reference Counting, where the developer is responsible for the life cycle of objects in use.
Automatic Reference Counting	A modern approach to manual reference counting takes the responsibility of keeping track of reference counts out of the hands of developers and passes it instead to the compiler.
Class Properties	Object-oriented programming languages recommend using public getter and setter methods to change member values while keeping the actual member variables private. Objective-C implements this concept using class properties.
Data Structures	Higher-level programming languages are designed with built-in data structures such as arrays and dictionaries that developers use to organize data to make their code fast and efficient. Objective-C includes the basic data structures `NSArray`, `NSSet`, and `NSDictionary`.
The Model-View-Controller Design Pattern	The Model-View-Controller design pattern is a high-level design pattern that separates all the components in a piece of software into three roles. These roles help to promote independence and reusability.
Delegates and Protocols	The Cocoa framework uses the concept of delegates and protocols to facilitate the Model-View-Controller design pattern by formalizing how components in different roles communicate and pass data to each other.
Objective-C Error Handling	All object-oriented programming languages include exceptions and errors. The way they are used, however, can vary widely. Understanding how Objective-C and Cocoa approach them is fundamental to writing iOS applications.

3

Starting a New App

WHAT YOU LEARN IN THIS CHAPTER:

➤ Creating a new project in Xcode

➤ Exploring Xcode's layout and editors

➤ Using Interface Builder to edit Storyboards

➤ Running your app in the simulator and on a device

WROX.COM CODE DOWNLOADS FOR THIS CHAPTER

You can find the wrox.com code downloads for this chapter at www.wrox.com/go/begios programming on the Download Code tab. The code is in the chapter 03 download and individually named according to the names throughout the chapter.

In Chapter 2, "Introduction to Objective-C," you learned about Objective-C, the language used to write iOS applications. In this chapter you learn about Xcode, the Integrated Development Environment used to actually create an iOS application. Xcode is similar to Microsoft Visual Studio or Eclipse. You start by creating a project; then you edit the code and user interface files within Xcode. It wasn't always this way. Just a few years ago, Xcode was strictly for code editing while you worked on your User Interface files in Interface Builder. Today Interface Builder is integrated within Xcode to make it more familiar to developers coming from other platforms.

CREATING A NEW APP IN XCODE

Xcode is the IDE for developing both iOS applications as well as Mac OS X desktop applications. To start the Bands app, create a new iOS project in Xcode.

Discussing Xcode Templates

Xcode offers a variety of project templates you can start with. In the previous section, you created the Bands project using the Single View Application. The Calculator app is an example of a single view application. Table 3-1 lists the other templates included by default in Xcode 5 and an example Apple application if one exists.

TABLE 3-1: Xcode Default Templates

TEMPLATE NAME	DESCRIPTION	EXAMPLE APP
Master-Details Application	An application that typically uses a table view to list objects and a navigation controller to transition to a details view of the object.	Contacts
Page-Based Application	An application that contains different views and allows the user to transition between them by swiping to the left or right. These apps have a series of dots along the bottom so the user knows how many views there are and which one they are on.	Compass
Tabbed Application	An application that has a tab bar along the bottom that is used to switch between the different views.	Music
Utility Application	An application with a main view and a secondary view with an info button to switch between the two.	iOS 6 Weather
OpenGL Game	A game application that uses OpenGL for drawing.	Infinity Blade
SpriteKit Game	A game application that uses SpriteKit for drawing.	Disco Bees
Empty	A project that contains only a window and an application delegate file.	N/A

It's important to think about what type of template makes sense for your application when you first create a project, because it gives you a head start. However, that doesn't mean you are stuck with that application architecture. Though you started the Bands app with the Single View Application template, you will modify it to be more of a Master Detail–type application as you add new features.

You can also modify the default templates or even add your own. If you are creating new projects often, you may want the default template to add files with your file naming conventions. This is an advanced topic and not recommended for beginners, but it's nice to know the option is there as you become an expert yourself.

Learning About Bundle Identifiers

The Bundle Identifier is the unique identifier for your application. This identifier is used throughout the Apple system, so you need to know it. The identifier is typically reverse-domain style with the company identifier you entered followed by your product name. An example of this using Wrox and Bands would be wrox.Bands. Though Xcode doesn't enable you to set this in the New Project steps, you can edit it after you create the project. You learn how to do this in Chapter 12, "Deploying Your iOS Apps."

Exploring the Xcode Project Layout

After you create your project, you can see the Xcode Workspace Window. The layout is similar to other IDEs. Figure 3-4 shows the Xcode IDE.

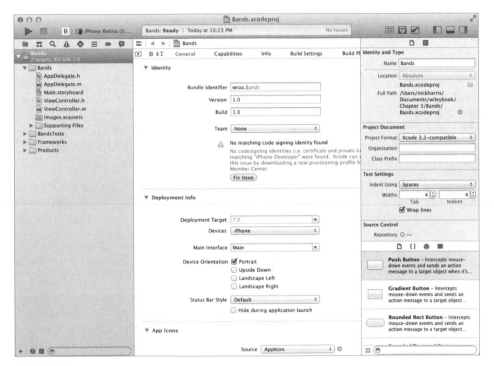

FIGURE 3-4

On the left is your navigation panel. The default view for this panel is the project navigator, which shows your project and its files, as well as any groups or folders you create. Yellow folders represent groups. They're used to group files together within the project, but they do not correspond to folders on disk. You can add folders, which map to folders on disk, which are shown as blue. Typically, groups are used instead of folders, but that's more of a developer preference. This panel also enables you to navigate your project using symbols as well as searching all files within the project. It also shows you all your breakpoints.

The center panel is the editor. Depending on the type of file selected, you see different editors. Selecting the project in the navigation panel brings up the settings editor. Files bring up the text editor, whereas user interface files bring up Interface Builder.

The right panel is the utility panel. Here you see additional information that supplements the editor panel. You can see how this panel is used as you continue the book.

The last panel is the debug area. It's typically hidden while you use the editor and then is shown while you debug the application. It contains your console as well as buttons to step through code along with variable information.

Discussing the UIKit Framework

Before you start building the user interface it is important to understand the components and frameworks you will use. All iOS applications are built using the UIKit framework that is part of Cocoa Touch. Apple uses a naming convention to help you know what framework a class or protocol is part of. The convention is to prepend the name of the class with the frameworks abbreviation. With the UIKit framework all classes and protocols start with UI.

The application itself is represented by the UIApplication object and its companion protocol UIApplicationDelegate. Every project you create using one of Xcode's templates will include a class called AppDelegate that implements the UIApplicationDelegate protocol. You use the methods of this protocol to know when important events in the life of the application occur. This includes when the application launches, becomes active, or is about to be terminated. The Bands app does not do anything with these events, but it's important for you to understand why the file is included when the project is created.

All of the user interface objects are also part of UIKit. You use them to build your application in a way that is visually familiar to other applications so the user knows how to interact with your application. With that knowledge it's time to start working on the user interface of the Bands app.

Discussing the Main Storyboard

Main.storyboard is the user interface file for your application. Storyboards were introduced to Xcode with the iOS 5 SDK. Storyboards enable you to build and view the entire flow of the application. The two main components of the Storyboard are Scenes and Segues. Scenes are views in your application's user interface. Typically, they have their own UIViewController subclass in your project. Segues represent how your app navigates from view to view. You learn more about using multiple scenes and segues in Chapter 5.

ADDING A LABEL TO A STORYBOARD

The most basic of user interface objects in any language is a text label. In iOS it's called a UILabel. The following Try It Out shows you how to add UIKit objects to a view in your Main.Storyboard.

TRY IT OUT Adding a UILabel to a Scene

1. Select the Main.storyboard from the Navigation pane.
2. At the bottom of the Utility pane, select the Objects tab represented by the cube.

3. In the search box at the very bottom of the screen, type **label** to filter the objects in the list.

4. Drag the label onto your scene in Interface Builder, as shown in Figure 3-5.

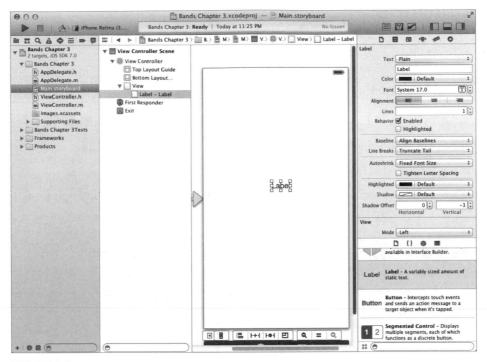

FIGURE 3-5

How It Works

The storyboard is the user interface file for the project. In the Model-View-Controller design pattern it is the "View" role. The project right now has only one scene that is represented by a single UIView object of the UIKit framework. You build the user interface of an application by adding other UIKit objects to the storyboard. In Xcode these objects are all listed in the Utility pane. You can use the search bar at the bottom of the pane to filter the list and quickly find the object you are looking for. In this Try It Out you added a UILabel object to the base UIView. This is how you will build all of the user interfaces for the Bands app.

Exploring Interface Builder

Interface Builder is the user interface editor in Xcode. The left side of the editor shows all the user interface objects and their hierarchy. Notice that the Label is listed under the View because it's a subview. Selecting objects in the hierarchy selects them in the scene shown in the main portion of the editor.

The Utilities pane in Interface Builder has a series of inspectors on top and the collection libraries on bottom. The most commonly used library is the Objects library, which lists all the UIKit objects used to build an iOS application.

Setting Attributes

After you add a UI object to your view, you need to set its attributes, which you learn how to do in the following Try It Out.

TRY IT OUT   Setting the Labels Text Attribute

1. Select the label.

2. On the Utilities tab, select the Attributes Inspector represented by the slider icon.

3. Change the text of the label by replacing Label with **Bands.**

4. In the view, drag the side boundary of the label to fit the new text, as shown in Figure 3-6.

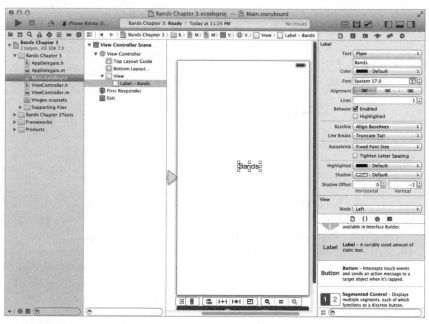

FIGURE 3-6

How It Works

All UIKit objects have attributes. These attributes can be set either at runtime or at design time. Changing the text from Label to **Bands** sets the text attribute of the label. Other attributes you can set for a label are all your typical text attributes such as color, font, and alignment.

Exploring the Inspectors

There are five other inspectors. The File inspector shows you attributes of the file. The Quick Help inspector shows you documentation of the selected object. The Identifier inspector enables you to set the parent class of an object, which you learn about in Chapter 5. The Size inspector enables you to change the size and origin of the object as well as its auto layout constraints. Finally, there is the Connections inspector, which Chapter 4, "Creating a User Input Form," discusses.

Aligning UI Objects

Interface Builder shows you guidelines as you add subviews. These guidelines, shown as dashed lines, are designed by Apple to show you the recommended spacing between objects as well as how they align to the boundaries of the view.

TRY IT OUT   Centering a UI Object

1. Select the label in the view.
2. Drag the label to the left side of the view until you see the left guideline appear.
3. Drag the label to the right side of the view until you see the right guideline appear.
4. Drag the label to the center of the screen until you see the horizontal and vertical centering guidelines.

How It Works

Interface Builder shows you the various guidelines as you move UI objects around in the view. You can use these to build place your objects in context to other objects and boundaries.

RUNNING IN THE SIMULATOR

Xcode includes the iOS simulator to help you quickly develop and prototype your app without needing to run on a device. Debugging with the simulator is faster than on a device and enables you access to some Xcode tools that aren't available to the device.

The simulator runs in its own window on your Mac. You can simulate iPhone 3.5-inch and 4-inch devices as well as iPads both in standard or retina display. You can also change the version of the OS the simulator runs.

> **NOTE** *Retina displays were first introduced with the iPhone 4. They have a higher resolution with more pixels per inch, making text and images appear sharper without looking pixelated.*

> **WARNING** *iOS devices are case-sensitive when using filenames. The simulator is not. If you run into issues with resources not loading correctly, make sure you use the case-sensitive filename.*

Choosing a Device

To launch the simulator, you first need to select the device you would like to test with, as shown in the following Try It Out.

TRY IT OUT   Running the App in the iPhone Retina (4-inch) Simulator

1. In Xcode, locate the scheme selector next to the Run button.
2. In the drop-down, select iPhone Retina (4-inch) in the Simulator section.
3. Click the Run button. The simulator launches; then runs your application, as shown in Figure 3-7.

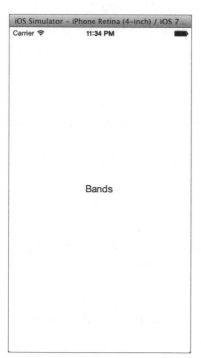

FIGURE 3-7

How It Works

Using the scheme selector, you selected to run the application in the simulator on an iPhone Retina 4-inch device. The app was then compiled, installed, and launched in the simulator using your selection.

Learning to Test on All Device Sizes

You must test your application on all devices you plan to support, because of the different screen sizes. You also need to keep these different sizes in mind while designing your user interface. The following Try It Out demonstrates a layout issue found only by testing with multiple devices.

TRY IT OUT   Running the App in the iPhone Retina (3.5-inch) Simulator

1. In Xcode, select the iPhone Retina (3.5-inch) device from the simulator section.

2. Click the Run button. The simulator switches to the iPhone Retina 3.5-inch device, as shown in Figure 3-8.

FIGURE 3-8

How It Works

What you have done here is switch the device type the simulator should use. As a result, the label you centered in Interface Builder is no longer centered in the simulated application. This is because the iPhone Retina 3.5 has less screen space. To keep the label centered, you need to use Auto Layout.

EXPLORING APPLICATION SETTINGS

Now that you have your application running, it's time to set its version number, icon, and other settings to make it complete. Xcode uses property list files, known as plists, to store this information. You can view your application's info plist by expanding Supporting Files group in the project navigator and selecting the `Bands-info.plist` file. Though you can edit your settings using the plist editor, you may find it easier to use Xcode's settings editor instead.

Setting Version and Build Numbers

Every iOS application, just like any desktop application, has a version and build number used to identify which version of the app is being run. The following Try It Out walks you through setting these using Xcode's settings editor.

TRY IT OUT Setting Properties Using the Info Property Editor

1. In the Project Navigator, select the project.

2. In the editor, select the General tab, and bring up the info property editor, as shown in Figure 3-15.

3. In the Identity section, set the Version to **1.0** and Build to **0.1**.

4. Select the `Bands-info.plist` file from the Project Navigator. You see the Bundle Version String, Short property set to 1.0 and the Bundle Version property set to 0.1, as shown in Figure 3-16.

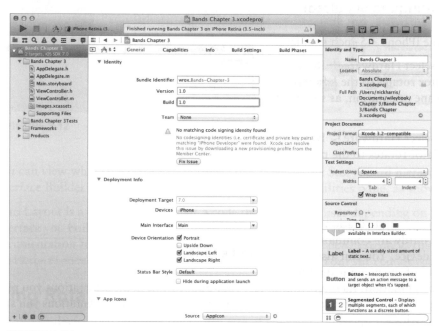

FIGURE 3-15

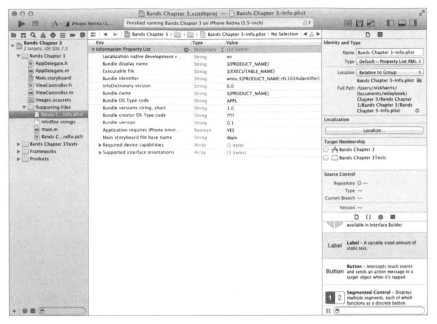

FIGURE 3-16

How It Works

The Xcode info property editor helps you change your application settings without needing to know the specific property names used in the underlying `Bands-info.plist` file.

Setting Supported Rotation Orientations

Supporting rotation in your application is optional. Designing an application that looks nice in both portrait and landscape can be challenging and may not be worth the effort. The following Try It Out shows how to support only Portrait orientation in your app.

TRY IT OUT   Setting Supported Rotation Orientations

1. In the Project Navigator, select the project.

2. In the Deployment Info section, check Portrait and uncheck Upside Down, Landscape Left, and Landscape Right.

3. Run the application in the iPhone 4-inch simulator.

4. Rotate the simulator to Landscape orientation. You see that the app no longer rotates to this orientation, as shown in Figure 3-17.

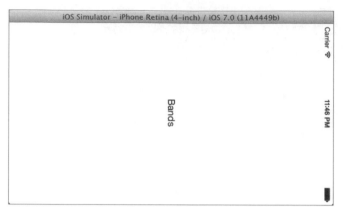

FIGURE 3-17

How It Works

In your application settings there is an array of supported orientations, which are listed under the Supported Interface Orientations property. By checking only Portrait in the info property editor, you remove all other orientations, leaving just Portrait in the array.

Setting the App Icon

An application isn't complete without an icon. The icon is one of the most important parts of your application. It's the first thing a user will see when browsing the App Store, so it needs to look nice as well as catch the user's eye. This book won't go into what makes for a good icon, but Apple does lay out some things to keep in mind in the Human Interface Guidelines at `https://developer.apple` `.com/library/ios/documentation/userexperience/conceptual/mobilehig/AppIcons.html`. If you can afford to, it is best to hire a designer to create your icon.

You will need icons of different sizes depending on what devices you plan on supporting. For iPhones and iPod touches with a retina display, you need an icon that is 120×120 pixels in size. If you plan on supporting non-retina display iPhones and iPod touches you need an icon that is half that size, 60×60. For retina display iPads and iPad minis you need an icon that is 152×152 while non-retina display iPad and iPad minis need an icon that is 76×76 in size. Since this book is primarily about coding an iOS application and not design you can use the simple 120×120 icon included with the sample code. The following Try It Out walks through setting the app icon in Xcode.

TRY IT OUT Setting the Bands App Icon

1. Download the `BandsIcon.png` file from `www.wrox.com` to your desktop.

2. In the Project Navigator, select the project.

3. In the App Icons section, click the arrow next to the Source drop-down to bring up the icon settings editor, as shown in Figure 3-18.

4. Drag the `BandsIcon.png` file onto Xcode, and drop it on the iPhone App iOS 7 placeholder.

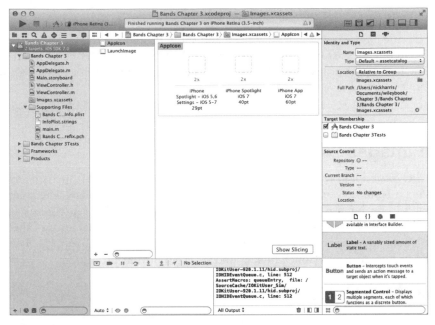

FIGURE 3-18

5. Run the application in the simulator.

6. Return to the home screen in the simulator by selecting Hardware ⇨ Home from the menu. You see the new icon on the simulator home screen, as shown in Figure 3-19.

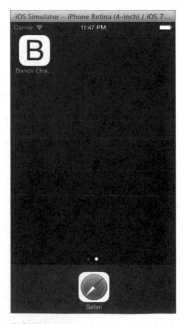

FIGURE 3-19

How It Works

Application icons have specific names used to identify them and show them properly. Instead of needing to know these names, Xcode uses asset catalogs. By dragging the file onto the Xcode icon settings editor, you have added the icon to the project, and Xcode has added it to its proper asset catalog, so the system knows how to show your app icon on the home screen.

Setting Launch Images

When iOS first launches your application, it may take a little bit of time before the app is ready to use. Instead of showing a blank screen, Apple requires you to supply a launch image. The image can be anything you want it to be, but it is recommended that you use an image that represents what your app will look like when it is ready to use. This creates a seamless visual experience to the user. You need to provide launch images for all device sizes and orientations your app supports. The following Try It Out shows how to create launch images and set them in your project.

TRY IT OUT   Creating and Setting Launch Images

1. Run your app in the iPhone 4-inch simulator.

2. Select File ➪ Save Screen Shot from the simulator menu. This creates a new PNG image on your desktop.

3. In Xcode, select your project from the Project Navigator.

4. In the Launch Images section, click the arrow next to the Source selector to bring up the launch image editor, as shown in Figure 3-20.

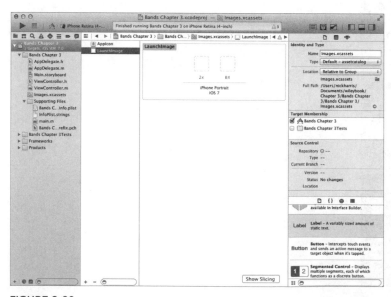

FIGURE 3-20

5. Drag the screen shot file from your desktop and drop it on the second placeholder. The project will automatically be saved once the image is dropped.

6. Run your application again using the iPhone 3.5-inch simulator.

7. Repeat step 2 to create another screen shot image on your desktop.

8. Drag the new screen shot file from your desktop, and drop it on the first placeholder. Again the project will automatically be saved once the image is dropped.

How It Works

Xcode determines if your application supports iPhone 4-inch displays by looking at what launch images are included. If no images are included, it assumes the app supports the 4-inch display. By using the screen shot feature of the simulator, you created image files that represent your user interface after the app is loaded and ready for use. Similar to icons, iOS uses specific names to know which launch images to use on different devices. Xcode saves you from having to know these names by again using the asset catalog, so the system knows which images to use without you memorizing the specific filenames.

RUNNING ON A DEVICE

Running your application in the simulator enables you to quickly prototype and test your app. But to actually get a feel for your application, you need to test using an actual device. To do this, first, you need to enroll in the iOS Developer Program. The developer program costs $99 a year, but it is necessary to test on physical devices as well as getting your app into the App Store. You also get access to all Apple's technical resources including the Apple Developer Forums. You can enroll from the iOS Dev Center at `https://developer.apple.com/devcenter/ios/`.

All apps that run on an iOS device require a provisioning profile. The provisioning profile is a form of Digital Rights Management (DRM). When you buy an app from the App Store, it gets installed using an App Store provisioning profile. When you test your app during development, you need to install a developer provisioning profile. Both types of provisioning profiles require a certificate, which is used to sign the profile. Xcode can handle this for you, as shown in the following Try It Out.

TRY IT OUT   Provisioning a Device for Testing

1. Connect your device to your Mac.

2. In Xcode, open the Organizer by selecting Window ➪ Organizer from the menu.

3. Select Devices from the top of the Organizer window, as shown in Figure 3-21.

4. Select your connected device, and click the Use for Development button in the main part of the window.

5. Select your account name from the dialog box that appears, then click Choose.

FIGURE 3-21

6. When the Certificate Not Found dialog displays, click Request to request a new certificate and wait for Xcode to complete the task.

7. In Xcode select iOS Device in the scheme selector, and click Run. Xcode installs the app on your device and runs it.

How It Works

You have now registered your device with your developer account, created a certificate, and then created a team provisioning profile. This profile is managed by Xcode and can now be used to test your application on your device.

SUMMARY

In this chapter you created your first iPhone application using Xcode. You learned about Xcode's layout as well as how to use different editors such as Interface Builder and the info properties editor. You also learned how to use the simulator to test your app on different devices and in different orientations, including using Auto Layout to make sure your user interface displays how you want it depending on the screen size and orientation of the device. Finally, you learned how to register a test device with your account in the iOS Developer Program and provisioned it to run your first iPhone application.

EXERCISES

1. What is the name of the pane on the left side of Xcode?

2. What is the Cocoa framework used to create an iOS applications user interface?

3. What type of file is used to store application settings?

4. What is the name of the Xcode feature you use to make sure your applications user interface is displayed correctly no matter what size device it is running on?

5. What is the name of the inspector used to change user interface object attributes in Interface Builder?

6. Change the color of the Bands label from black to light gray.

7. Add a new label with text **Bottom** aligned with the bottom and center guidelines of the scene with an auto layout constraint keeping it at the bottom.

8. Change the version number to 1.1.

➤ WHAT YOU LEARNED IN THIS CHAPTER

TOPIC	KEY CONCEPTS
Creating an Xcode Project	All iOS applications are built in Xcode. The Xcode project organizes all of the code files, art assets, configuration files and settings.
Building a User Interface	The user interface is the "view" role in the Model-View-Controller design pattern. It's the part of the application the user interacts with. In Xcode the user interface is built using storyboards with scenes and segues showing the flow of the application.
Using Auto Layout	iOS devices come in different sizes. They are also handheld devices that the user can rotate which changes the screen dimensions. Apple has designed its Auto Layout feature in Xcode to ensure your user interface is displayed correctly no matter what device or orientation it is being viewed in.
Changing App Settings	There are many settings to an iOS application. They are stored in property list files, also known as plist files. Xcode includes editors you can use to change these settings so you don't need to know the keys and valid setting options, though you can edit the plist files directly if you choose.
Running in the Simulator	The iOS simulator is an essential tool in developing iOS applications. It allows you to test your application using any iOS device quickly without needing test devices connected to your development machine.
Running on a Device	In order to test your application on a physical iOS device, it needs to be registered and provisioned with Apple through your developer account. Provisioning a test device can be done within Xcode.

Creating a User Input Form

WHAT YOU LEARN IN THIS CHAPTER:

- ➤ Creating a model object and adding properties
- ➤ Building an interactive user interface
- ➤ Saving and retrieving data

WROX.COM CODE DOWNLOADS FOR THIS CHAPTER

You can find the wrox.com code downloads for this chapter at www.wrox.com/go/begios programming on the Download Code tab. The code is in the chapter 04 download and individually named according to the names throughout the chapter.

In the last chapter you learned how to create a simple iOS application. Though some applications display only information, most require a way for the user to add and edit data. In this chapter, you continue building the Bands app by giving the user a way to add a band and save it.

If you have created desktop applications or web apps, you're familiar with data input forms. You are also familiar with the objects or classes that represent this data within the code. Typically, you present the user with an interface including text fields, switches, and selectors they can use to enter and manipulate the data objects. iOS applications are no different. In Visual Studio you add user interface objects to a dialog or window and then double-click them to associate methods that handle events as the user manipulates the data. Xcode handles this a bit differently, although the concepts are the same.

The first step is adding the model object, which represents a band.

INTRODUCING THE BAND MODEL OBJECT

As discussed in Chapter 2, "Introduction to Objective-C," iOS applications use the Model View Controller design pattern. In the Bands app, the model represents a band. Eventually, you'll have multiple bands represented by the model, so the first step is creating a class that encapsulates all the properties of a band within the application.

The band object needs the following properties:

➤ **Name** — The name of the band.

➤ **Notes** — Any notes the user would like to attach to the band.

➤ **Rating** — How the user rates the band on a scale of 1–10.

➤ **Touring Status** — Whether the band is currently touring or if it is disbanded.

➤ **Have Seen** — Whether the user has seen the band in concert.

Creating the Band Model Object

The WBABand class will represent the Band model object. The name of the class follows Apples naming convention by adding a three letter prefix to the beginning of the class name. The prefix is a combination of the company name Wrox and the Bands app name, as Apple suggests. You can read more about Apple naming conventions in the Apple Developer Library at https://developer.apple.com/library/mac/documentation/Cocoa/Conceptual/ CodingGuidelines/CodingGuidelines.html.

TRY IT OUT Creating the WBABand Class

1. In Xcode, open the Bands project you created in Chapter 3.

2. Select File ➪ New ➪ File; then select Objective-C class, as shown in Figure 4-1.

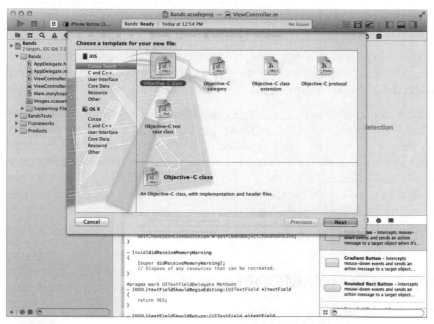

FIGURE 4-1

3. In the next dialog, name the class **WBABand** and set its subclass to **NSObject**, as shown in Figure 4-2.

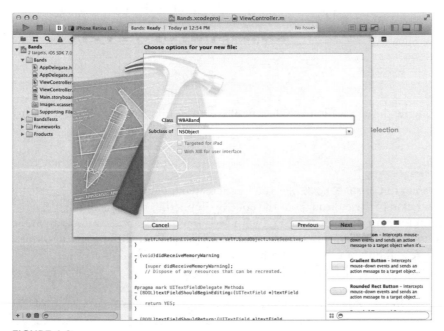

FIGURE 4-2

4. Save the file with the rest of the project files, and ensure it's added to the Bands target. Click Create.

How It Works

You created a new class named WBABand, which is a subclass of NSObject. As discussed in Chapter 2, NSObject is the base class for almost all classes in iOS applications. This enables you to use instances of WBABand in NSArrays, which you cover in Chapter 5, "Using Table Views."

Creating Enumerations

Before you add the properties to the WBABand class you need to declare an enumeration to represent the three different states of touring that a band can have: Touring, Not Touring. and Disbanded.

Enumerations are common in most programming languages. They enable you to declare a type, which consists of named elements. The elements represent simple integers but enable you to use their names in the code to make it readable.

Creating an Enumeration

1. In Xcode, select the `WBABand.h` file from the Project Navigator.

2. In the code editor, add the following code to the top of the file after the imports section:

```
typedef enum {
    WBATouringStatusOnTour,
    WBATouringStatusOffTour,
    WBATouringStatusDisbanded,
} WBATouringStatus;
```

3. Save the file and compile the application by selecting Project ➪ Build from the menu to ensure there are no errors.

How It Works

By adding the `typedef enum` to the `WBABand.h` file, you have created a new type named `WBATouringStatus`, which you can use throughout the code by importing the `WBABand.h` file. The typical naming convention for enumerations is to start with the same prefix abbreviation you are using for class names followed by the name of the enumeration type with the differentiating value at the end. This helps the readability of your code both for yourself and for any other developer who may work on the application. By default the elements are assigned their integer values based on their placement in the list. For the `WBATouringStatus`, `WBATouringStatusOnTour` has a value of 0, `WBATouringStatusOffTour` has a value of 1, and `WBATouringStatusDisbanded` has a value of 2.

Adding Properties to the Band Model Object

Now that you have declared the `WBATouringStatus` enumeration, you have all the types you need to add all the properties of the `WBABand` class to the code. For the properties to be accessible in the code, add them as properties to the `WBABand.h` class, as described in the following Try It Out.

Adding Properties to a Class

1. Select the `WBABand.h` file from the Project Navigator.

2. Add the following code to the interface:

```
@property (nonatomic, strong) NSString *name;
@property (nonatomic, strong) NSString *notes;
@property (nonatomic, assign) int rating;
@property (nonatomic, assign) WBATouringStatus touringStatus;
@property (nonatomic, assign) BOOL haveSeenLive;
```

3. Save the file and compile the application by selecting Project ➪ Build from the menu to ensure there are no errors.

How It Works

As you learned in Chapter 2, properties enable you to add member variables to an Objective-C class. The code you added creates all the member variables for the WBABand class. By declaring the enumeration types in the previous section, you could declare a property using that type in the class interface.

You now have the WBABand class created and ready to be used as the model for the Bands app. The next step you learn is how to build a user interface to allow your users to add objects and edit them.

BUILDING AN INTERACTIVE USER INTERFACE

In the previous chapter you added a UILabel to a UIView and set its properties in Xcode using the Attributes Inspector. This is known as setting properties at design time. All user interface objects can be created and set this way, but they cannot be changed in code. To refer to the user interface objects in code you need to learn about the IBOutlet keyword.

Learning About IBOutlet

The IBOutlet keyword stands for Interface Builder Outlet. Xcode uses this keyword to connect objects in the code to objects in the user interface. With the Model-View-Controller design pattern, a UIView is controlled by a UIViewController. The Single View Application template you used to create the Band project included the ViewController class, which is set as the UIViewController for the UIView in the Storyboard. This is where you declare the IBOutlet objects you want to connect to the UIKit objects you add to the UIView, as shown in the following Try It Out.

> **NOTE** When referring to user interface objects, this book will use the name you see in Xcode where appropriate but otherwise will refer to them by their UIKit names. For instance, when you add a new user interface object from the Object library or interact with the Storyboard hierarchy, the user interface objects are labeled by common names such as Label or Text Field in Xcode. In those situations the book will refer to them as Label or Text Field. In most other situations they will be referred to by their UIKit names. If a Try It Out connects an IBOutlet property in code to a UIKit object the How It Works section will use the property name.

TRY IT OUT   Connecting an IBOutlet

1. In Xcode, drag a UILabel onto the UIView, use the Interface Builder guidelines to align it at the top and center of the UIView, and then set its text to **Band**.

2. Select the ViewController.h file from the Project Navigator.

3. Add the following code to the interface section:

```
@interface ViewController : UIViewController

@property (nonatomic, weak) IBOutlet UILabel *titleLabel;

@end
```

4. Return to the Main.storyboard, and select the View Controller from the Storyboard hierarchy on the left of the editor.

5. Control-drag the line that is shown to the UILabel until both the View Controller and the UILabel are highlighted and connected, as shown in Figure 4-3.

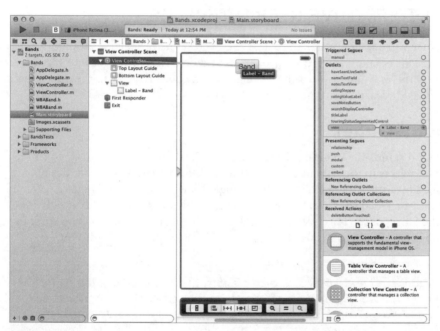

FIGURE 4-3

6. Release the mouse button; then select titleLabel from the Outlets dialog.

7. Select the ViewController.m file from the Project Navigator.

8. Add the following code to the viewDidLoad method:

```
- (void)viewDidLoad
{
    [super viewDidLoad];
    // Do any additional setup after loading the view, typically from a nib.

    NSLog(@"titleLabel.text = %@", self.titleLabel.text);
}
```

9. Run the application in the simulator. You see titleLabel.text = Band in the console.

How It Works

In the `ViewController` class interface you declared a `UILabel` property with the `IBOutlet` keyword and named it `titleLabel`. You then used Interface Builder to connect the `titleLabel` in the code to the `UILabel` in the `UIView`. Finally, you printed the text property of the `titleLabel` to the console at runtime showing the connection was successfully made.

> **NOTE** `IBOutlet` *properties are always created as weak properties instead of strong. This is because the Storyboard is the owner of the object. The code only needs a weak reference to the object.*

Using UITextField and UITextFieldDelegate

`UILabel` is one of the most basic of `UIKit` objects; however, the bands app needs to enable users to type in text of their own for the band name. For a single line of text you use a `UITextField`. Keeping with the Model-View-Controller design pattern, the `UITextField` will ask its controller how it should act. It does this using the `UITextFieldDelegate` protocol. In the Bands app, the controller for the `UITextField` is the `ViewController` class, so it needs to implement the `UITextFieldDelegate`, as you will see in the following Try It Out.

TRY IT OUT Adding a UITextField

1. In the `Main.storyboard`, add a new `UILabel` to the `UIView` and use the Interface Builder guidelines to align it to the left side of the `UIView`. Then set its text to **Name:**.

2. Find and drag a new Text Field from the Objects library to the `UIView`, and align it under the Name `UILabel`, stretched to the left and right guidelines of the `UIView`, as shown in Figure 4-4.

3. Select `ViewController.h` from the Project Navigator, and add the following code to the interface:

```
#import "WBABand.h"

@interface ViewController : UIViewController <UITextFieldDelegate>

@property (nonatomic, strong) WBABand *bandObject;
@property (nonatomic, weak) IBOutlet UILabel *titleLabel;
@property (nonatomic, weak) IBOutlet UITextField *nameTextField;

@end
```

4. Return to the `Main.storyboard`, and select the View Controller from the Storyboard hierarchy on the left of the editor.

5. Connect the `nameTextField` to the `UITextField` following the same steps as in the previous section.

6. Select the `UITextField` in the `UIView`. Then use the same Control-drag procedure, and drag the line back to the View Controller in the Storyboard hierarchy.

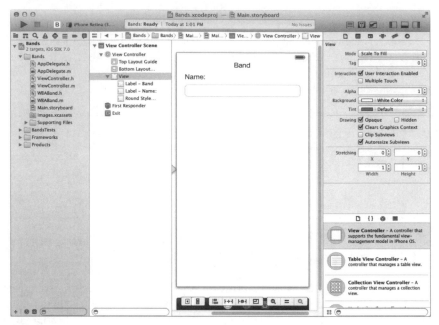

FIGURE 4-4

7. Release the mouse button; then select delegate in the dialog.

8. Select the `ViewController.m` file from the Project Navigator.

9. Add the following code to the `viewDidLoad` method:

```
- (void)viewDidLoad
{
    [super viewDidLoad];
    // Do any additional setup after loading the view, typically from a nib.

    NSLog(@"titleLabel.text = %@", self.titleLabel.text);

    self.bandObject = [[BandObject alloc] init];
}
```

10. Add the following code to the implementation:

```
- (BOOL)textFieldShouldBeginEditing:(UITextField *)textField
{
    return YES;
}

- (BOOL)textFieldShouldReturn:(UITextField *)textField
{
    self.bandObject.name = self.nameTextField.text;
    [self.nameTextField resignFirstResponder];
    return YES;
}

- (BOOL)textFieldShouldEndEditing:(UITextField *)textField
```

```
    {
        self.bandObject.name = self.nameTextField.text;
        [self saveBandObject];
        [self.nameTextField resignFirstResponder];
        return YES;
    }
```

11. Run the application in the iPhone 4-inch simulator, and select the UITextField. The software keyboard becomes visible, as shown in Figure 4-5.

12. Enter **My Band** in the UITextField; then tap the Return key on the software keyboard. The text is entered into the UITextField and the software keyboard is hidden.

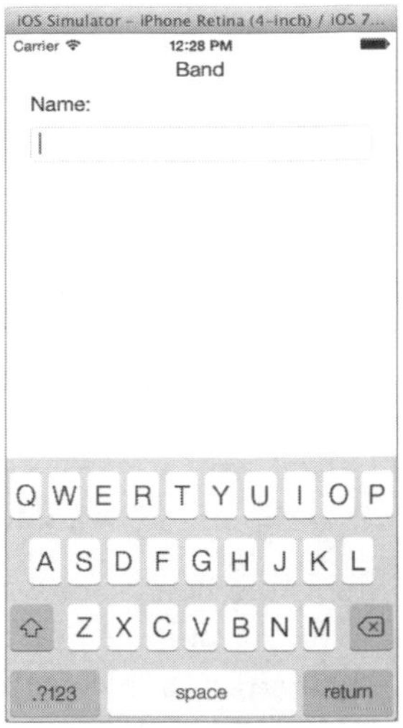

How It Works

In the ViewController.h file you added an IBOutlet property for the UITextField named nameTextField along with a WBABand property named bandObject to represent the model. You also declared that the ViewController class implements the UITextFieldDelegate protocol.

FIGURE 4-5

Using Interface Builder you added a UILabel and UITextField to the UIView so the user can enter the name of a band. After connecting the UITextField to the nameTextField, you then set its delegate as the ViewController class. You could do this because you declared that the ViewController class implements the UITextFieldDelegate.

Finally, you added code to the ViewController class implementation. In the viewDidLoad method you added code to initialize the bandObject. Then you added methods that implement the UITextFieldDelegate.

The UITextFieldDelegate protocol enables you to handle events that get triggered as the user interacts with the nameTextField. The first method of the protocol you implemented is the textFieldShouldBeginEditing: method, which tells the system that the nameTextField should become the first responder. Being the first responder means that it is the first object to handle any events raised by user interaction. Because you have made a UITextField the first responder, the system shows the software keyboard. You're not doing any data verification in this code, so you should always return YES. In other applications you may want to validate other pieces of data and prevent the UITextField from becoming the first responder. In those cases, you would return NO.

The second UITextFieldDelegate protocol method you implemented was the textFieldShouldReturn: method. This method gets triggered when the user taps the Return key on the keyboard. In that implementation, the first thing you did was set the name property of the bandObject. The next line resigns the nameTextField as the first responder. Because the first responder is no longer a UITextField, the system hides the keyboard.

The last method of the UITextFieldDelegate protocol you implemented was the textFieldShouldEndEditing: method. This gets called when another object attempts to become the first responder. Its implementation is the same as textFieldShouldReturn:.

> **COMMON MISTAKES** *If the keyboard does not hide when you test your app and you press the Return key, make sure you have implemented the* `textFieldShouldReturn:` *method and that it resigns the* `nameTextField` *as the first responder. Also make sure that the delegate of the* `nameTextField` *has been connected to the* `ViewController` *class. Missing either of those will cause the keyboard to remain onscreen.*

Using UITextView and UITextViewDelegate

For the Bands app, each band has notes associated with it that the user can type in. These notes can be multiple lines. For text that needs multiple lines you use a `UITextView`. A `UITextView` is similar in implementation to a `UITextField`. It asks its controller how it should act through the `UITextViewDelegate` protocol. Just like the `UITextField`, the `ViewController` class will be the delegate for the `UITextView`.

TRY IT OUT   Adding a UITextView

1. In the Main.storyboard, add a new `UILabel` to the `UIView` using Interface Builder guidelines to align it to the left side of the `UIView`. Then set its text to **Notes:**.

2. Find and drag a new Text View from the Objects library onto the `UIView`. Align it under the Notes `UILabel` and stretch it to the left and right guidelines of the `UIView`; then set its height to 90 pixels.

3. In the Attributes Inspector, change the background color of the `UITextView` to Light Gray.

4. Select `ViewController.h` from the Project Navigator, and add the following code to the interface:

   ```
   @interface ViewController : UIViewController <UITextFieldDelegate,
   UITextViewDelegate>

   @property (nonatomic, strong) WBABand *bandObject;
   @property (nonatomic, weak) IBOutlet UILabel *titleLabel;
   @property (nonatomic, weak) IBOutlet UITextField *nameTextField;
   @property (nonatomic, weak) IBOutlet UITextView *notesTextView;

   @end
   ```

5. Return to the Main.storyboard, and select the `View Controller` from the Storyboard hierarchy on the left side of the editor.

6. Connect the `notesTextView` to the `UITextView` following the same steps as in the previous section.

7. Connect the delegate of the `notesTextView` to the `ViewController` using the same steps as in the previous section.

8. Select the `ViewController.m` file from the Project Navigator.

9. Add the following code to the implementation:

```
- (BOOL)textViewShouldBeginEditing:(UITextView *)textView
{
    return YES;
}

- (BOOL)textViewShouldEndEditing:(UITextView *)textView
{
    self.bandObject.notes = self.notesTextView.text;
    [self.notesTextView resignFirstResponder];
    return YES;
}
```

10. Run the application in the iPhone 4-inch simulator. When you tap the notesTextView, the keyboard appears and enables you to enter text.

11. Tap the Return button to add a line break to the text.

How It Works

The UITextView and UITextViewDelegate are similar to the UITextField and UITextFieldDelegate. The textViewShouldBeginEditing: method of the UITextViewDelegate protocol tells the system that the notesTextView should become the first responder, which will show the keyboard. The other UITextViewDelegate protocol method you implemented was the textViewShouldEndEditing: method, which gets triggered when another object wants to become the first responder. In its implementation, you set the notes property of the bandObject with the text entered in the notesTextView then resign the notesTextView as the first responder.

The difference between a UITextField and a UITextView is that the Return key in a UITextView adds a line break to the text instead of triggering a delegate method. This presents a problem. How does the user tell a UITextView they are done entering text?

Using UIButton and IBAction

The simplest way for the user to tell a UITextView they are done entering text is to add a UIButton, which when touched resigns the UITextView as the first responder. A UIButton, however, does not have a corresponding UIButtonDelegate. Instead you have to connect the touch event to a method in your code. To make that method visible in Interface Builder you use the IBAction keyword, which is short for Interface Builder Action.

TRY IT OUT   Adding a UIButton

1. Select the Main.storyboard from the Project Navigator to open Interface Builder.

2. Find and drag a new Button from the Object library, and align it on the right side of the UIView in line with the Notes UILabel.

3. In the Attributes Inspector, change the text of the UIButton to **Save**.

4. Also in the Attributes Inspector, uncheck the Enabled checkbox.

5. Select `ViewController.h` from the Project Navigator, and add the following code to the interface:

```
@interface ViewController : UIViewController <UITextFieldDelegate,
UITextViewDelegate>

@property (nonatomic, strong) WBABand *bandObject;
@property (nonatomic, weak) IBOutlet UILabel *titleLabel;
@property (nonatomic, weak) IBOutlet UITextField *nameTextField;
@property (nonatomic, weak) IBOutlet UITextView *notesTextView;
@property (nonatomic, weak) IBOutlet UIButton *saveNotesButton;

- (IBAction)saveNotesButtonTouched:(id)sender;

@end
```

6. Select `ViewController.m`, and add the following code to the implementation:

```
- (BOOL)textViewShouldBeginEditing:(UITextView *)textView
{
    self.saveNotesButton.enabled = YES;
    return YES;
}

- (BOOL)textViewShouldEndEditing:(UITextView *)textView
{
    self.bandObject.notes = self.notesTextView.text;
    [self.notesTextView resignFirstResponder];
    self.saveNotesButton.enabled = NO;
    return YES;
}

- (IBAction)saveNotesButtonTouched:(id)sender
{
    [self textViewShouldEndEditing:self.notesTextView];
}
```

7. Return to the `Main.storyboard`, and connect the `saveNotesButton` to the `UIButton`.

8. Control-drag back to the View Controller in the Storyboard hierarchy, and select `saveNotesButtonTouched:` from the dialog.

9. Run the application in the iPhone 4-Inch simulator. When you select the `notesTextView`, the `saveNotesButton` becomes enabled. When you tap the `saveNotesButton`, it becomes disabled and the keyboard is hidden.

How It Works

By creating the `IBAction` method `saveNotesButtonTouched:`, you could connect it to the touch event of the `saveNotesButton`. You also used the `enabled` attribute of the `saveNotesButton` to indicate to the user that it's associated with the `notesTextView`. When the `saveNotesButton` is enabled and tapped, the `saveNotesButtonTouched:` method is called, which resigns the `notesTextView` as the first responder hiding the keyboard.

Using UIStepper

Many times while building a user interface, you need a user interface object that increases or decreases an integer. You can use a UIStepper for this. A UIStepper is a simple control with a minus button on the left and a plus button on the right. Tapping either adjusts its value up or down. You can use a UIStepper to represent the rating property of the bandObject.

TRY IT OUT Adding a UIStepper

1. In the Main.storyboard add a new UILabel and use the Interface Builder guidelines to align it on the left side of the UIView. Then set its text to **Rating:**.

2. Find and drag a new Stepper from the Object library, and use the Interface Builder guidelines to align it on the left side of the UIView underneath the Rating UILabel.

3. In the Attributes Inspector set the minimum value to 0, the maximum value to 10, the current value to 0, and the step value to 1.

4. Add another UILabel to the UIView, and align it on the Interface Builder guidelines to the right side of the UIView and vertically centered with the UIStepper; then set its text to 0, as shown in Figure 4-6.

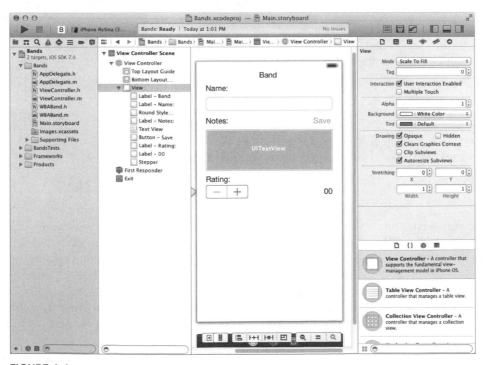

FIGURE 4-6

5. Select `ViewController.h` from the Project Navigator, and add the following code to the interface:

```
@interface ViewController : UIViewController <UITextFieldDelegate,
UITextViewDelegate>

@property (nonatomic, strong) WBABand *bandObject;
@property (nonatomic, weak) IBOutlet UILabel *titleLabel;
@property (nonatomic, weak) IBOutlet UITextField *nameTextField;
@property (nonatomic, weak) IBOutlet UITextView *notesTextView;
@property (nonatomic, weak) IBOutlet UIButton *saveNotesButton;
@property (nonatomic, weak) IBOutlet UIStepper *ratingStepper;
@property (nonatomic, weak) IBOutlet UILabel *ratingValueLabel;

- (IBAction)saveNotesButtonTouched:(id)sender;
- (IBAction)ratingStepperValueChanged:(id)sender;

@end
```

6. Select `ViewController.m` and add the following code to the implementation:

```
- (IBAction)ratingStepperValueChanged:(id)sender
{
    self.ratingValueLabel.text =
[NSString stringWithFormat:@"%g", self.ratingStepper.value];
    self.bandObject.rating = (int)self.ratingStepper.value;
}
```

7. Return to `Main.storyboard`, and connect the `ratingStepper` to the `UIStepper` and the `ratingValueLabel` to `UILabel` on the right side of the `UIView`.

8. Connect the `ratingStepperValueChanged:` method to the `ratingStepper`.

9. Run the application in the iPhone 4-Inch simulator. When you tap the plus and minus buttons of the `ratingStepper`, its value displays in the `ratingValueLabel`, as shown in Figure 4-7.

FIGURE 4-7

How It Works

A `UIStepper` has properties for its minimum and maximum values along with the amount the value should be "stepped" when the user taps the plus and minus buttons. By setting these values you configured the `ratingStepper` to go to a value as high as 10 and as low as 0, changing by a value of 1 on each step. You also created an `IBAction` method to connect the code to the Value Changed event of the `ratingStepper`. When the `ratingStepper` value changes, the `ratingStepperValueChanged:` is triggered and updates the text of the `ratingLabel` reflecting the current value. Because the value of a `UIStepper` is a double, you need to cast it to an `int` before setting the `rating` property of the `bandObject`.

Using UISegmentedControl

The next property of the WBABand class that you add to the interface is the Touring State. For this you use a UISegmentedControl. The UISegmentedControl has the same look as the UIStepper you added in the last section except you have control over how many segments it has and what the text or image of those segments should be. Each segment acts as its own button and can either stay selected when tapped or it can be "momentary" like the buttons in the UIStepper control. For the Touring State, use a UISegmentedControl that stays selected.

TRY IT OUT

1. In the Main.storyboard, add a new UILabel using Interface Builder guidelines to align the label on the left side of the UIView. Then set its text to **Touring Status:**.

2. Find and drag a new Segmented Control from the Object library, and use the Interface Builder guidelines to stretch it to both the left and right sides of the UIView underneath the Touring Status UILabel.

3. In the Attributes Inspector, set the number of segments to 3.

4. Set the Title of Segment 0 to **On Tour**.

5. Use the segment selector to choose Segment 1, and set its title to **Off Tour**.

6. Use the segment selector to choose Segment 2, and set its title to **Disbanded**.

7. Select ViewController.h from the Project Navigator, and add the following code to the interface:

```
@interface ViewController : UIViewController <UITextFieldDelegate,
UITextViewDelegate>

@property (nonatomic, strong) WBABand  *bandObject;
@property (nonatomic, weak) IBOutlet UILabel *titleLabel;
@property (nonatomic, weak) IBOutlet UITextField *nameTextField;
@property (nonatomic, weak) IBOutlet UITextView *notesTextView;
@property (nonatomic, weak) IBOutlet UIButton *saveNotesButton;
@property (nonatomic, weak) IBOutlet UIStepper *ratingStepper;
@property (nonatomic, weak) IBOutlet UILabel *ratingValueLabel;
@property (nonatomic, weak) IBOutlet UISegmentedControl
*touringStatusSegmentedControl;

- (IBAction)saveNotesButtonTouched:(id)sender;
- (IBAction)ratingStepperValueChanged:(id)sender;
- (IBAction)tourStatusSegmentedControlValueChanged:(id)sender;

@end
```

8. Select ViewController.m, and add the following code to the implementation:

```
- (IBAction)tourStatusSegmentedControlValueChanged:(id)sender
{
    self.bandObject.touringStatus =
self.touringStatusSegmentedControl.selectedSegmentIndex;
}
```

9. Go back to Main.Storyboard, and connect the
`touringStatusSegmentedControl` to the `UISegmentedControl` .

10 Connect the `touringStatusSegmentedControl` to the
`tourStatusSegmentedControlValueChanged:` method.

11. Run the application in the iPhone 4-Inch simulator. As you tap the
segments of the `touringStatusSegmentedControl`, you see them
become selected while deselecting the others, as shown in Figure 4-8.

How It Works

You added a `UISegmentedControl` to the `UIView` and set it to
have three segments correlating to the three touring status values in
the `WBATouringStatus` enumeration. You then connected it to the
`touringStatusSegmentedControl` in the `ViewController` class. Like a
`UIButton`, a `UISegmentedControl` does not have a corresponding delegate
protocol, so in order to know when the user interacts with it you added an
`IBAction` method named `tourStatusSegmentedControlValueChanged:`.
It gets triggered when the selected segment changes. In its implementation
you can use the `selectedSegmentIndex` property to set the `touringStatus` property of the `bandObject` because both the segments and the `WBATouringStatus` enumeration are 0 based.

FIGURE 4-8

Using UISwitch

The last property of the `WBABand` class you need to add to the user interface is the `haveSeen` property using a `UISwitch`. A `UISwitch` is what you would expect it to be: a user interface object that is either on or off. It too does not have a corresponding delegate, so you need one more `IBAction` method to know when the user interacts with it.

TRY IT OUT Adding a UISwitch

1. In the `Main.storyboard`, add a new `UILabel` using Interface Builder guidelines to align it on the left side of the `UIView`. Then set its text to **Have Seen:**.

2. Find and drag a new Switch from the Objects library, and add it to the `UIView`, aligning it with the vertical center of the Have Seen `UILabel` and the right side of the `UIView`.

3. Select `ViewController.h` from the Project Navigator, and add the following code to the interface:

```
@interface ViewController : UIViewController <UITextFieldDelegate,
UITextViewDelegate>

@property (nonatomic, strong) WBABand *bandObject;
@property (nonatomic, weak) IBOutlet UILabel *titleLabel;
@property (nonatomic, weak) IBOutlet UITextField *nameTextField;
@property (nonatomic, weak) IBOutlet UITextView *notesTextView;
@property (nonatomic, weak) IBOutlet UIButton *saveNotesButton;
@property (nonatomic, weak) IBOutlet UIStepper *ratingStepper;
```

```
@property (nonatomic, weak) IBOutlet UILabel *ratingValueLabel;
@property (nonatomic, weak) IBOutlet UISegmentedControl
*touringStatusSegmentedControl;
@property (nonatomic, weak) IBOutlet UISwitch *haveSeenLiveSwitch;

- (IBAction)saveNotesButtonTouched:(id)sender;
- (IBAction)ratingStepperValueChanged:(id)sender;
- (IBAction)tourStatusSegmentedControlValueChanged:(id)sender;
- (IBAction)haveSeenLiveSwitchValueChanged:(id)sender;

@end
```

4. Select `ViewController.m` from the Project Navigator, and add the following code to the implementation:

```
- (IBAction)haveSeenLiveSwitchValueChanged:(id)sender
{
    self.bandObject.haveSeenLive = self.haveSeenLiveSwitch.on;
}
```

5. Return to `Main.Storyboard`, and connect the `haveSeenLiveSwitch` property and `haveSeenLiveSwitchValueChanged:` method to the `UISwitch`.

6. Run the application in the iPhone 4-inch simulator. You can toggle the `haveSeenLiveSwitch` off and on to change the value of the `haveSeen` property of the `bandObject`, as shown in Figure 4-9.

How It Works

In the Storyboard you added a new `UISwitch` to the `UIView`. You then declared an `IBOutlet` named `haveSeenLiveSwitch` and an `IBAction` method named `haveSeenLiveSwitchValueChanged:`, that you connected to the `UISwitch`. In the implementation you set the `haveSeenLive` property of the `bandObject` to the value of the `haveSeenLiveSwitch`.

FIGURE 4-9

SAVING AND RETRIEVING DATA

Giving the user the ability to enter data into your app is great but not useful unless you can save the data, retrieve it, and present it back to the user. There are many ways to do this in an iOS application, but the simplest is to use `NSUserDefaults`. The documented use for `NSUserDefaults` is to save preferences for an application, but because of its simplicity, it's often used to save small amounts of data as well. You can use it to save and retrieve an instance of the `WBABand` class.

Implementing the NSCoding Protocol

Before you can save an instance of the `WBABand` class, you need to declare that the `WBABand` class implement the `NSCoding` protocol and then add the protocol's two methods, `initWithCoder:` and encodeWithCoder:, to the WBABand class implementation. These methods give the class a way to encode and decode itself so that it can be archived and saved to persistent storage.

TRY IT OUT Implementing the NSCoding Protocol

1. Select the WBABand.h file from the Project Navigator, and add the following code to the interface:

```
@interface WBABand : NSObject <NSCoding>

@property (nonatomic, strong) NSString *name;
@property (nonatomic, strong) NSString *notes;
@property (nonatomic, weak) int rating;
@property (nonatomic, weak) WBATouringStatus touringStatus;
@property (nonatomic, weak) BOOL haveSeenLive;

@end
```

2. Select the WBABand.m file from the Project Navigator, and add the following code to the implementation:

```
static NSString *nameKey = @"BANameKey";
static NSString *notesKey = @"BANotesKey";
static NSString *ratingKey = @"BARatingKey";
static NSString *tourStatusKey = @"BATourStatusKey";
static NSString *haveSeenLiveKey = @"BAHaveSeenLiveKey";

@implementation WBABand

-(id) initWithCoder:(NSCoder*)coder
{
    self = [super init];

    self.name = [coder decodeObjectForKey:nameKey];
    self.notes = [coder decodeObjectForKey:notesKey];
    self.rating = [coder decodeIntegerForKey:ratingKey];
    self.touringStatus = [coder decodeIntegerForKey:tourStatusKey];
    self.haveSeenLive = [coder decodeBoolForKey:haveSeenLiveKey];

    return self;
}

- (void)encodeWithCoder:(NSCoder *)coder
{
    [coder encodeObject:self.name forKey:nameKey];
    [coder encodeObject:self.notes forKey:notesKey];
    [coder encodeInteger:self.rating forKey:ratingKey];
    [coder encodeInteger:self.touringStatus forKey:tourStatusKey];
    [coder encodeBool:self.haveSeenLive forKey:haveSeenLiveKey];
}

@end
```

How It Works

The NSCoding protocol gives an instance of a class a way to encode itself for archiving as well as initializing itself from an archive. In the interface of the WBABand class you declared that it implements this protocol by adding it to its protocol list. The protocol has two methods, encodeWithCoder: and initWithCoder: that you then added to the WBABand class implementation. Both of these methods take an instance of an NSCoder object as an argument which does the actual archiving and unarchiving of the data. How the archiving and unarchiving is implemented in the NSCoder object is not important to the WBABand class. All it needs to do is call the various encode and decode methods of it to package up its member variables using a key-value paring. The primitive data types all have their own encode and decode methods. For the integer and enumeration member variables of the WBABand class you use the encodeInteger:forKey: and decodeIntegerForKey: methods. For the haveSeenLive boolean property you use the encodeBool:forKey: and decodeBoolForKey: methods. For member variables that are instances of NSObject you use the encodeObject:forKey: and decodeObjectForKey: methods. The keys are always an NSString instance. You declared all of the keys as static NSString instances at the beginning of the WBABand.m file before the actual implementation of the class. With these two methods of the NSCoding protocol implemented, the WBABand class is ready to be saved in persistent storage.

Saving Data

To save an instance of the WBABand class to persistent storage you will use the standardUserDefaults, which is a global instance of the NSUserDefaults class. It works a bit like NSCoder in that it uses a key-value paring to save both primitive types and NSObject instances to disk. In order to save an instance of the WBABand class it first needs to be archived into an NSData object, which is an object-oriented wrapper around a byte buffer. To do this you use the NSKeyedArchiver class, which is a subclass of NSCoder. When you call the archiveDataWithRootObject: method it will call the encodeWithCoder: method you implemented in the WBABand class to create an NSData archive. The archive is then stored in the standardUserDefaults using the setObject:forKey: method.

TRY IT OUT   Saving Data Using NSUserDefaults

1. Select the ViewController.h file from the Project Navigator, and add the following code to the interface:

```
@interface ViewController : UIViewController <UITextFieldDelegate,
UITextViewDelegate>

@property (nonatomic, strong) WBABand *bandObject;
@property (nonatomic, weak) IBOutlet UILabel *titleLabel;
@property (nonatomic, weak) IBOutlet UITextField *nameTextField;
@property (nonatomic, weak) IBOutlet UITextView *notesTextView;
@property (nonatomic, weak) IBOutlet UIButton *saveNotesButton;
@property (nonatomic, weak) IBOutlet UIStepper *ratingStepper;
@property (nonatomic, weak) IBOutlet UILabel *ratingValueLabel;
@property (nonatomic, weak) IBOutlet UISegmentedControl
```

```
*touringStatusSegmentedControl;
@property (nonatomic, weak) IBOutlet UISwitch *haveSeenLiveSwitch;

- (IBAction)saveNotesButtonTouched:(id)sender;
- (IBAction)ratingStepperValueChanged:(id)sender;
- (IBAction)tourStatusSegmentedControlValueChanged:(id)sender;
- (IBAction)haveSeenLiveSwitchValueChanged:(id)sender;

- (void)saveBandObject;

@end
```

2. Select the `ViewController.m` file from the Project Navigator, and add the following code before the implementation:

```
#import "ViewController.h"

static NSString *bandObjectKey = @"BABandObjectKey";

@implementation ViewController
```

3. Add the following code to the `ViewController` implementation:

```
- (void)saveBandObject
{
    NSData *bandObjectData =
[NSKeyedArchiver archivedDataWithRootObject:self.bandObject];
    [[NSUserDefaults standardUserDefaults]
setObject:bandObjectData forKey:bandObjectKey];
}
```

4. Add a call to the `saveBandObject` method after setting any of the properties in the previous methods:

```
- (BOOL)textFieldShouldReturn:(UITextField *)textField
{
    self.bandObject.name = self.nameTextField.text;
    [self saveBandObject];
    [self.nameTextField resignFirstResponder];
    return YES;
}

- (BOOL)textViewShouldEndEditing:(UITextView *)textView
{
    self.bandObject.notes = self.notesTextView.text;
    [self saveBandObject];
    [self.notesTextView resignFirstResponder];
    self.saveNotesButton.enabled = NO;
    return YES;
}

- (IBAction)ratingStepperValueChanged:(id)sender
{
    self.ratingValueLabel.text = [NSString stringWithFormat:@"%g",
```

```
    self.ratingStepper.value];
        self.bandObject.rating = (int)self.ratingStepper.value;
        [self saveBandObject];
}

- (IBAction)tourStatusSegmentedControlValueChanged:(id)sender
{
        self.bandObject.touringStatus =
    self.touringStatusSegmentedControl.selectedSegmentIndex;
        [self saveBandObject];
}

- (IBAction)haveSeenLiveSwitchValueChanged:(id)sender
{
        self.bandObject.haveSeenLive = self.haveSeenLiveSwitch.on;
        [self saveBandObject];
}
```

5. Build the project and make sure there are no errors.

How It Works

You first declared a new method in the `ViewController` class interface named `saveBandObject`. In its implementation you archive the `bandObject` using the `archivedDataWithRootObject:` method of the `NSKeyedArchiver`. You then set the archive in the `standardUserDefaults` using the `setObject:forKey:` method. The key is an `NSString` named `bandObjectKey` that you declared as static in the `ViewController.m` file. The `standardUserDefaults` saves to disk at periodic intervals so you do not need to do anything more to get the object written to disk. Finally, you added calls to `saveBandObject` to all of the `IBAction` methods to make sure what gets written to disk reflects any changes the user made.

Retrieving Saved Data

Retrieving stored data from `NSUserDefaults` is basically the reverse of saving. You retrieve the object from `standardUserDefaults` using the `objectForKey:` method and the same `bandObjectKey`. This returns you back the `NSData` archive. You then use the `unarchiveObjectWithData:` method of the `NSKeyedUnarchiver` class to unarchive the data and get back the `WBABand` instance.

TRY IT OUT Retrieving Data from NSUserDefaults

1. Select the `ViewController.h` file from the Project Navigator, and add the following code to the interface:

```
@interface ViewController : UIViewController <UITextFieldDelegate,
UITextViewDelegate>

@property (nonatomic, strong) WBABand *bandObject;
@property (nonatomic, weak) IBOutlet UILabel *titleLabel;
@property (nonatomic, weak) IBOutlet UITextField *nameTextField;
```

```
@property (nonatomic, weak) IBOutlet UITextView *notesTextView;
@property (nonatomic, weak) IBOutlet UIButton *saveNotesButton;
@property (nonatomic, weak) IBOutlet UIStepper *ratingStepper;
@property (nonatomic, weak) IBOutlet UILabel *ratingValueLabel;
@property (nonatomic, weak) IBOutlet UISegmentedControl
*touringStatusSegmentedControl;
@property (nonatomic, weak) IBOutlet UISwitch *haveSeenLiveSwitch;

- (IBAction)saveNotesButtonTouched:(id)sender;
- (IBAction)ratingStepperValueChanged:(id)sender;
- (IBAction)tourStatusSegmentedControlValueChanged:(id)sender;
- (IBAction)haveSeenLiveSwitchValueChanged:(id)sender;

- (void)saveBandObject;
- (void)loadBandObject;
- (void)setUserInterfaceValues;

@end
```

2. Select the `ViewController.m` file from the Project Navigator, and add the following code to the implementation:

```
- (void)loadBandObject
{
    NSData *bandObjectData = [[NSUserDefaults standardUserDefaults]
objectForKey:bandObjectKey];

    if(bandObjectData)
        self.bandObject =
[NSKeyedUnarchiver unarchiveObjectWithData:bandObjectData];
}

- (void)setUserInterfaceValues
{
    self.nameTextField.text = self.bandObject.name;
    self.notesTextView.text = self.bandObject.notes;
    self.ratingStepper.value = self.bandObject.rating;
    self.ratingValueLabel.text = [NSString stringWithFormat:@"%g",
self.ratingStepper.value];
    self.touringStatusSegmentedControl.selectedSegmentIndex =
self.bandObject.touringStatus;
    self.haveSeenLiveSwitch.on = self.bandObject.haveSeenLive;
}
```

3. Modify the `viewDidLoad` method with the following code:

```
- (void)viewDidLoad
{
    [super viewDidLoad];
    // Do any additional setup after loading the view, typically from a nib.

    NSLog(@"titleLabel.text = %@", self.titleLabel.text);

    [self loadBandObject];

    if(!self.bandObject)
```

```
        self.bandObject = [[BandObject alloc] init];

    [self setUserInterfaceValues];
}
```

4. Run the application in the iPhone 4-inch simulator, and enter some data.

5. Restart the application. The data you entered will be reloaded.

How It Works

In the `ViewController` interface you declared two new methods named `loadBandObject` and `setUserInterfaceValues`. In the implementation of the `loadBandObject` you first attempt to retrieve an `NSData` archive from the `standardUserDefaults` using the `bandObjectKey`. If there is no archive this call will return `nil`. If there is, the code then calls the `unarchiveObjectWithData:` method of the `NSKeyedUnarchiver` class to unarchive the `WBABand` instance and set the `bandObject` property.

In the `viewDidLoad` method of the `ViewController` you added a call to `loadBandObject`, and a check to see if the `bandObject` property was set using archived data. If the `bandObject` is `nil`, the code instantiates a new instance of the `WBABand` class. Finally you added a call to the `setUserInterfaceValues` method whose implementation sets up the user interface using the member values of the `bandObject`.

Deleting Saved Data

To delete data you have saved to `standUserDefaults`, all you need to do is set the object for the key to `nil`. Adding delete to the user interface is a little more difficult. Before you delete any data you need to verify with user that they actually want it deleted. The best way to do this in an iOS application is to use a `UIActionSheet`, which has a "destructive" button that will be red when presented to the user. This way user knows they are about to permanently delete the data.

A `UIActionSheet` also has its own delegate. When a user taps a button in a `UIActionSheet` it tells its delegate about it using the `actionSheet:clickedButtonAtIndex:` method of the `UIActionSheetDelegate` protocol. For the Bands app the `ViewController` class will act as the delegate so it needs to implement this protocol.

TRY IT OUT Deleting Data from NSUserDefaults

1. In the `Main.storyboard`, add a new `UIButton` to the bottom of the `UIView`, set its text to **Delete**, and add an auto layout constraint to anchor the button to the bottom of the view, as shown in Figure 4-10.

2. Select `ViewController.h` from the Project Navigator, and add the following code:

```
@interface ViewController : UIViewController <UITextFieldDelegate,
UITextViewDelegate, UIActionSheetDelegate>

@property (nonatomic, strong) WBABand *bandObject;
```

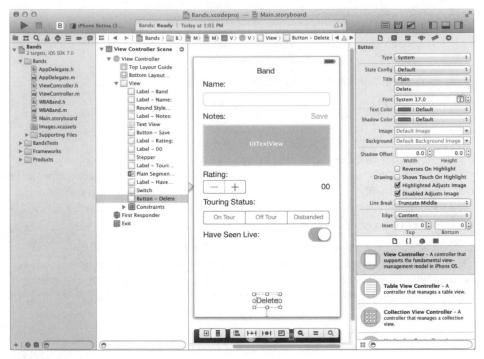

FIGURE 4-10

```
@property (nonatomic, weak) IBOutlet UILabel *titleLabel;
@property (nonatomic, weak) IBOutlet UITextField *nameTextField;
@property (nonatomic, weak) IBOutlet UITextView *notesTextView;
@property (nonatomic, weak) IBOutlet UIButton *saveNotesButton;
@property (nonatomic, weak) IBOutlet UIStepper *ratingStepper;
@property (nonatomic, weak) IBOutlet UILabel *ratingValueLabel;
@property (nonatomic, weak) IBOutlet UISegmentedControl
*touringStatusSegmentedControl;
@property (nonatomic, weak) IBOutlet UISwitch *haveSeenLiveSwitch;

- (IBAction)saveNotesButtonTouched:(id)sender;
- (IBAction)ratingStepperValueChanged:(id)sender;
- (IBAction)tourStatusSegmentedControlValueChanged:(id)sender;
- (IBAction)haveSeenLiveSwitchValueChanged:(id)sender;
- (IBAction)deleteButtonTouched:(id)sender;

- (void)saveBandObject;
- (void)loadBandObject;
- (void)setUserInterfaceValues;

@end
```

3. Select the WBABand.m file from the Project Navigator, and add the following code to the implementation:

```
- (IBAction)deleteButtonTouched:(id)sender
{
    UIActionSheet *promptDeleteDataActionSheet = [[UIActionSheet alloc]
initWithTitle:nil delegate:self cancelButtonTitle:@"Cancel"
destructiveButtonTitle:@"Delete Band" otherButtonTitles:nil];
    [promptDeleteDataActionSheet showInView:self.view];
}

- (void)actionSheet:(UIActionSheet *)actionSheet
clickedButtonAtIndex:(NSInteger)buttonIndex
{
    if(actionSheet.destructiveButtonIndex == buttonIndex)
    {
        self.bandObject = nil;
        [self setUserInterfaceValues];

        [[NSUserDefaults standardUserDefaults] setObject:nil forKey:bandObjectKey];
    }
}
```

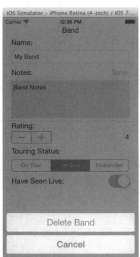

FIGURE 4-11

4. Run the application in the iPhone 4-inch simulator. When you tap the
Delete button the UIActionSheet will be presented asking if you want
to delete the band, as shown in Figure 4-11. Tapping delete will delete
the data from standardUserDefaults.

How It Works

To allow the user to delete a WBABand instance from the
standardUserDefaults, you first added a new UIButton to the UIView. In
the ViewController interface you added a new IBAction method named
deleteButtonTouched: and connected it to the new UIButton.

The implementation of the deleteButtonTouched: method creates a
new UIActionSheet instance named promptDeleteDataActionSheet. A
UIActionSheet can have a Cancel button, a Destructive button, and any
number of other buttons you would like to add. All of these buttons are
optional. For the promptDeleteDataActionSheet you set the text of the
Cancel button to **Cancel** and the text of the destructive button to **Delete
Band**. You also set the ViewController as its delegate.

To know which button the user clicked, you implemented the actionSheet:clickedButtonAtIndex:
method of the UIActionSheetDelegate protocol. In its implementation you used the
destructiveButtonIndex property of the actionSheet argument and compared it to the
buttonIndex argument. If they are equal, you know the user selected the Delete Band button, so
the code uses the same bandObjectKey to set the object in standardUserDefaults to nil.

SUMMARY

In this chapter you implemented the WBABand class that will be the model for the Bands app, including the code needed to save and retrieve instances of it from persistent storage. You also learned how to use various UIKit objects to build a user interface, as well as how to use the IBOutlet and IBAction keywords as well as delegates to both set and retrieve values from the user interface. These are all important lessons in building an iOS application. They may be a bit much to fully grasp at this point, but you are well on your way! The next chapter expands on these lessons by adding multiple bands to the model, listing them in a table, and navigating between the table and the user interface you just finished creating.

EXERCISES

1. What keyword do you use to connect a UIKit property in a class to a UIKit object in Interface Builder?

2. What keyword do you use to connect an event of a UIKit object in Interface Builder to a method in a class?

3. What does it mean to be the first responder?

4. What protocol do you implement in a class that allows it to be used with the NSKeyedArchiver class?

➤ WHAT YOU LEARNED IN THIS CHAPTER

TOPIC	KEY CONCEPTS
Creating the WBABand class	iOS applications are built using the Model-View-Controller design pattern. For the Bands app the WBABand class is the model for a Band object.
Using IBOutlets	To connect user interface objects in Interface Builder to code you use the IBOutlet keyword. IBOutlet stands for Interface Builder Outlet.
Showing and hiding the software keyboard	The software keyboard of an iOS devices is how a user inputs text into an app. The system knows when to show and hide the keyboard depending on what user interface object is the first responder. The first responder in an app is the first object that has the option to handle a user interaction.
Implementing IBActions	Methods that get triggered when a user interaction event occurs use the IBAction keyword. IBAction stands for Interface Builder Action.
Storing model objects in NSUserDefaults	There are many ways to save data to persistent storage in an iOS app. The simplest way is to use NSUserDefaults.

5

Using Table Views

WHAT YOU LEARN IN THIS CHAPTER:

➤ Adding a UITableView

➤ Creating a data source

➤ Editing data in a UITableView

➤ Presenting modal views

➤ Using segues

WROX.COM CODE DOWNLOADS FOR THIS CHAPTER

You can find the wrox.com code downloads for this chapter at www.wrox.com/go/begiosprogramming on the Download Code tab. The code is in the chapter 05 download and individually named according to the names throughout the chapter.

In this chapter you learn how to use the UITableView. The UITableView is a little different from what you would expect a table to be. They consist of a scroll view with single-row cells instead of a table with multiple columns and rows. A better way to think of them is a scrolling list of cells.

The UITableView is probably the most used view in iOS applications. This is because of their versatility. You can use a UITableView and basic UITableViewCells for a standard look and feel, or you can use a custom UITableViewCell with varying cell heights and content for more complex user interfaces.

An example of a UITableView using basic UITableViewCells is Apple's Settings app. You can see a more complex example in popular apps such as Facebook and Twitter.

6. In the Attributes Inspector, change the Title from Root View Controller to **Bands**.

7. Run the app in the iPhone 4-inch simulator. You can now see the table view, as shown in Figure 5-3.

How It Works

When you add a Navigation Controller from the Object library to a Storyboard, it has a UITableView set as its root UIViewController by default. The Storyboard relationship with the two dots and a line signifies this. The arrow that you moved from the View Controller to the Navigation Controller tells the Storyboard which scene to initially show when the app launches. By pointing it at the Navigation Controller, the UITableView is now shown on launch instead of the View Controller.

FIGURE 5-3

Now that you have the UITableView added to the Storyboard, you need to add the UITableViewController class. When you initially created the project, the View Controller already had its ViewController class in the project and was connected to the UIView in the Storyboard. For the UITableView you need to do this manually.

TRY IT OUT Adding a UITableViewController

1. From the Xcode menu select File ➪ New ➪ File.

2. Select the Objective-C class from the dialog, and click Next.

3. Name the Class **WBABandsListTableViewController** and set its Subclass to UITableViewController, as shown in Figure 5-4.

4. In the next dialog, select the Bands directory where the other class files of the project are located to keep all the class files of the project together.

5. Select the Main.storyboard from the Project Navigator.

6. Select the Table View Controller from the Storyboard hierarchy.

7. Select the Identity Inspector in the Utilities pane.

8. Set the Class for the Table View Controller to the WBABandsListTableViewController class you just created.

9. Control-drag from the UITableView in the Storyboard to the Bands List Table View Controller in the Storyboard hierarchy, and set it as the dataSource.

10. Control-drag again from the UITableView to the Bands List Table View Controller and set it as the delegate.

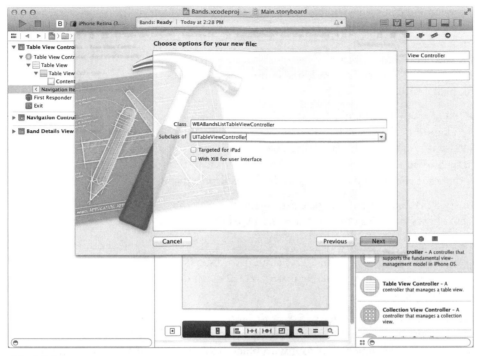

FIGURE 5-4

How It Works

When you add a new class to your project in Xcode, you have the opportunity to set what it's a subclass of. When you add the WBABand class in Chapter 4, "Creating a User Input Form," you created it as a subclass of NSObject. In this Try It Out you add a new class that is a subclass of UITableViewController. This means your WBABandsListTableViewController has an IBOutlet to a UITableView and implements the UITableViewDelegate and UITableViewDataSource protocols. For Xcode to know which class to associate with the UITableView in the Storyboard, you need to change its Identity to the class you created. Finally, you connect the dataSource and delegate of the UITableView to the WBABandsListTableViewContoller class. Now when the app runs, it calls your delegate to get the information it needs to display and control the UITableView.

Learning About Cells

The UITableViewCell object represents a cell in a UITableView. Unlike the UITableView, though, they do not have a delegate, and if you use a predefined style for your cell, you won't need to add a code file. Predefined cells are versatile, so you should consider using them first before creating a custom cell.

There are four predefined cell styles you can use: basic, left detail, right detail, and subtitle. All the predefined cells have a `textLabel` that is a `UILabel` and an `accessoryView` that is a `UIView`.
The right detail, left detail, and subtitle styles add a `UILabel` named `detailsTextLabel`. The basic, right detail, and subtitles also include a `UIImageView` named `imageView`.

The basic style cell, as shown in Figure 5-5, displays the `imageView` on the left. The `textLabel` is black text left-aligned with the cell, whereas the `accessoryView` is aligned on the far right. The `accessoryView` can be set using a `UIView` you define or one of the standard types. In the following figures, the `accessoryView` uses the standard checkmark type.

The right detail style cell, as shown in Figure 5-6, is the same as the basic style cell but shows the `detailsTextLabel` as gray text right-aligned next to the `accessoryView`.

The subtitle style cell, as shown in Figure 5-7, is similar to the basic and right detail styles except it moves the `detailsTextLabel` under the `textLabel` and is black text.

FIGURE 5-5

The left detail style cell, as shown in Figure 5-8, is different than the other three. It does not have an `imageView`. It also shows the `textLabel` with blue text that is right-aligned to the first third of the cell with the details label left-aligned next to it with black text. (Unfortunately, you won't notice the color difference on a figure in a black-and-white book, but you get the idea.)

For the Bands app you use a basic cell style.

FIGURE 5-6

FIGURE 5-7

FIGURE 5-8

Apple spent a good amount of time making sure that cells scroll smoothly. One of the features it added to accomplish this is cell reuse. This means the system keeps only a handful of cells in memory and simply changes the data presented instead of creating and deallocating new cells each time the user scrolls the table.

A `UITableView` uses methods of the `UITableViewDataSource` protocol to know how many sections are in the table, how many rows are in each section as well as getting the actual `UITableViewCells` to display. You will implement these methods in the `WBATableViewController` class in the next Try It Out.

TRY IT OUT Displaying a UITableViewCell

1. Select the `Main.storyboard` from the Project Navigator.

2. Select the Table View Cell from the Storyboard hierarchy.

3. Set the Style of the cell to Basic in the Attributes Inspector.

4. Set the Identifier to **Cell**.

5. Select the `WBABandsListTableViewController.m` file from the Project Navigator.

6. Find the `numberOfSectionsInTableView:` method, and change the return value to 1, as shown in the following code:

```
- (NSInteger)numberOfSectionsInTableView:(UITableView *)tableView
{
    // Return the number of sections.
    return 1;
}
```

7. Find the `tableView:numberOfRowsInSection:` method, and change the return value to 10, as shown in the following code:

```
- (NSInteger)tableView:(UITableView *)tableView
numberOfRowsInSection:(NSInteger)section
{
    // Return the number of rows in the section.
    return 10;
}
```

8. Find the `tableView:cellForRowAtIndexPath:` method, and add the following code:

```
- (UITableViewCell *)tableView:(UITableView *)tableView
cellForRowAtIndexPath:(NSIndexPath *)indexPath
{
    static NSString *CellIdentifier = @"Cell";
    UITableViewCell *cell =
[tableView dequeueReusableCellWithIdentifier:CellIdentifier
forIndexPath:indexPath];

    // Configure the cell...
    cell.textLabel.text = [NSString stringWithFormat:@"%d", indexPath.row];

    return cell;
}
```

9. Run the app in the iPhone 4-inch simulator. You can see 10 numbered cells (0–9) in the table, as shown in Figure 5-9.

How It Works

The `UITableView` in the Storyboard has a prototype cell associated with it. The first thing you do is set its style to Basic and its identifier to Cell. Next you modify three of the `UITableViewDataSource` protocol methods. The first is the `numberOfSectionsInTableView:` method, which tells the `UITableView` there is one section. The second, `tableView:numberOfRowsInSection:`, tells the `UITableView` there are 10 rows in that section. The last is the `table View:cellForRowAtIndexPath:` method, which dequeues a `UITableViewCell` with an identifier of "Cell" if one exists, or creates a new one. The code then sets the `textLabel` to the row number of the `indexPath`. A `NSIndexPath` simply has the section number and row number of the cell the table is going to present.

FIGURE 5-9

> **NOTE** *If you run the app and the* `UITableView` *does not display the cells correctly, make sure you have the Identity of the table set to the* `WBABandsListTableViewController` *class and that the* `dataSource` *and* `delegate` *are connected correctly.*

IMPLEMENTING THE BANDS DATA SOURCE

In the last chapter you added a single `WBABand` data model object and used `NSUserDefaults` to store it. In this section you expand on that by storing as many `WBABand` objects as the user wants to add to the app. You also need to keep in mind how the bands will display in the `UITableView`. This way you can use the storage as the data source for the table.

Creating the Band Storage

The easiest storage option to use to support sections is an `NSMutableDictionary`. As described in Chapter 2, "Introduction to Objective-C," an `NSMutableDictionary` is a key/value data storage object. For the Bands storage, the first letter of the bands is the key, and the value is an `NSMutableArray` with all the bands that have that first letter.

Because you section the bands by the first letters of their names, it also makes sense to sort them in alphabetical order. To do this you need a way to compare two bands by their first names. All subclasses of `NSObject` have a `compare:` method. You need to override this method in the `WBABand` class to compare bands by their names.

Finally, you also need to implement another `NSMutableArray` of first letters used. You learn why in the Implementing Sections and Index section of this chapter, but it makes sense to implement the code for it now while adding the code for the `WBABand` data storage in the following Try It Out.

TRY IT OUT Adding Band Object Storage

1. Select the WBABand.m file from the Project Navigator, and add the following code to the implementation:

```
- (NSComparisonResult)compare:(WBABand *)otherObject
{
    return [self.name compare:otherObject.name];
}
```

2. Select the WBABandsListTableViewController.h file from the Project Navigator, and add the following code:

```
@class WBABand;
@interface WBABandsListTableViewController : UITableViewController

@property (nonatomic, strong) NSMutableDictionary *bandsDictionary;
@property (nonatomic, strong) NSMutableArray *firstLettersArray;

- (void)addNewBand:(WBABand *)WBABand;
- (void)saveBandsDictionary;
- (void)loadBandsDictionary;

@end
```

3. Select the WBABandsListTableViewController.m file from the Project Navigator.

4. Add the WBABand.h file to the imports with the following code:

```
#import "WBABand.h"
```

5. Add the following code before the implementation:

```
static NSString *bandsDictionarytKey = @"BABandsDictionarytKey";
```

6. Add the following code to the implementation:

```
- (void)addNewBand:(WBABand *)bandObject
{
    NSString *bandNameFirstLetter = [bandObject.name substringToIndex:1];
    NSMutableArray *bandsForLetter = [self.bandsDictionary
objectForKey:bandNameFirstLetter];

    if(!bandsForLetter)
        bandsForLetter = [NSMutableArray array];

    [bandsForLetter addObject:bandObject];
    [bandsForLetter sortUsingSelector:@selector(compare:)];
    [self.bandsDictionary setObject:bandsForLetter forKey:bandNameFirstLetter];

    if(![self.firstLettersArray containsObject:bandNameFirstLetter])
    {
        [self.firstLettersArray addObject:bandNameFirstLetter];
        [self.firstLettersArray sortUsingSelector:@selector(compare:)];
```

```
        }

        [self saveBandsDictionary];
}

- (void)saveBandsDictionary
{
    NSData *bandsDictionaryData = [NSKeyedArchiver
archivedDataWithRootObject:self.bandsDictionary];
    [[NSUserDefaults standardUserDefaults] setObject:bandsDictionaryData
forKey:bandsDictionarytKey];
}


- (void)loadBandsDictionary
{
    NSData *bandsDictionaryData = [[NSUserDefaults standardUserDefaults]
objectForKey:bandsDictionarytKey];

    if(bandsDictionaryData)
    {
        self.bandsDictionary = [NSKeyedUnarchiver
unarchiveObjectWithData:bandsDictionaryData];
        self.firstLettersArray = [NSMutableArray
arrayWithArray:self.bandsDictionary.allKeys];
        [self.firstLettersArray sortUsingSelector:@selector(compare:)];
    }
    else
    {
        self.bandsDictionary = [NSMutableDictionary dictionary];
        self.firstLettersArray = [NSMutableArray array];
    }
}
```

7. Modify the `viewDidLoad` method with the following code:

```
- (void)viewDidLoad
{
    [super viewDidLoad];

    [self loadBandsDictionary];
}
```

How It Works

The first code you implement overrides the `compare:` method for the `WBABand` class to compare two instances using the name property. Next, you declare the `NSMutableDictionary` to hold all the bands and the `NSMutableArray` for the first letters of the band names. You also declare the methods for adding, saving, and loading the bands from `NSUserDefaults`.

In the implementation of the `addNewBand:` method, you get the first letter of the band name using the `substring` method. Next, you look in the dictionary to see if you already have a band with that first letter. If so, you would find an `NSMutableArray` for the letter. If not, you create a new one. You then add the band to the array and sort it. You then look for the first letter in the `firstLettersArray`. If it is not there, you add it in and then sort that array as well.

Finally, you add code to save and retrieve the dictionary to NSUserDefaults. The code to do this is the same as when you save a single WBABand instance, because the WBABand class implements the NSCoding protocol, as does the NSMutableDictionary.

Adding Bands

In the last chapter you built the user interface for adding a band. The scene is no longer visible, though, since adding the Navigation Controller to the project. Instead you can present it from the WBABandsListTableViewController. The user will tap a button you will place on the UINavigationItem when they want to add a new band.

First you need to make some modifications to the ViewController class, starting with renaming it following the Apple naming conventions. Xcode makes this easy using its Refactor feature.

TRY IT OUT   Renaming a Class Using Xcode Refactoring

1. Select the ViewController.h class from the Project Navigator.

2. Right click on the ViewController class name to bring up the context menu as shown in Figure 5-10 and select Refactor ⇨ Rename...

3. Rename the class **WBABandDetailsViewController** and click Preview.

4. Review the changes then click Save.

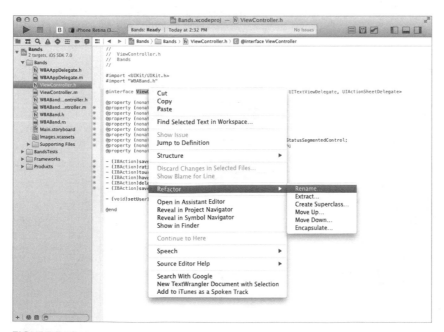

FIGURE 5-10

5. Xcode will prompt you to enable snapshots, which are a lightweight type of version control. Whether or not you want to use them is up to you.

6. Compile the project and verify there are no errors.

How It Works

The refactor feature in Xcode is very handy. Renaming a class can be tricky, since you need to find every place in the project where the name is used and change it. The Refactor feature finds all of them for you. You can see how many places are being changed in the preview before you click Save.

Snapshots in Xcode give you a way to rollback the entire project should the refactoring go wrong. The decision to use them is up to you. If you are not using any other type of source control like Git or Mercurial, then you should use them.

> **NOTE** The `AppDelegate` class should also be renamed to `WBAAppDelegate`. You won't be modifying any code in this class, but the sample code does have it renamed.

Changing the name of the class to `WBABandDetailsViewController` also changes how its scene appears in the Storyboard. With multiple scenes in a Storyboard, Interface Builder uses the dock of each to show a friendly name, as shown in Figure 5-11. This book will use these friendly names to refer to different scenes in the Storyboard for readability. For example the Band Details View Controller will be referred to as the Band Details scene.

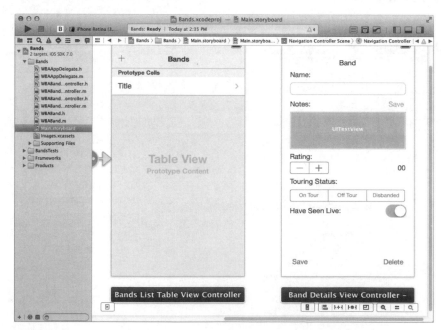

FIGURE 5-11

The next step is to clean up the code and add a Save button to the Band Details scene. There is no longer a need to store just a single WBABand instance in NSUserDefaults, so that code can be removed. You also need a way to tell the WBATableViewController that users want to save the new band they just added.

TRY IT OUT Cleaning Up the WBABandDetailsViewController

1. Select the Main.storyboard from the Project Navigator.

2. In the Band Details View Controller move the Delete UIButton to be aligned with the right guideline of the UIView.

3. Drag a new UIButton onto the view, set its text to **Save**, and align it with the Delete UIButton and the left guideline of the view, as shown in Figure 5-12.

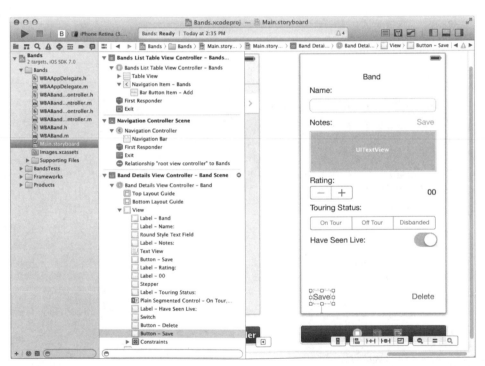

FIGURE 5-12

4. Add an auto layout constraint to anchor the Save UIButton to the bottom of the UIView.

5. Select the WBABandDetailsViewController.h file from the Project Navigator, and add the following code:

```
@interface WBABandDetailsViewController : UIViewController <UITextFieldDelegate,
UITextViewDelegate, UIActionSheetDelegate>

@property (nonatomic, strong) WBABand *bandObject;
```

```
@property (nonatomic, weak) IBOutlet UILabel *titleLabel;
@property (nonatomic, weak) IBOutlet UITextField *nameTextField;
@property (nonatomic, weak) IBOutlet UITextView *notesTextView;
@property (nonatomic, weak) IBOutlet UIButton *saveNotesButton;
@property (nonatomic, weak) IBOutlet UIStepper *ratingStepper;
@property (nonatomic, weak) IBOutlet UILabel *ratingValueLabel;
@property (nonatomic, weak) IBOutlet UISegmentedControl
*touringStatusSegmentedControl;
@property (nonatomic, weak) IBOutlet UISwitch *haveSeenLiveSwitch;
@property (nonatomic, assign) BOOL saveBand;

- (IBAction)saveNotesButtonTouched:(id)sender;
- (IBAction)ratingStepperValueChanged:(id)sender;
- (IBAction)tourStatusSegmentedControlValueChanged:(id)sender;
- (IBAction)haveSeenLiveSwitchValueChanged:(id)sender;
- (IBAction)deleteButtonTouched:(id)sender;
- (IBAction)saveButtonTouched:(id)sender;

- (void)saveBandObject;
- (void)loadBandObject;
- (void)setUserInterfaceValues;

@end
```

6. Remove the following lines from the interface:

```
- (void)saveBandObject;
- (void)loadBandObject;
```

7. Select the WBABandDetailsViewController.m file from the Project Navigator, and add the following code to the implementation:

```
- (IBAction)saveButtonTouched:(id)sender
{
    if(self.bandObject.name && self.bandObject.name.length > 0)
    {
        self.saveBand = YES;
        [self dismissViewControllerAnimated:YES completion:nil];
    }
    else
    {
        UIAlertView *noBandNameAlertView = [[UIAlertView alloc]
initWithTitle:@"Error" message:@"Please supply a name for the band"
delegate:nil cancelButtonTitle:@"OK" otherButtonTitles:nil];
        [noBandNameAlertView show];
    }
}
```

8. Modify the actionSheet:clickedButtonAtIndex: method with the following code:

```
- (void)actionSheet:(UIActionSheet *)actionSheet
clickedButtonAtIndex:(NSInteger)buttonIndex
{
    if(actionSheet.destructiveButtonIndex == buttonIndex)
    {
```

```
                self.bandObject = nil;
                self.saveBand = NO;

                [self dismissViewControllerAnimated:YES completion:nil];
        }
}
```

9. Remove the `saveBandObject` and `loadBandObject` methods along with all calls to those methods throughout the implementation.

10. Select the `Main.storyboard` from the Project Navigator.

11. Connect the Save `UIButton` to the `saveButtonTouched:` method you added to the `WBABandDetailsViewController`.

How It Works

In the Storyboard you added a Save `UIButton` to the Band Details scene. In the `WBABandDetailsViewController` class you declared a new boolean named `saveBand` as well as a new `IBAction` method named `saveButtonTouched:`,which you then connected to the Save `UIButton`. When users tap Save, this method validates that the `bandObject` has a name then sets the `saveBand` flag to TRUE before calling `dismissViewControllerAnimated:completion:`, which does nothing at this point but will dismiss the view after you complete the next Try It Out. If the `bandObject` does not have a name, the code uses a `UIAlertView` to tell users that a name is required.

The code is now ready. The last step is presenting the Band Details scene from the Bands List. In iOS apps it is customary to use a `UIBarButtonItem` with the + icon to add new data. You use `UIBarButtonItem` when adding buttons to a `UINavigationItem`. The Bands app will use this approach in the following Try It Out.

TRY IT OUT   Adding Band Objects

1. Select the `Main.storyboard` from the Project Navigator.

2. Drag a new Bar Button Item from the Object library to the left side of the `UINavigationItem`.

3. In the Attributes Inspector, change the button style to **Add**, which changes the icon to a +, as shown in Figure 5-13.

4. Select the Band Details scene.

5. In the Identity Inspector, set the Storyboard ID to **bandDetails**.

6. Select the `WBABandsListTableViewController.h` file from the Project Navigator, and add the following code:

```
@class WBABand, WBABandDetailsViewController;
@interface WBABandsListTableViewController : UITableViewController

@property (nonatomic, strong) NSMutableDictionary *bandsDictionary;
@property (nonatomic, strong) NSMutableArray *firstLettersArray;
```

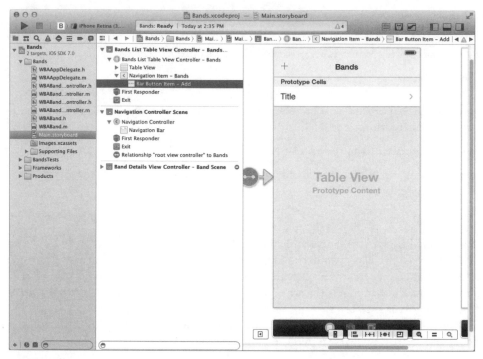

FIGURE 5-13

```objc
@property (nonatomic, strong) WBABandDetailsViewController
*bandDetailsViewController;

- (void)addNewBand:(WBABand *)bandObject;
- (void)saveBandsDictionary;
- (void)loadBandsDictionary;

- (IBAction)addBandTouched:(id)sender;

@end
```

7. Select the `WBABandsListTableViewController.m` file from the Project Navigator.

8. Add the `WBABandDetailsViewController.h` file to the imports with the following code:

```objc
#import "WBABandsListTableViewController.h"
#import "WBABand.h"
#import "WBABandDetailsViewController.h"
```

9. Add the following code to the implementation:

```objc
- (void)viewWillAppear:(BOOL)animated
{
```

```
    [super viewWillAppear:animated];

    if(self.bandDetailsViewController && self.bandDetailsViewController.saveBand)
    {
        [self addNewBand:self.bandDetailsViewController.bandObject];
        self.bandDetailsViewController = nil;
    }
}

- (IBAction)addBandTouched:(id)sender
{
    UIStoryboard *mainStoryboard = [UIStoryboard storyboardWithName:@"Main"
bundle:nil];
    self.bandDetailsViewController = (WBABandDetailsViewController *)
[mainStoryboard instantiateViewControllerWithIdentifier:@"bandDetails"];

    [self presentViewController:self.bandDetailsViewController animated:YES
completion:nil];
}
```

10. Select the `Main.storyboard` from the Project Navigator.

11. Connect the Add button to the `addBandTouched:` method you added to the `WBABandsListTableViewController`.

12. Run the app in the iPhone 4-inch simulator. When you tap the Add button, the Band Details scene displays.

How It Works

The first thing you do is add a button to the `UINavigationItem`. A `UINavigationItem` has both a left and a right button. Typically, the left button is used for navigating back up the navigation stack, but because this is the root `UIViewController`, you can use the left button for adding bands.

The main lesson is how to show and dismiss a modal view. You first set the Storyboard identity of the Band Details scene. In the `addBandTouched:` method you use an instance of the Storyboard and the scenes Storyboard ID to initialize a copy of the `WBABandDetailsViewController`. You set it as a property of the `WBABandsListTableViewController` to get to the `bandObject` after the view is dismissed. Finally, you use `presentViewController:animated:` and `dismissViewControllerAnimated:` to show and hide the band info view.

Displaying Bands

Now that you have implemented the Bands data source along with a way to add new bands, it's time to display the bands in the `UITableView`. Most of the hard work is done. You just need to modify the `UITableViewDataSource` methods to use the Bands dictionary and reload the `UITableView` data when a new band is added.

TRY IT OUT Displaying Band Names

1. Select the `WBABandsListTableViewController.m` file from the Project Navigator.

2. Modify the `numberOfSectionsInTableView:` method with the following code:

```
- (NSInteger)numberOfSectionsInTableView:(UITableView *)tableView
{
    // Return the number of sections.
    return self.bandsDictionary.count;
}
```

3. Modify the `tableView:numberOfRowsInSection:` method with the following code:

```
- (NSInteger)tableView:(UITableView *)tableView
numberOfRowsInSection:(NSInteger)section
{
    // Return the number of rows in the section.
    NSString *firstLetter = [self.firstLettersArray objectAtIndex:section];
    NSMutableArray *bandsForLetter = [self.bandsDictionary
objectForKey:firstLetter];
    return bandsForLetter.count;
}
```

4. Modify the `tableView:cellForRowAtIndexPath:` method with the following code:

```
- (UITableViewCell *)tableView:(UITableView *)tableView
cellForRowAtIndexPath:(NSIndexPath *)indexPath
{
    static NSString *CellIdentifier = @"Cell";
    UITableViewCell *cell = [tableView
dequeueReusableCellWithIdentifier:CellIdentifier forIndexPath:indexPath];

    NSString *firstLetter = [self.firstLettersArray
objectAtIndex:indexPath.section];
    NSMutableArray *bandsForLetter = [self.bandsDictionary
objectForKey:firstLetter];
    WBABand *bandObject = [bandsForLetter objectAtIndex:indexPath.row];

    // Configure the cell...
    cell.textLabel.text = bandObject.name;

    return cell;
}
```

5. Modify the `viewWillAppear:` method with the following code:

```
- (void)viewWillAppear:(BOOL)animated
{
    [super viewWillAppear:animated];

    if(self.bandDetailsViewController)
    {
        if(self.bandDetailsViewController.saveBand)
```

```
        {
            [self addNewBand:self.bandDetailsViewController.bandObject];
            [self.tableView reloadData];
        }
        self.bandDetailsViewController = nil;
    }
}
```

FIGURE 5-14

6. Run the app in the iPhone 4-inch simulator. When you add a new band, it displays in the table, as shown in Figure 5-14.

How It Works

The UITableViewDataSource methods use an NSIndexPath to refer to rows in the table. An NSIndexPath has a section and row number. NSMutableDictionary is a key/value collection, not a sorted set, so it doesn't have an objectAtIndex: method you can use with an NSIndexPath. Because of this you need to use the firstLetterArray to get the correct key to use with the Bands dictionary. It may seem like more work than it's worth, but the firstLetterArray is also used to implement section headers and the index, so it's worth the effort.

In the code you modify the numberOfSectionsInTableView: to return the number of items in the Bands dictionary. In the tableView:numberOfRows InSection: method, you use the section number to get the correct key from the firstLettersArray, then use that key to get the bands array for that key, and use its count for the number of rows. The tab leView:cellForRowAtIndexPath: is modified to also use the section to get the correct key from the firstLettersArray. You then use the row of the index path to get the correct WBABand instance to configure the cell with.

Finally, you add a viewWillAppear: method to the WBATableViewController. This method is part of the UIViewControllerDelegate and gets called when the view is about to appear. In the Bands app it is called when the app first starts but also after the WBABandDetailsViewController is dismissed. To know which occurred, you look at the bandDetailsViewController property you set prior to presenting the WBABandDetailsViewController. If it's set, you check if the user tapped Save by looking at the saveBand property. If true, you save the new bandObject and reload the tableView. Finally, you set the bandDetailsViewController to nil, so the save code is not triggered twice by accident.

IMPLEMENTING SECTIONS AND INDEX

As users of the Bands app add more and more bands, it becomes harder to find the band they want in the UITableView. To help them out you've already alphabetically ordered the bands. Adding sections and the section index can help as well. The sections break up the bands visually while the index gives the user a shortcut to jump to the different sections.

Adding Section Headers

Section headers are simple to add because of the data storage architecture you implemented using both the dictionary and the first letters array. There is a single method in the `UITableViewDataSource` protocol, which returns the section header for the section.

TRY IT OUT Displaying First Letter Section Headers

1. Select the `WBABandsListTableViewController.m` file from the Project Navigator.

2. Add the following code to the implementation:

```
- (NSString *)tableView:(UITableView *)tableView
titleForHeaderInSection:(NSInteger)section
{
    return [self.firstLettersArray objectAtIndex:section];
}
```

3. Run the app in the iPhone 4-inch simulator. You see section headers corresponding to the first letters of the band names, as shown in Figure 5-15.

How It Works

As the `UITableView` is loaded and scrolled, it calls its data source and looks for header titles for each section using the `tableView:titleForHeaderInSection:` method. Your code simply returns the letter in the `firstLettersArray` at the index matching the section number.

FIGURE 5-15

Showing the Section Index

The section index is slightly more complicated because you need to supply both the titles for the index and the section that corresponds with the title. You need to implement two more methods of the `UITableViewDataSource` to accomplish this.

TRY IT OUT Displaying First Letter Section Index

1. Select the `WBABandsListTableViewController.m` file from the Project Navigator.

2. Add the following code to the implementation:

```
- (NSArray *)sectionIndexTitlesForTableView:(UITableView *)tableView
{
    return self.firstLettersArray;
}

- (int)tableView:(UITableView *)tableView sectionForSectionIndexTitle:
```

```
(NSString *)title atIndex:(NSInteger)index
{
    return [self.firstLettersArray indexOfObject:title];
}
```

3. Run the app in the iPhone 4-inch simulator. You see the section index on the right side of the UITableView, as shown in Figure 5-16.

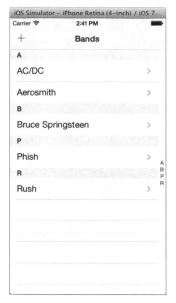

FIGURE 5-16

How It Works

The first method you implement is sectionIndexTitlesForTableView. This method tells the UITableView what strings to put in the index. The tableView:sectionForSectionIndexTitle: method tells the UITableView what section to jump to based on the title in the index that was touched.

EDITING TABLE DATA

UITableView also give you a way to edit the underlying data source. You can control which rows are editable along with the type of editing that can be done. The most used is deleting data, but you could also give your user a way to reorder the data in the data model. Because the Band app displays the band names alphabetically, it doesn't make sense to allow the user to move cells around.

Deleting a band does make sense, though. To do this you need to enable edit mode for both the table and each individual row.

Enabling Edit Mode

`UITableView` has an edit mode built in. `UITableViewController` also has a built-in button you can add to the `UINavigationItem` to toggle into edit mode named `editButtonItem`. Since the `WBABandsListTableViewController` is a subclass of the `UITableViewController`, you can access the `editButtonItem` from `self`.

When a table goes into edit mode, it asks its delegate which rows are editable. You can control which rows are editable by implementing the `tableView:canEditRowAtIndexPath:` method. If this method is not implemented, the table will not allow any of the rows to be editable.

Implementing the Allow Edit Method

1. Select the `WBABandsListTableViewController.m` file from the Project Navigator.

2. Add the following code to the `viewDidLoad` method:

```
- (void)viewDidLoad
{
    [super viewDidLoad];

    [self loadBandsDictionary];

    self.navigationItem.rightBarButtonItem = self.editButtonItem;
}
```

3. Add the following method to the implementation:

```
- (BOOL)tableView:(UITableView *)tableView canEditRowAtIndexPath:
(NSIndexPath *)indexPath
{
    return YES;
}
```

4. Run the app in the iPhone 4-inch simulator. When you tap the Edit button, you see the delete option in each cell next to the band name, as shown in Figure 5-17.

FIGURE 5-17

How It Works

When the view is loaded, the code you add sets the right button of the `UINavigationItem` to the `editButtonItem` built into the `UITableViewController`. The `tableView:canEditRowAtIndexPath:` always returns YES, meaning that all rows in the `UITableView` are editable.

Deleting Cells and Data

You probably noticed that when the UITableView goes into edit mode and you attempt to delete a row, nothing happens. This is because you need to implement one last method of the UITableViewDelegate, the tableView:commitEditingStyle:forRowAtIndexPath: method.

TRY IT OUT Implementing the Commit Edit Method

1. Select the WBABandsListTableViewController.h file from the Project Navigator, and add the following code to the interface:

```
@class WBABand, WBABandDetailsViewController;
@interface WBABandsListTableViewController : UITableViewController

@property (nonatomic, strong) NSMutableDictionary *bandsDictionary;
@property (nonatomic, strong) NSMutableArray *firstLettersArray;
@property (nonatomic, strong) WBABandDetailsViewController
*bandDetailsViewController;

- (void)addNewBand:(WBABand *)bandObject;
- (void)saveBandsDictionary;
- (void)loadBandsDictionary;
- (void)deleteBandAtIndexPath:(NSIndexPath *)indexPath;

- (IBAction)addBandTouched:(id)sender;

@end
```

2. Select the WBABandsListTableViewController.m file from the Project Navigator, and add the following methods to the implementation:

```
- (void)tableView:(UITableView *)tableView
commitEditingStyle:(UITableViewCellEditingStyle)editingStyle
forRowAtIndexPath:(NSIndexPath *)indexPath
{
    if (editingStyle == UITableViewCellEditingStyleDelete)
    {
        [self deleteBandAtIndexPath:indexPath];
    }
}

- (void)deleteBandAtIndexPath:(NSIndexPath *)indexPath
{
    NSString *sectionHeader = [self.firstLettersArray
objectAtIndex:indexPath.section];
    NSMutableArray *bandsForLetter = [self.bandsDictionary
objectForKey:sectionHeader];
    [bandsForLetter removeObjectAtIndex:indexPath.row];

    if(bandsForLetter.count == 0)
    {
        [self.firstLettersArray removeObject:sectionHeader];
        [self.bandsDictionary removeObjectForKey:sectionHeader];
        [self.tableView deleteSections:
```

```
[NSIndexSet indexSetWithIndex:indexPath.section]
withRowAnimation:UITableViewRowAnimationFade];
    }
    else
    {
        [self.bandsDictionary setObject:bandsForLetter forKey:sectionHeader];
        [self.tableView deleteRowsAtIndexPaths:@[indexPath]
withRowAnimation:UITableViewRowAnimationFade];
    }

    [self saveBandsDictionary];
}
```

How It Works

In the implementation you first look to see if the editing style is a delete. If it is you call the
`deleteBandAtIndexPath:` method. It uses the `indexPath` to again get the key to the `bandsForLetter`
array. It then removes the `WBABand` instance by calling the `removeObjectAtIndex:` method using the
row of the `indextPath`. Next, you check to see if there are any bands left for the first letter. If there
are no more bands, you delete the entire section from the table. If there are, you delete only the row in
the section.

> **WARNING** It is very important to delete the section and not just the row if
> there are no more bands for that letter. Failing to do so leaves a section in the
> `UITableView` with no rows. This will cause the app to crash. Also be sure to
> make all the changes to the data source prior to deleting the section or the
> row. The app will crash in that situation as well.

Modifying Data

Users of the Bands app will want to modify band info along with adding and deleting it. The best
way to do this is to show the Band Details scene when the user taps the band name in
the `UITableView`. You can implement a segue in the Storyboard to do this.

A *segue* is a way of transitioning from one view to the next. Modal and push segues are the two
most common. A *modal segue* presents the view over the parent view, the same as using
`presentViewController:animated:completion:`, as you did with the Add button. You could have
used a segue for this, but learning how to present and dismiss views in code is a valuable lesson.

A *push segue* can be used with a `UINavigationController`. The view slides in from the right
and adds a `UINavigationItem` to the top of the view with a back button, which enables the user
to return to the parent `UIViewController`. It does this by using a navigation stack. As you segue
from one `UIViewController` to the next, the `UIViewControllers` get pushed onto the navigation stack. The back button pops each `UIViewController` off until you get back to the root
`UIViewController`. This makes it easy for users to know where they are in the app. Storyboards
make it easy for you as the developer to visualize how the user can navigate through the app.

TRY IT OUT   Implementing a Push Segue

1. Select the Main.storyboard from the Project Navigator.

2. In the Band Details scene, move all the subviews down 20 pixels except for the Save and Delete buttons.

3. Control-drag from the prototype cell to the Band Details scene, and select Push from the segue pop-up menu that appears. The segue is represented by an arrow from the Bands List scene to the Band Details scene. The Band Details scene also now has a UINavigationItem.

4. Select the UINavigationItem and set its title to **Band** in the Attributes Inspector.

5. Select the WBABandsListTableViewController.h file from the Project Navigator, and add the following code to the interface:

```
@class WBABand, WBABandDetailsViewController;
@interface WBABandsListTableViewController : UITableViewController

@property (nonatomic, strong) NSMutableDictionary *bandsDictionary;
@property (nonatomic, strong) NSMutableArray *firstLettersArray;
@property (nonatomic, strong) WBABandDetailsViewController
*bandDetailsViewController;

- (void)addNewBand:(WBABand *)bandObject;
- (void)saveBandsDictionary;
- (void)loadBandsDictionary;
- (void)deleteBandAtIndexPath:(NSIndexPath *)indexPath;
- (void)updateBandObject:(WBABand *)bandObject
atIndexPath:(NSIndexPath *)indexPath;

- (IBAction)addBandTouched:(id)sender;

@end
```

6. Select the WBABandsListTableViewController.m file from the Project Navigator.

7. Add the following code to the viewDidLoad method:

```
- (void)viewDidLoad
{
    [super viewDidLoad];

    [self loadBandsDictionary];

    self.navigationItem.rightBarButtonItem = self.editButtonItem;
    self.clearsSelectionOnViewWillAppear = NO;
}
```

8. Modify the viewWillAppear: method with the following code:

```
- (void)viewWillAppear:(BOOL)animated
{
    [super viewWillAppear:animated];

    if(self.bandDetailsViewController)
```

```
    {
        NSIndexPath *selectedIndexPath = [self.tableView indexPathForSelectedRow];

        if(self.bandDetailsViewController.saveBand)
        {
            if(selectedIndexPath)
            {
                [self updateBandObject:self.bandDetailsViewController.bandObject
atIndexPath:selectedIndexPath];
                [self.tableView deselectRowAtIndexPath:selectedIndexPath
animated:YES];
            }
            else
                [self addNewBand:self.bandDetailsViewController.bandObject];
            [self.tableView reloadData];
        }
        else if (selectedIndexPath)
        {
            [self deleteBandAtIndexPath:selectedIndexPath];
        }

        self.bandDetailsViewController = nil;
    }
}
```

9. Add the following methods to the implementation:

```
- (void)updateBandObject:(WBABand *)bandObject
atIndexPath:(NSIndexPath *)indexPath
{
    NSIndexPath *selectedIndexPath = [self.tableView indexPathForSelectedRow];
    NSString *sectionHeader = [self.firstLettersArray
objectAtIndex:selectedIndexPath.section];
    NSMutableArray *bandsForSection = [self.bandsDictionary
objectForKey:sectionHeader];
    [bandsForSection removeObjectAtIndex:indexPath.row];
    [bandsForSection addObject:bandObject];
    [bandsForSection sortUsingSelector:@selector(compare:)];
    [self.bandsDictionary setObject:bandsForSection forKey:sectionHeader];
    [self saveBandsDictionary];
}


- (void)prepareForSegue:(UIStoryboardSegue *)segue sender:(id)sender
{
    NSIndexPath *selectedIndexPath = [self.tableView indexPathForSelectedRow];
    NSString *sectionHeader = [self.firstLettersArray
objectAtIndex:selectedIndexPath.section];
    NSMutableArray *bandsForSection = [self.bandsDictionary
objectForKey:sectionHeader];
    WBABand *bandObject = [bandsForSection objectAtIndex:selectedIndexPath.row];
    self.bandDetailsViewController = segue.destinationViewController;
    self.bandDetailsViewController.bandObject = bandObject;
    self.bandDetailsViewController.saveBand = YES;
}
```

10. Select the WBABandDetailsViewController.m file from the Project Navigator.

11. Modify the `saveButtonTouched:` method with the following code:

```
- (IBAction)saveButtonTouched:(id)sender
{
    if(!self.bandObject.name || self.bandObject.name.length == 0)
    {
        UIAlertView *noBandNameAlertView = [[UIAlertView alloc]
initWithTitle:@"Error" message:@"Please supply a name for the band"
delegate:nil cancelButtonTitle:@"OK" otherButtonTitles:nil];
        [noBandNameAlertView show];
    }
    else
    {
        self.saveBand = YES;

        if(self.navigationController)
            [self.navigationController popViewControllerAnimated:YES];
        else
            [self dismissViewControllerAnimated:YES completion:nil];
    }
}
```

12. Modify the `actionSheet:clickedButtonAtIndex:` method with the following code:

```
- (void)actionSheet:(UIActionSheet *)actionSheet
clickedButtonAtIndex:(NSInteger)buttonIndex
{
    if(actionSheet.destructiveButtonIndex == buttonIndex)
    {
        self.bandObject = nil;
        self.saveBand = NO;

        if(self.navigationController)
            [self.navigationController popViewControllerAnimated:YES];
        else
            [self dismissViewControllerAnimated:YES completion:nil];
    }
}
```

13. Run the app in the iPhone 4-inch simulator. You can now see the accessoryView for each row is set to a chevron. When a row is selected, you can segue to the Band Details scene with all the UI objects set according to the `bandObject`.

How It Works

By Control-dragging from the prototype cell to the Band Details scene, you create a segue. When the app runs, tapping a cell starts the segue, which first calls the `prepareForSegue:sender:` method. In this method you get the `NSIndexPath` of the selected row in the `tableView` and set the `bandObject` of the `WBABandDetailsViewController` with the `bandObject` in the data source.

In the `WBABandDetailsViewController`, you change how it is dismissed based on if it has a `UINavigationController`. If it does, you call `popViewControllerAnimated:` to return back to the `WBABandsListViewController`. When it appears, it looks to see if it has a row selected. If it does, it knows to either update a band if `saveBand` is true or delete the band if not.

SUMMARY

UITableViews are powerful. They can show a lot of data in a scrollable view and enable the user to edit that data. Apple has given you many tools to do these actions. You learned how to add a UITableView to a Storyboard and set up its UITableViewController identity class, UITableViewDataSource, and UITableViewDelegate. You modified the Bands app to give it the ability to store many WBABand instances in the data model and display them in the new Bands List scene. You also learned how to use the UINavigationItem of a UINavigationController to add data to the Bands app, enable edit mode to delete the data, and to segue from the Bands List scene to the Band Details scene. With the UITableView as the main scene of the app that segues to a details scene, you have transitioned the Bands app from a Single View Application to a Master-Details application.

EXERCISES

1. What is the difference between the UITableViewDataSource protocol and the UITableViewDelegate protocol?

2. What are the four built-in UITableViewCell styles?

3. Modify the UITableViewCell to a right detail style, and show the band rating as the detailTextLabel.

4. What method can you use to show a UIViewController that animates up from the bottom of the bottom of the screen?

5. What is the UIKit object that is added to the top of each UIView when using a UINavigationController?

6. What type of segue is used to transition between the Bands List scene and the Band Details scene?

➤ WHAT YOU LEARNED IN THIS CHAPTER

TOPIC	KEY CONCEPTS
UITableView	The UITableView is one of the most important views in iOS development. It's a scrollable list of cells that can show all of the objects in your data model. The Bands app uses one to show all of the bands the user has added to the app.
UITableViewCell	Each row in a UITableView is represented by a UITableView Cell. They can have a custom design you create, or you can use one of the standard cell styles provided by Apple.
UITableViewDataSource	The UITableView gets the data from the data model via its controller using the UITableViewDataSource protocol. You use this to tell the table how many sections it has and how many rows are in each section, as well as create the actual UITableViewCells to display.
UITableViewDelegate	Users can edit the data model of an application from within a UITableView. When in edit mode users can move or delete rows. When this happens the table will communicate with its controller using the UITableViewDelegate protocol.
UINavigationController	The UINavigationController allows your application to push or pop new views onto the navigation stack using segues. When you use it with a UITableView, you can transition from the list of data model objects to the details of a single object.

6

Integrating the Camera and Photo Library in iOS Apps

WHAT YOU LEARN IN THIS CHAPTER:

➤ Taking pictures with the camera

➤ Importing pictures from the Photo Library

➤ Using gesture recognizers for advanced user interactions

WROX.COM CODE DOWNLOADS FOR THIS CHAPTER

You can find the wrox.com code downloads for this chapter at www.wrox.com/go/begios programming on the Download Code tab. The code is in the chapter 06 download and individually named according to the names throughout the chapter.

Even before the iPhone came onto the market in 2007, camera phones were already gaining in popularity. Digital cameras had been around for a while and were far superior to any camera phone on the market, so many people owned both. This continued even after the release of the first iPhone, iPhone 3G, and iPhone 3GS. It began to change with improvements to the built-in camera in the iPhone 4. Photo-sharing services started releasing data showing that the most popular camera used to take pictures was the iPhone 4. Today, the camera on a smartphone has become one of the top selling points, with manufacturers building far superior cameras than digital cameras produced as recently as a few years ago.

Pictures can also add to the usability of an app. The Contacts app from Apple is a good example of this. When you add contacts, you have the option to assign a picture to them. When you receive a phone call from contacts, their picture displays on the screen. In the old days of landlines and caller ID, you needed to have the phone number of a person memorized to know who was calling. That eventually evolved to showing the name of the person or business the number was registered to, but that still involved reading. Glancing at your phone and seeing the face of the person who is calling can speed up recognition.

The Bands app adopts this idea by adding an optional picture to each band. Users can choose a picture from the photo library or take a picture with the camera. To implement this, you learn not only how to use the camera, but also how to add a UIImageView to the user interface and create gesture recognizers so that the user can interact with it.

ADDING AN IMAGE VIEW AND GESTURE RECOGNIZER

Before you add the code to choose or take pictures, first you need to add a place to display the image in the Band Details scene and give users a way to interact with it to set it. In iOS, images display using a UIImageView. As its name implies, a UIImageView is a subclass of UIView that displays an image. In code a UIImage represents the image. A UIImage can be a JPEG, a bitmap, a TIFF, an icon, a Windows cursor, or a PNG. Though not officially documented, the PNG format is the preferred format because it is a lossless format. This makes the image appear vivid on retina display devices.

Images and pictures come in an endless array of sizes. UIViews have a mode attribute that dictates how their contents display. If the content of the UIView is larger than the UIView, the system uses the mode to determine how to adjust the aspect ratio of the content. Because UIImageView is a subclass of UIView, it uses this mode to determine how to resize the image. Following are the modes:

➤ **Scale to Fill** — Setting the mode to Scale to Fill alters the aspect ratio of the image to fill the entire UIImageView. This can result in images looking distorted.

➤ **Aspect Fit** — The Aspect Fit mode keeps the same aspect ratios of the original image but resizes it so the entire image displays in the UIImageView. This can result in parts of the UIImageView being empty.

➤ **Aspect Fill** — The Aspect Fill mode also resizes the image but ensures there is no empty space. This can result in parts of the image being outside the bounds of the UIImageView and therefore not shown.

➤ **Center** — Center mode does not resize the image and simply centers the image in the UIImageView. With pictures taken from the camera, this can result in large portions of the picture not being shown.

For the Bands app you can use the Aspect Fit mode so that the entire picture is always visible.

The UIView class also has a userInteractionEnabled property that tells the system if the user can interact with it through touches. A UIView that has this property set to false never recognize touches. For example, a UIButton with an IBAction connected to it can never trigger the action if its userInteractionEnabled property is false. By default, a UIImageView has this attribute set to false.

Enabling User Interactions with a UIImageView

The Bands app can have an optional picture the user can set for each band. The first step in adding this functionality is to add a UIImageView to the Band Details scene. Because a UIImageView does not allow user interaction by default, you also need to set its userInteractionEnabled property to true. This is a simple check box in Interface Builder, as you see in the following Try It Out.

TRY IT OUT Adding an Image View

1. Select the `Main.storyboard` from the Project Navigator.

2. In the Band Details scene, move the Name `UILabel` to the right 70 pixels to make room for the `UIImageView`.

3. Resize the Name `UITextField` to be 210 pixels and aligned with the Name `UILabel` to finish making room for the `UIImageView`.

4. Drag a new Image View from the Object library onto the view, and set its size to be 64 pixels by 64 pixels.

5. Align it with the left guideline of the `UIView` and the top of the Name `UILabel`, and set its background color to light gray.

6. Set the Mode of the `UIImageView` to Aspect Fit in the Attributes Inspector.

7. Check the Allow User Interaction box in the Attributes Inspector.

8. Drag a new `UILabel` onto the view, and set its boundaries to be the same as the `UIImageView`.

9. In the Attributes Inspector, change its text to **Add Photo**, its alignment to Center using the center alignment button, and the number of lines to 2, as shown in Figure 6-1.

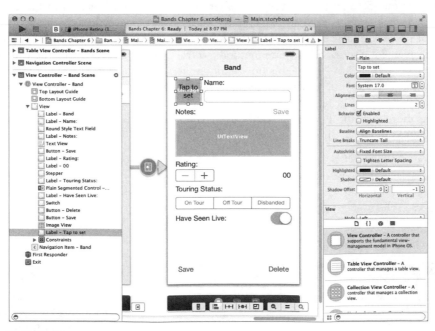

FIGURE 6-1

10. Select the `WBABandDetailsViewController.h` file from the Project Navigator, and add `IBOutlet` properties for the `UIImageView` and `UILabel` using the following code:

```
@property (nonatomic, assign) IBOutlet UIImageView *bandImageView;
@property (nonatomic, assign) IBOutlet UILabel *addPhotoLabel;
```

11. Open the Storyboard again and connect the `bandImageView` and `addPhotoLabel` properties in the `WBABandDetailsViewController` to the `UIImageView` and `UILabel`.

How It Works

What you did was make room for and then add the `UIImageView` you can use to not only display the picture for the band but also to set it. You also set its mode to Aspect Fit, so the entire picture displays. When checked, the User Interaction Allowed property in the Attributes Inspector sets the `enable UserInteraction` property of the `UIImageView` to true. This allows the `UIImageView` to accept touches from users. The default background for a `UIImageView` whose `image` property is not set is transparent. You change it to light gray so that the users know there is a user interface object there. Finally, you added a `UILabel` over the top of the `UIImageView`. The text for the label, "Add Photo," lets the users know it's a `UIImageView` and that they can interact with it. The text is the same as what users see in the Contacts app. Using the same text enables the users to easily recognize the purpose of that part of the user interface.

Learning About Gesture Recognizers

In previous chapters, you used `IBActions` to respond when the user taps various user interface objects. Not all user interface objects allow being connected to `IBActions`, even though all subviews of `UIView` can accept touches if their `userInteractionEnable` property is set to true. In the past, you would need to implement a series of delegate methods to track which subview is being touched and how many touches it received (which means how many fingers the user has touching the phone). The number of taps was given to you, so detecting that a subview was tapped twice with two fingers was relatively easy to implement but required a lot of code. Detecting if users swiped their finger across a subview was more difficult. First, you would need to do all the math to detect that a swipe had taken place as well as in which direction it went.

With the introduction of iPhoneOS 3.2, Apple added the `UIGestureRecognizer` classes to make these user interactions easier to implement. There are seven `UIGestureRecognizer` classes you can use, as listed in Table 6-1. You can add as many gesture recognizers to a single `UIView` as you want; though you need to keep the user experience in mind when doing so.

TABLE 6-1: Types of Gesture Recognizers

GESTURE RECOGNIZER	DESCRIPTION
`UITapGestureRecognizer`	Detects when the user taps a `UIView`. You can set how many touches and taps are required for the gesture to be recognized. For example, in the Maps app you can double-tap the map with one finger to zoom in. You can also double-tap the map with two fingers to zoom out.

`UIPinchGestureRecognizer`	Detects when the user pinches two fingers together or spreads them apart. This is typically used for zooming in or out. In the Maps app you can pinch two fingers together to zoom out or you can spread two fingers apart to zoom in.
`UIRotateGestureRecognizer`	Detects when the user uses two fingers moving in a circular motion. In the Maps app if you use two fingers and rotate them, the map rotates.
`UISwipeGestureRecognizer`	Detects when the user moves any number of touches across the view in a particular direction. The best example of this is when you unlock an iOS device by swiping the screen from left to right.
`UIPanGestureRecognizer`	Detects when the user drags any number of fingers around a view. In the Maps app you can pan around the map by touching the screen and dragging your finger.
`UIScreenEdgePanGestureRecognizer`	Detects when the user begins a dragging gesture close to the edge of the screen. In iOS 7 you use this gesture from the bottom of the screen to bring up the Control Center.
`UILongPressGestureRecognizer`	Detects when the user touches one or more fingers on the view and then holds the position for a set amount of time. An example of this is holding a finger down in the Maps app to add a pin to the map.

Some gesture recognizers have additional properties you can set (refer to Table 6-1). For example, the tap gesture can be set to recognize a minimum number of times the user taps the screen and also the minimum number of fingers doing the tapping. These default to one each, but you can adjust that using the `numberOfTapsRequired` and `numberOfTouchesRequired` properties. If the `numberOfTapsRequired` is two and the `numberOfTouchesRequired` is three, the user would need to double-tap the screen using three fingers. The swipe gesture has a direction property you need to set so that the system knows in which direction the user must swipe for the gesture to be recognized.

If a `UIView` has another `UIView` that overlaps it but does not recognize a particular gesture, the gesture is passed down to the `UIView` underneath it. In the following Try It Out you add both a `UITapGestureRecognizer` and a `UISwipeGestureRecognizer` to the `UIImageView` for the band picture. Those gestures can be recognized even though there is a `UILabel` on top of the `UIImageView`.

TRY IT OUT Implementing Gesture Recognizers

1. Select the `WBABandDetailsViewController.h` file from the Project Navigator, and add the following method declarations to the interface:

```
- (void)bandImageViewTapDetected;
- (void)bandImageViewSwipeDetected;
```

2. Select the `WBABandDetailsViewController.m` file from the Project Navigator, and add the following code to the implementation:

```
- (void)bandImageViewTapDetected
{
    NSLog(@"band image tap detected");
}

- (void)bandImageViewSwipeDetected
{
    NSLog(@"band image swipe detected");
}
```

3. Add the following code to the `viewDidLoad` method:

```
- (void)viewDidLoad
{
    [super viewDidLoad];
    // Do any additional setup after loading the view, typically from a nib.

    NSLog(@"titleLabel.text = %@", self.titleLabel.text);

    if(!self.bandObject)
        self.bandObject = [[WBABand alloc] init];


    [self setUserInterfaceValues];

    UITapGestureRecognizer *bandImageViewTapGestureRecognizer =
[[UITapGestureRecognizer alloc] initWithTarget:self
action:@selector(bandImageViewTapDetected)];
    bandImageViewTapGestureRecognizer.numberOfTapsRequired = 1;
    bandImageViewTapGestureRecognizer.numberOfTouchesRequired = 1;
    [self.bandImageView addGestureRecognizer:bandImageViewTapGestureRecognizer];

    UISwipeGestureRecognizer *bandImageViewSwipeGestureRecognizer =
[[UISwipeGestureRecognizer alloc] initWithTarget:self
action:@selector(bandImageViewSwipeDetected)];
    bandImageViewSwipeGestureRecognizer.direction =
UISwipeGestureRecognizerDirectionRight;
    [self.bandImageView addGestureRecognizer:bandImageViewSwipeGestureRecognizer];
}
```

How It Works

You first declared two methods to the interface of the `WBABandDetailsViewController` named `bandImageViewTapDetected` and `bandImageViewSwipeDetected`. In their implementation you simply log a message to the debug console. This is just to verify that they are being called when the `UIImageView` is either tapped or swiped.

The main lesson of this Try It Out was creating the two `UIGestureRecognizers`. The first was the `UITapGestureRecognizer`. When you create it you use the `initWithTarget:action:` method. For the target you pass in `self` referring to the `WBABandDetailsViewController`. For the action you use the `@selector` followed by the `bandImageViewTapDetected` method name. This code tells the system that when the `UITapGestureRecognizer` is triggered, it should call the `bandImageViewTapDetected` method found in the `WBABandDetailsViewController`. This is the code equivalent of connecting an `IBAction` to a `UIKit` object. You then set the `numberOfTapsRequired` property and the `numberOfTouchesRequired` property both to 1. This tells the system to trigger the gesture when one finger taps once on the `UIView` to which the gesture is assigned. You assign the `bandImageViewTapGestureRecognizer` to the `bandImageView` by calling the `addGestureRecognizer:` method.

Next you declared a new `UISwipeGestureRecognizer` using the same `initWithTarget:action:` method but using the `bandImageViewSwipeDetected` method for the `@selector`. `UISwipeGestureRecognizer` requires setting its `direction` property, which you do using the `UISwipeGestureRecognizerDirectionRight` constant. You use the `addGestureRecognizer` method of the `bandImageView` again to add the gesture to the `UIImageView`. When users swipe from left to right across the `bandImageView`, the `bandImageViewSwipeDetected` method is called.

SELECTING A PICTURE FROM THE PHOTO LIBRARY

The Bands app gives users two ways to set the picture for a band. They can either choose a picture they have saved in the photo library or use the camera to take a picture. The photo library in the iOS simulator is empty by default. Before you start adding code to pick a photo, you need to add a photo to the library. The following Try It Out walks you through doing this in the iOS simulator.

> **NOTE** Not all iOS devices have a camera. The iPhone has always had a camera, but early versions of the iPad and iPod touch did not. The simulator also does not support a camera. You can also restrict access to the camera using parental controls. All iOS devices do have a photo library to which the user can save pictures from e-mails and web pages.

TRY IT OUT Save an Image from Safari to the Photo Library in the iPhone Simulator

1. From the Xcode menu select Xcode ➪ Open Developer Tool ➪ iOS Simulator.
2. Start Safari in the simulator.
3. From the favorites menu, select ESPN or surf to any web page that has a picture on it.
4. After the picture loads, long-press the picture to bring up the action sheet.
5. Select Save Image from the action sheet.
6. Go back to the home screen by selecting Hardware ➪ Home from the menu.
7. Open the Photos app. You'll see the picture you just saved.

How It Works

iOS allows you to save pictures from other apps into your photo library. In this Try It Out you saved a picture from Mobile Safari using a `UILongPressGestureRecognizer`. You can also save pictures you receive in an e-mail or text message the same way. Third party apps can also implement a way to save pictures they display into the photo library. You will learn how to do this in Chapter 7, "Integrating Social Media."

Learning About UIImagePickerController

You use `UIImagePickerController` to interact with both the camera and the photo library. This is the standard controller all apps use, so the user experience is the same no matter which app the user has open. The controller is self-contained but uses the `UIImagePickerControllerDelegate` to let your code know what image the user has selected or if the user canceled the action. Your app is responsible only for presenting and dismissing the controller.

For added security, Apple has accessibility controls around the photo library. This means users must explicitly grant your app access to their photo library before you can import images from it. When your app first presents the image picker and tries to access the library, users will be prompted to allow access, as shown in Figure 6-2.

If they deny access they will have no images to choose from. Instead users need to simply cancel the image picker. The next time the image picker is presented, it enables users to know that they have denied access for this app, as shown in Figure 6-3.

FIGURE 6-2

Determining Device Capabilities

Before presenting the image picker, you need to set its source type. The source type can be the camera, photo library, or saved photos album represented by the `UIImagePickerControllerSourceTypeCamera`, `UIImagePickerControllerSourceTypePhotoLibrary`, and the `UIImagePickerControllerSourceTypeSavedPhotoAlbum` enumeration values. If you try to present the image picker with a source type that is not supported by the device, your app will crash. Apple will test these scenarios when you submit your app for approval. Any crash will cause your app to be rejected.

To determine if a source type is available, you use the `isSourceTypeAvailable:` static method of the `UIImagePickerController` passing in the enumeration for the source type you would like to check. If the method returns true, you can present the controller with that source type. If it returns false you must do something different to prevent your app from crashing.

FIGURE 6-3

Allowing Picture Editing

A useful feature of the `UIImagePickerController` is that it enables users to move and scale the picture they selected before having it returned to your code. It's a simple boolean you can set before presenting the picker, but it also means that you don't have to implement your own editing interface. When an image is picked, the `imagePickerController:didFinishPickingMediaWithInfo:` method of the `UIImagePickerControllerDelegate` protocol is called. It has a dictionary that contains both the original image and the edited image, and information about what was edited. Table 6-2 lists the dictionary keys returned in the info dictionary.

TABLE 6-2: Media Info Dictionary Keys

INFO DICTIONARY KEY	DESCRIPTION
`UIImagePickerControllerMediaType`	The type of media picked. Its value is an `NSString` that will be either the `kUTTypeImage` or `kUTTypeMovie` constants.
`UIImagePickerControllerOriginalImage`	A `UIImage` of the original image selected.
`UIImagePickerControllerEditedImage`	A `UIImage` of the edited image.
`UIImagePickerControllerCropRect`	An `NSValue` containing a `CGRect` that represents the rectangle used when editing and cropping the original image.
`UIImagePickerControllerMediaURL`	An `NSURL` of the file system URL of the movie selected when the media type is `kUTTypeMovie`.
`UIImagePickerControllerReferenceURL`	An `NSURL` of the file system URL of the original image or movie.
`UIImagePickerControllerMediaMetadata`	An `NSDictionary` with the meta data associated with a new picture taken by the camera. This can be used to save the image to the photo library.

The following Try It Out demonstrates how this works by presenting the `UIImagePickerController` for the photo library.

TRY IT OUT   Displaying the Photo Library Image Picker

1. Select the `WBABandDetailsViewController.h` file from the Project Navigator.

2. Add the `UIImagePickerControllerDelegate` and `UINavigationControllerDelegate` protocols to the interface using the following code:

```
@interface WBABandDetailsViewController : UIViewController <UITextFieldDelegate,
UITextViewDelegate, UIActionSheetDelegate,
UIImagePickerControllerDelegate, UINavigationControllerDelegate>
```

3. Add the following method declaration to the interface:

```
- (void)presentPhotoLibraryImagePicker;
```

4. Select the WBABandDetailsViewController.m file from the Project Navigator.

5. Add the following method to the implementation:

```
- (void)presentPhotoLibraryImagePicker
{
    UIImagePickerController *imagePickerController =
[[UIImagePickerController alloc] init];
    imagePickerController.sourceType =
UIImagePickerControllerSourceTypePhotoLibrary;
    imagePickerController.delegate = self;
    imagePickerController.allowsEditing = YES;
    [self presentViewController:imagePickerController animated:YES completion:nil];
}
```

6. Add the following UIImagePickerControllerDelegate methods to the implementation:

```
- (void)imagePickerController:(UIImagePickerController *)picker
didFinishPickingMediaWithInfo:(NSDictionary *)info
{
    UIImage *selectedImage =
[info objectForKey:UIImagePickerControllerEditedImage];
    if(selectedImage == NULL)
        selectedImage = [info objectForKey:UIImagePickerControllerOriginalImage];

    self.bandImageView.image = selectedImage;
    self.addPhotoLabel.hidden = YES;

    [picker dismissViewControllerAnimated:YES completion:nil];
}

- (void)imagePickerControllerDidCancel:(UIImagePickerController *)picker
{
    [picker dismissViewControllerAnimated:YES completion:nil];
}
```

7. Modify the bandImageViewTapDetected method with the following code:

```
- (void)bandImageViewTapDetected
{
    if([UIImagePickerController
isSourceTypeAvailable:UIImagePickerControllerSourceTypePhotoLibrary])
    {
        [self presentPhotoLibraryImagePicker];
    }
    else
    {
        UIAlertView *photoLibraryErrorAlert = [[UIAlertView alloc]
initWithTitle:@"Error" message:@"There are no" delegate:nil
cancelButtonTitle:@"OK" otherButtonTitles:nil];
        [photoLibraryErrorAlert show];
    }
}
```

8. Run the app in the iPhone 4-inch simulator. Tapping the empty image view now shows the Photo Library Image Picker.

How It Works

You first declared that the `WBABandDetailsViewController` implements both the `UIImagePickerControllerDelegate` and the `UINavigationControllerDelegate`. You needed to declare the `UINavigationControllerDelegate` because the `UIImagePickerController` implements it. You did not need to implement any of its methods, but you will get a build error if it is not present.

Next, you declared and implemented a method to show the `UIImagePickerController` with its source type set to `UIImagePickerControllerSourceTypePhotoLibrary`. You also set its delegate to the `WBABandDetailsViewController` using `self` and set the `allowsEditing` flag to true before presenting the `UIImagePickerController` modally over the `WBABandDetailsViewController`.

Then you implemented the two methods of the `UIImagePickerControllerDelegate`. The `imagePicker Controller:didFinishPickingMediaWithInfo:` method is called when users select an image from the photo library. You get the image by first looking at the `UIImagePickerControllerEditedImage` value in the media `info` `NSDictionary`. If this value is `NULL`, you then get the image from the `UIImagePickerControllerOriginalImage` value. Using that image, you set the `UIImageView` and hide the `addPhotoLabel` using its `hidden` property before dismissing the `UIImagePickerController`.

The other delegate method you implemented, `imagePickerControllerDidCancel:`, gets called when the user cancels the `UIImagePickerController`, in which case you simply dismiss it.

The last thing you did was modifying the `bandImageViewTapDetectedMethod`. In the new code you first make sure the photo library is available on the device. If it is, call the `presentPhotoLibraryIm-agePicker` to display the `UIImagePickerController`; if not, notify the user that no photo library is available.

Saving Band Images

You can now present the image picker for the photo library, choose an image, and set the `image` property of the `UIImageView` with the picture. You need to add the code to save the picture with the rest of the `WBABand` instance in `standardUserDefaults`. Similar to the `WBABand` instance, you cannot save a `UIImage` directly into `standardUserDefaults`. You first need to serialize it into an `NSData` object. You can use one of two helper functions to do this. The `UIImageJPEGRepresentation` can take the `UIImage` and a compression ratio to serialize the picture in the JPEG format. In the Bands app you can use the `UIImagePNGRepresentation` method instead. It takes the `UIImage` and serializes it into the PNG format. After the image is converted to `NSData`, it can be saved in `standardUserDefaults` with the rest of the `WBABand` instance. To load the picture back, you simply retrieve the `NSData` and create the `UIImage` with the `initWithData` method.

TRY IT OUT Saving Images in NSUserDefaults

1. Select the `WBABand.h` file from the Project Navigator, and add the following property:

   ```
   @property (nonatomic, strong) UIImage *bandImage;
   ```

2. Select the `WBABand.m` file from the Project Navigator.

it's what they actually want to do. When deleting a band, you implemented a UIActionSheet with a destructive button. You also implemented the UIActionSheetDelegate in the WBABandDetailsViewController to handle whichever option users selected.

When users swipe to delete the band picture, you should again use a UIActionSheet with a destructive button. Because the WBABandDetailsViewController already implements the UIActionSheetDelegate, you need to know which action sheet users interact with. The UIActionSheet has a tag property, which is an integer. You can set the tag property then check it in UIActionSheetDelegate methods to determine the context of the UIActionSheet.

To make your code easier to follow, you should declare the values you will use for the tag property as a constant. There are a couple ways to do this. One way is to use the #define C preprocessor command. The Coding Guidelines for Cocoa (which you can find at https://developer.apple.com/library/mac/documentation/Cocoa/Conceptual/CodingGuidelines) discourage this approach, although many developers use it. The recommended approach is to use an enumeration, which you will use in the following Try It Out.

TRY IT OUT Implementing the Swipe to Delete Gesture

1. Select the WBABandDetailsViewController.h file from the Project Navigator.

2. Add the following code before the interface:

```
typedef enum {
    WBAActionSheetTagDeleteBand,
    WBAActionSheetTagDeleteBandImage,
} WBAActionSheetTag;
```

3. Select the WBABandDetailsViewController.m file from the Project Navigator.

4. Modify the bandImageViewSwipeDetected method with the following code:

```
- (void)bandImageViewSwipeDetected
{
    if(self.bandObject.bandImage)
    {
        UIActionSheet *deleteBandImageActionSheet =
[[UIActionSheet alloc] initWithTitle:nil delegate:self
cancelButtonTitle:@"Cancel" destructiveButtonTitle:@"Delete Picture"
otherButtonTitles:nil];
        deleteBandImageActionSheet.tag = WBAActionSheetTagDeleteBandImage;
        [deleteBandImageActionSheet showInView:self.view];
    }
}
```

5. Modify the actionSheet:clickedButtonAtIndex: method with the following code:

```
- (void)actionSheet:(UIActionSheet *)actionSheet
clickedButtonAtIndex:(NSInteger)buttonIndex
{
    if(actionSheet.tag == WBAActionSheetTagDeleteBandImage)
    {
        if(buttonIndex == actionSheet.destructiveButtonIndex)
        {
```

```
            self.bandObject.bandImage = nil;
            self.bandImageView.image = nil;
            self.addPhotoLabel.hidden = NO;
        }
    }
    else if(actionSheet.tag == WBAActionSheetTagDeleteBand)
    {
        if(actionSheet.destructiveButtonIndex == buttonIndex)
        {
            self.bandObject = nil;
            self.saveBand = NO;

            if(self.navigationController)
                [self.navigationController popViewControllerAnimated:YES];
            else
                [self dismissViewControllerAnimated:YES completion:nil];
        }
    }
}
```

6. Run the code in the iPhone 4-inch simulator. Swiping the image view now prompts you to delete the picture.

How It Works

You added a new enumeration named `WBAActionSheetTag` with two values, `WBAActionSheetTagDeleteBand` and `WBAActionSheetTagDeleteBandImage`, to the interface file of the `WBABandDetailsViewController` class to use with the `tag` property of a `UIActionSheet` when prompting the users.

You then modified the `bandImageViewSwipeDetected` method to show a `UIActionSheet` with its tag set to `WBAActionSheetTagDeleteBandImage`. This prompts users to verify that they want to delete the picture.

In the `actionSheet:clickedButtonAtIndex:` method of the `UIActionSheetDelegate` protocol, you can now use the tag to determine the context in which the `UIActionSheet` was displayed. If its tag is `WBAActionSheetTagDeleteBandImage`, you know the user has swiped the band picture. If the `buttonIndex` is the `destructiveButtonIndex`, you know the user has confirmed they would like to delete the band picture. You set both the `image` property of the `bandImageView` and the `bandImage` property of the `bandObject` to `nil`. Finally you set the `hidden` property of the `addPhotoLabel` back to false so that it again is shown to the users.

TAKING A PICTURE WITH THE CAMERA

Presenting the `UIImagePickerController` to use the camera is similar to presenting it for the photo library. You first check to make sure the camera is available on the device and simply change the `sourceType` of the `UIImagePickerController` to `UIImagePickerControllerSourceTypeCamera`. Just because the device has a camera does not mean that is what users want to use to set the band picture. They may still want to select a picture in their photo library.

Unfortunately, Apple does not have a built-in way to prompt users if they want to choose a saved picture or take a new picture. Most apps that enable both have adopted prompting users with a `UIActionSheet` much like you have already implemented when users try to delete something, as you will see in the following Try It Out.

TRY IT OUT Presenting the Camera

1. Select the `WBABandDetailsViewController.h` file from the Project Navigator.

2. Modify the `WBAActionSheetTag` enum with the following code:

```
typedef enum {
    WBAActionSheetTagDeleteBand,
    WBAActionSheetTagDeleteBandImage,
    WBAActionSheetTagChooseImagePickerSource,
} WBAActionSheetTag;
```

3. Add a new enum using the following code:

```
typedef enum {
    WBAImagePickerSourceCamera,
    WBAImagePickerSourcePhotoLibrary
} WBAImagePickerSource;
```

4. Add the following method declaration:

```
- (void)presentPhotoLibraryImagePicker;
```

5. Select the `WBABandDetailsViewController.m` file from the Project Navigator.

6. Modify the `bandImageViewTapDetected` method with the following code:

```
- (void)bandImageViewTapDetected
{
    if([UIImagePickerController
isSourceTypeAvailable:UIImagePickerControllerSourceTypeCamera])
    {
        UIActionSheet *chooseCameraActionSheet = [[UIActionSheet alloc]
initWithTitle:nil delegate:self cancelButtonTitle:@"Cancel"
destructiveButtonTitle:nil otherButtonTitles:@"Take with Camera",
@"Choose from Photo Library", nil];
        chooseCameraActionSheet.tag = WBAActionSheetTagChooseImagePickerSource;
        [chooseCameraActionSheet showInView:self.view];
    }
    else if([UIImagePickerController
isSourceTypeAvailable:UIImagePickerControllerSourceTypePhotoLibrary])
    {
        [self presentPhotoLibraryImagePicker];
    }
    else
    {
        UIAlertView *photoLibraryErrorAlert = [[UIAlertView alloc]
                    initWithTitle:@"Error" message:@"There are no" delegate:nil
                    cancelButtonTitle:@"OK" otherButtonTitles:nil];
        [photoLibraryErrorAlert show];
    }
}
```

5. Modify the `actionSheet:clickedButtonAtIndex:` method with the following code:

```
- (void)actionSheet:(UIActionSheet *)actionSheet
clickedButtonAtIndex:(NSInteger)buttonIndex
{
    if(actionSheet.tag == WBAActionSheetTagChooseImagePickerSource)
    {
        if(buttonIndex == WBAImagePickerSourceCamera)
        {
            [self presentCameraImagePicker];
        }
        else if (buttonIndex == WBAImagePickerSourcePhotoLibrary)
        {
            [self presentPhotoLibraryImagePicker];
        }
    }
    else if(actionSheet.tag == WBAActionSheetTagDeleteBandImage)
    {
        if(buttonIndex == actionSheet.destructiveButtonIndex)
        {
            self.bandObject.bandImage = nil;
            self.bandImageView.image = nil;
            self.addPhotoLabel.hidden = NO;
        }
    }
    else if(actionSheet.tag == WBAActionSheetTagDeleteBand)
    {
        if(buttonIndex == actionSheet.destructiveButtonIndex)
        {
            self.bandObject = nil;
            self.saveBand = NO;

            if(self.navigationController)
                [self.navigationController popViewControllerAnimated:YES];
            else
                [self dismissViewControllerAnimated:YES completion:nil];
        }
    }
}
```

6. Add the following code to the implementation:

```
- (void)presentCameraImagePicker
{
    UIImagePickerController *imagePickerController =
[[UIImagePickerController alloc] init];
    imagePickerController.sourceType = UIImagePickerControllerSourceTypeCamera;
    imagePickerController.delegate = self;
    imagePickerController.allowsEditing = YES;
    [self presentViewController:imagePickerController
animated:YES completion:nil];
}
```

7. Run the app on a test device with a camera. When you tap the image view, you're prompted to take a picture with the camera or choose from the library. Selecting Take with Camera allows you to take a new picture using the camera.

How It Works

You first added a `WBAActionSheetTagChooseImagePickerSource` value to the `WBAActionSheetTag` enumeration. You also added a new enumeration named `WBAImagePickerSource` to keep track of the button index of the options shown when prompting users with devices that have both a camera and a photo library. It has two values, `WBAImagePickerSourceCamera` and `WBAImagePickerSourcePhotoLibrary`. You then declared a new method in the interface named `presentCameraImagePicker`.

In the implementation you modified the `bandImageViewTapDetected` method to first check if the device has a camera by using the `isSourceTypeAvailable:` static method of the `UIImagePickerController` class and the `UIImagePickerControllerSourceTypeCamera` constant. If it returns true, you prompt the users to choose either the camera or the photo library using a new `UIActionSheet` with its `tag` property set to `WBAActionSheetTagChooseImagePickerSource`. This `UIActionSheet` is different from ones you have used before. There is no need for a destructive button, so you set the `destructiveButtonTitle` argument to `nil` when creating the `UIActionSheet`. To add the "Take with Camera" and "Choose from Photo Library" buttons, you pass them in using a C Style array in the `otherButtonTitles` argument. A C Style array lists all of the values followed by a `nil`.

In the `actionSheet:didClickButtonAtIndex:` method you added code to handle a `UIActionSheet` with its `tag` set to `WBAActionSheetTagChooseImagePickerSource`. If the `buttonIndex` is equal to `WBAImagePickerSourceCamera`, the code calls the `presentCameraImagePicker` method. If the `buttonIndex` is equal to `WBAImagePickerSourcePhotoLibrary`, the code calls the `presentPhotoLibraryImagePicker` method.

Finally you implemented the `presentCameraImagePicker` method. It creates and shows the `UIImagePickerController` virtually the same as the `presentPhotoLibraryImagePicker`, except it sets the `sourceType` to `UIImagePickerControllerSourceTypeCamera`. When the `UIImagePicker Controller` is displayed the users can now take a picture using the camera of the device.

> **NOTE** To test the camera code, you need to test on a device that has a camera. There is no other way to test this code. Though it can be a barrier, you need to test any app you write on a device prior to submitting it for approval, so it's a good habit to get into as early in the development process as possible.

SUMMARY

The camera and the photo library are valuable features of iOS devices. They can help you add to the user experiences of your apps, but you need to make sure that the device on which your app runs supports them.

In this chapter you learned how to add a `UIImageView` to your user interface and how to implement a `UITapGestureRecognizer` and `UISwipeGestureRecognizer` so that users can interact with it.

You also learned how to use the `UIImagePickerController` to check what capabilities the device has and to also interact with the camera or photo library to set the picture associated with a band.

While implementing this feature, you learned more about using the `UIActionSheet`. You learned how to hide the destructive button and add your own options as well as how to tell the context in which the `UIActionSheet` was shown when the `actionSheet:didClickButtonAtIndex:` method of the `UIActionSheetDelegate` protocol gets called. In the next chapter you will expand on this by giving users options to share their bands using e-mail, text messaging, and social media.

EXERCISES

1. How would you change the tap gesture recognizer to require two fingers tapping the image to set the band picture?

2. What are the three source types of the UIImagePickerController?

3. What happens if you try to present the image picker on a device that does not support the source type?

4. What property can you set on a UIActionSheet so that your delegate method knows how to handle the button index that was clicked?

Sending e-mails was the first form of social networking Apple added in iOS 3. When iOS 5 was introduced, it included built-in support for sending messages to Twitter. iOS 6 added Facebook support, whereas iOS 7 added both Flickr and Vimeo. Instead of developers needing to know the networking details of each of these services, integration with these services was instead built in to iOS.

In this chapter you add the ability to share bands through e-mail and text messages, as well as through Facebook, Twitter, and Flickr.

SENDING E-MAILS AND TEXT MESSAGES

The most basic form of social networking is sending e-mails and text messages. Almost all users of iOS devices have an e-mail address configured on their device. Prior to iPhone OS 3, users could send e-mails only using the built-in Mail app. Apple began including the `MessageUI.framework` with the release of iPhone OS 3, enabling all third-party apps the capability to compose and send e-mails from within the app as well as setting the subject of the e-mail, the body, and the recipients.

Text messages are also a basic form of social networking. The first iPhone had text messaging through the Messages app; though iPod touches and iPads did not, because text messages were thought of more as part of your cell phone plan. That changed with the release of iMessages in iOS 5. iMessages enables anyone with an Apple account to send text messages to other Apple accounts for free. If you use an iPhone, you can also send text messages to people who do not have an Apple account but have a text-messaging plan. Both use the Messages app or the message composer while inside third-party apps.

Using the E-mail Composer

The capability to show the e-mail composer from within a third-party app was first introduced in iPhone OS 3 with the inclusion of the `MessageUI.framework`. A framework is best thought of as a DLL in Windows or a Jar file in Java. Some frameworks such as `UIKit` are automatically added to any new project you create using the project templates. Others need to be added before you can use them. The `MessageUI.framework` is one that needs to be added. You will learn how to do this in the following Try It Out. After it's included in your project, you have access to the `MFMailComposeViewController` and `MFMailComposeViewControllerDelegate`.

The `MFMailComposeViewController`, like the `UIImagePickerController`, is a self-contained view. You don't need to code your own user interface for writing e-mails nor do you need any special networking code to send them. Instead you create the `MFMailComposeViewController`, set whatever properties you want, such as the e-mail body and subject, and then present it within your app. To know when the user either sends the e-mail or taps the Cancel button, you need to register as the `MFMailComposeViewController` delegate and implement the `mailComposeController:didFinishWithResult:error` method of the `MFMailComposeViewControllerDelegate` protocol.

The features of the Bands app, as discussed in Chapter 1, "Building a Real World iOS App — Bands," will eventually include searching for a band on the web, finding local record stores and searching for tracks of a band in iTunes. These are all activity options the users will initiate from the Band Details scene. Options in an iOS app are generally presented to the users with a `UIActionSheet`. In

Chapter 6, "Integrating the Camera and Photo Library in iOS Apps," you used a UIActionSheet to prompt the user to choose between using the camera or selecting an image from the photo library. The activity options will be presented in the same manner. The recommended way to do this is to add a UIBarButtonItem to the UINavigationItem with its Identifier set to Action. The icon for this type of UIBarButtonItem is a box with an arrow pointing up and out of it. The Bands app will implement this approach to show the activity options to users.

TRY IT OUT Presenting the MFMailComposeViewController

1. Select the Project in the Project Navigator.

2. Select the General tab in the editor.

3. In the Linked Frameworks and Libraries section, click the Add button.

4. Search for and find the MessageUI.framework, and add it to the project.

5. Select the WBABand.h file from the Project Navigator, and add the following method declaration to the interface:

```
- (NSString *)stringForMessaging;
```

6. Select the WBABand.m file from the Project Navigator, and add the following method to the implementation:

```
- (NSString *)stringForMessaging
{
    NSMutableString *messageString = [NSMutableString stringWithFormat:@"%@\n",
    self.name];

    if(self.notes.length > 0)
        [messageString appendString:[NSString stringWithFormat:@"Notes: %@\n",
    self.notes]];
    else
        [messageString appendString:@"Notes: \n"];

    [messageString appendString:[NSString stringWithFormat:@"Rating: %d\n",
    self.rating]];

    if(self.touringStatus == WBATouringStatusOnTour)
        [messageString appendString:@"Touring Status: On Tour\n"];
    else if (self.touringStatus == WBATouringStatusOffTour)
        [messageString appendString:@"Touring Status: Off Tour\n"];
    else if (self.touringStatus == WBATouringStatusDisbanded)
        [messageString appendString:@"Touring Status: Disbanded\n"];

    if(self.haveSeenLive)
        [messageString appendString:@"Have Seen Live: Yes"];
    else
        [messageString appendString:@"Have Seen Live: No"];

    return messageString;
}
```

7. Select the `WBABandDetailsViewController.h` file from the Project Navigator.

8. Add the following import to the class imports:

```
#import <MessageUI/MFMailComposeViewController.h>
```

9. Add a new constant to the `WBAActionSheetTag` using the following code:

```
typedef enum {
    WBAActionSheetTagDeleteBand,
    WBAActionSheetTagDeleteBandImage,
    WBAActionSheetTagChooseImagePickerSource,
    WBAActionSheetTagActivity,
} WBAActionSheetTag;
```

10. Add a new enumeration using the following code:

```
typedef enum {
    WBAActivityButtonIndexEmail,
} WBAActivityButtonIndex;
```

11. Add the following protocol to the interface:

```
@interface WBABandDetailsViewController : UIViewController <UITextFieldDelegate,
UITextViewDelegate, UIActionSheetDelegate, UIImagePickerControllerDelegate,
UINavigationControllerDelegate, MFMailComposeViewControllerDelegate>
```

12. Add the following `IBAction` to the interface:

```
- (IBAction)activityButtonTouched:(id)sender;
```

13. Add the following method declaration to the interface:

```
- (void)emailBandInfo;
```

14. Select the `Main.storyboard` from the Project Navigator.

15. Add a new Bar Button Item from the Object library to the `UINavigationItem` of the Band Details scene, and set its identifier to Action, as shown in Figure 7-1.

16. Connect the button to the `activityButtonTouched:` method.

17. Select the `WBABandDetailsViewController.m` file from the Project Navigator.

18. Add the following methods to the implementation:

```
- (IBAction)activityButtonTouched:(id)sender
{
    UIActionSheet *activityActionSheet = [[UIActionSheet alloc]
initWithTitle:nil delegate:self cancelButtonTitle:@"Cancel"
destructiveButtonTitle:nil otherButtonTitles:@"Mail", @"Message", nil];

    activityActionSheet.tag = WBAActionSheetTagActivity;
    [activityActionSheet showInView:self.view];
}

- (void)emailBandInfo
{
```

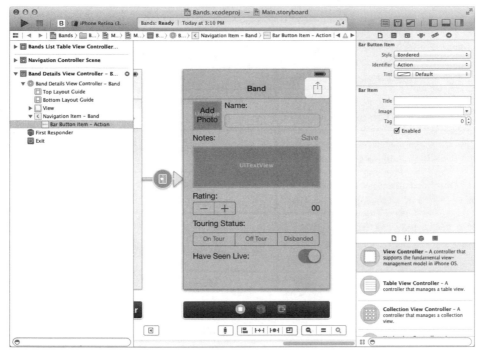

FIGURE 7-1

```
    MFMailComposeViewController *mailComposeViewController =
[[MFMailComposeViewController alloc] init];
    mailComposeViewController.mailComposeDelegate = self;

    [mailComposeViewController setSubject:self.bandObject.name];
    [mailComposeViewController setMessageBody:
[self.bandObject stringForMessaging] isHTML:NO];

    if(self.bandObject.bandImage)
        [mailComposeViewController addAttachmentData:
UIImagePNGRepresentation(self.bandObject.bandImage)
mimeType:@"image/png" fileName:@"bandImage"];

    [self presentViewController:mailComposeViewController
animated:YES completion:nil];
}

- (void)mailComposeController:
(MFMailComposeViewController *)controller
didFinishWithResult:(MFMailComposeResult)result error:(NSError *)error
{
    [controller dismissViewControllerAnimated:YES completion:nil];
    if(error)
    {
```

```
        UIAlertView *emailErrorAlertView = [[UIAlertView alloc]
initWithTitle:@"Error" message:error.localizedDescription delegate:nil
cancelButtonTitle:@"OK" otherButtonTitles:nil];
        [emailErrorAlertView show];
    }
}
```

19. Modify the `activitySheet:clickedButtonAtIndex:` method with the following code:

```
- (void)actionSheet:(UIActionSheet *)actionSheet
clickedButtonAtIndex:(NSInteger)buttonIndex
{
    if(actionSheet.tag == WBAActionSheetTagActivity)
    {
        if(buttonIndex == WBAActivityButtonIndexEmail)
        {
            [self emailBandInfo];
        }
    }
    else if(actionSheet.tag == WBAActionSheetTagChooseImagePickerSource)
    {
        if(buttonIndex == WBAImagePickerSourceCamera)
        {
            [self presentCameraImagePicker];
        }
        else if (buttonIndex == WBAImagePickerSourcePhotoLibrary)
        {
            [self presentPhotoLibraryImagePicker];
        }
    }
    else if(actionSheet.tag == WBAActionSheetTagDeleteBandImage)
    {
        if(buttonIndex == actionSheet.destructiveButtonIndex)
        {
            self.bandObject.bandImage = nil;
            self.bandImageView.image = nil;
            self.tapToSetLabel.hidden = NO;
        }
    }
    else if (actionSheet.tag == WBAActionSheetTagDeleteBand)
    {
        if(actionSheet.destructiveButtonIndex == buttonIndex)
        {
            self.bandObject = nil;
            self.saveBand = NO;

            if(self.navigationController)
                [self.navigationController popViewControllerAnimated:YES];
            else
                [self dismissViewControllerAnimated:YES completion:nil];
        }
    }

}
```

20. Run the code in the iPhone 4-inch simulator. When selecting the Email button, you see the MFMailComposeViewController screen prefilled with the band message string and band image, as shown in Figure 7-2.

How It Works

You started by adding the MessageUI.framework to the project using the General settings editor and the Linked Frameworks and Libraries section. This tells the compiler to include the framework when building the project. Next, you implemented a helper method in the WBABand class that returns a string representing all the properties of the band.

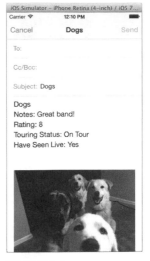

FIGURE 7-2

In the WBABandDetailsViewController header you imported the MFMessageComposeViewController.h file. Next you added a new WBAActionSheetTagActivity value to the WBAActionSheetTag enumeration to be used with the activity options UIActionSheet. You also added a new enumeration named WBAActivityButtonIndex with a WBAActivityButtonIndexEmail constant to keep track of the activity option button indexes in the UIActionSheet. You then declared that the WBABandDetailsViewController implements the MFMessageComposeViewControllerDelegate. You also declared a new IBAction named actionButtonTouched: and an emailBandInfo method.

In the Storyboard, you added a new UIBarButtonItem to the UINavigationItem of the Band Details scene and set its identity to Action. The Action identifier uses the standard action icon, which signals to the user that tapping it performs some sort of action on the data in the scene. You then connected it to the actionButtonTapped: method you previously declared in the WBABandDetailsViewController interface.

Next, you modified code in the WBABandDetailsViewController implementation. The actionButtonTapped: method creates a new UIActionSheet with an e-mail option button and its tag set to the new WBAActionSheetTagActivity constant. In the actionSheet:clickedButton AtIndex: method, you look for this tag then check to see if the buttonIndex is equal to the new WBAActivityButtonIndexEmail. If it is, the code calls the emailBandInfo method.

The emailBandInfo method first initializes a new MFMailComposeViewController and sets its delegate to the WBABandDetailsViewController using self. Next, it sets the subject of the e-mail to the band's name using the setSubject: method. You set the e-mail body using the setMessageBody:isHTML: method using the stringForMessaging helper method of the bandObject. Because the string is not HTML, you pass in NO for the isHTML argument. If the bandObject has the bandImage property set, that gets added to the e-mail using the addAttachmentData:mimeType: filename method. The bandImage property is a UIImage, which needs to be serialized to NSData to be attached to an e-mail. You use the UIImagePNGRepresentation function to do this. The mimeType is set to "image/png" and the fileName is set to "bandImage."

You present the MFMailComposeViewController using the presentViewController:animated: completion: method. When the user sends the e-mail or taps the Cancel button, the mailComposeControllerDidFinish:withResult:error: method of the MFMailComposeViewControllerDelegate protocol gets called. In its implementation you dismiss the MFMailComposeViewController using the dismissViewControllerAnimated:completion: method and then check to see if the error argument is set. If it is, you notify the users that an error occurred using a UIAlertView.

> **NOTE** The `MFMailComposeViewController` *does allow you to send an e-mail with HTML formatting by supplying an HTML string and setting the* `isHTML` *flag to true.*

Using the Message Composer

Sending text messages and iMessages is similar to sending e-mails. Instead of using the `MFMailComposeViewController`, you use the `MFMessageComposeViewController` and `MFMessageComposeViewControllerDelegate`. Text and iMessages also support attaching the band image to the message, but it's done a bit differently than with e-mail. Instead of setting the mime type of the image, you need to use its Universal Type Identifier. These identifiers were created by Apple and are included in the `MobileCoreServices.framework`. This is another framework that is not included in the Project templates, so you need to add it manually, the same as the `MessageUI.framework`.

> **NOTE** *The ability to attach images in text and iMessages in code was introduced in iOS 7. Users could attach images to text messages and iMessages through the Photo app, but there was no way to add them in a third-party app. If your app needs to support iOS 6, you need to check which version of iOS the device is running before attempting to add the image. Failing to do so can cause your app to crash in iOS 6.*

TRY IT OUT Presenting the MFMessageComposeViewController

1. Add the `MobileCoreServices.framework` to the project following the same steps from the previous section.

2. Select the `WBABandDetailsViewController.h` file from the Project Navigator.

3. Add the following to the imports:

   ```
   #import <MessageUI/MFMessageComposeViewController.h>
   ```

4. Add the following to the protocols of the interface:

   ```
   @interface WBABandDetailsViewController : UIViewController <UITextFieldDelegate,
   UITextViewDelegate, UIActionSheetDelegate, UIImagePickerControllerDelegate,
   UINavigationControllerDelegate, MFMailComposeViewControllerDelegate,
   MFMessageComposeViewControllerDelegate>
   ```

5. Add the following method declaration to the interface:

   ```
   - (void)messageBandInfo;
   ```

6. Add the following value to the `WBAActivityButtonIndex` enumeration:

   ```
   typedef enum {
       WBAActivityButtonIndexEmail,
       WBAActivityButtonIndexShare,
   } WBAActivityButtonIndex;
   ```

7. Select the `WBABandDetailsViewController.m` file from the Project Navigator.

8. Add the following methods to the implementation:

```
- (void)messageBandInfo
{
    MFMessageComposeViewController *messageComposeViewController =
[[MFMessageComposeViewController alloc] init];
    messageComposeViewController.messageComposeDelegate = self;

    [messageComposeViewController setSubject:self.bandObject.name];
    [messageComposeViewController setBody:
[self.bandObject stringForMessaging]];

    if(self.bandObject.bandImage)
        [messageComposeViewController addAttachmentData:
UIImagePNGRepresentation(self.bandObject.bandImage)
typeIdentifier:(NSString *)kUTTypePNG filename:@"bandImage.png"];

    [self presentViewController:messageComposeViewController
animated:YES completion:nil];
}

- (void)messageComposeViewController:
(MFMessageComposeViewController *)controller
didFinishWithResult:(MessageComposeResult)result
{
    [controller dismissViewControllerAnimated:YES completion:nil];
    if(result == MessageComposeResultFailed)
    {
        UIAlertView *emailErrorAlertView = [[UIAlertView alloc]
initWithTitle:@"Error" message:@"The message failed to send" delegate:nil
cancelButtonTitle:@"OK" otherButtonTitles:nil];
        [emailErrorAlertView show];
    }
}
```

9. Modify the `activityButtonTouched:` method with the following code:

```
- (IBAction)activityButtonTouched:(id)sender
{
    UIActionSheet *activityActionSheet = nil;

    if([MFMessageComposeViewController canSendText])
        activityActionSheet = [[UIActionSheet alloc] initWithTitle:nil
delegate:self cancelButtonTitle:@"Cancel" destructiveButtonTitle:nil
otherButtonTitles:@"Mail", @"Message", nil];
    else
        activityActionSheet = [[UIActionSheet alloc] initWithTitle:nil
delegate:self cancelButtonTitle:@"Cancel" destructiveButtonTitle:nil
otherButtonTitles:@"Mail", nil];

    activityActionSheet.tag = WBAActionSheetTagActivity;
    [activityActionSheet showInView:self.view];
}
```

10. Modify the `activitySheet:clickedButtonAtIndex:` with the following code:

```
- (void)actionSheet:(UIActionSheet *)actionSheet
clickedButtonAtIndex:(NSInteger)buttonIndex
{
    if(actionSheet.tag == WBAActionSheetTagActivity)
    {
        if(buttonIndex == WBAActivityButtonIndexEmail)
        {
            [self emailBandInfo];
        }
        else if (buttonIndex == WBAActivityButtonIndexMessage)
        {
            [self messageBandInfo];
        }
    }
    else if(actionSheet.tag == WBAActionSheetTagChooseImagePickerSource)
    {
        if(buttonIndex == WBAImagePickerSourceCamera)
        {
            [self presentCameraImagePicker];
        }
        else if (buttonIndex == WBAImagePickerSourcePhotoLibrary)
        {
            [self presentPhotoLibraryImagePicker];
        }
    }
    else if(actionSheet.tag == WBAActionSheetTagDeleteBandImage)
    {
        if(buttonIndex == actionSheet.destructiveButtonIndex)
        {
            self.bandObject.bandImage = nil;
            self.bandImageView.image = nil;
            self.tapToSetLabel.hidden = NO;
        }
    }
    else if (actionSheet.tag == WBAActionSheetTagDeleteBand)
    {
        if(actionSheet.destructiveButtonIndex == buttonIndex)
        {
            self.bandObject = nil;
            self.saveBand = NO;

            if(self.navigationController)
                [self.navigationController popViewControllerAnimated:YES];
            else
                [self dismissViewControllerAnimated:YES completion:nil];
        }
    }
}
```

11. Run the app on a test device that has text messaging available. When you tap the Messages option, you can see the text message compose screen.

How It Works

Before implementing the `MFMailComposeViewController` you first added the `MobileCoreServices` `.framework` to the Bands project. This framework is required in order to use the Universal Type Identifier constants. You also added the `WBAActivityButtonIndexShare` constant to the `WBAActivityButtonIndex` enumeration to use when presenting the e-mail and messaging options to users.

In the implementation you first imported the `MobileCoreServices.h` file, which allows you to use the Universal Type Identifier constants in the code. Next you modified the `activityButtonTouched:` method to use the `canSendText` static method of the `MFMessageComposeViewController` class to make sure the users device is able to send text messages or iMessages. If it returns true, you then present the `UIActivitySheet` with both the Mail and Message options. If not you only show the Mail option. If you attempt to use the `MFMessageComposeViewController` on a device that does not support it your app will crash, so this check is very important.

The method you declared for sending messages, `messageBandInfo`, is almost identical to the `emailBandInfo` method you added in the previous section. Instead of using the `MFMailComposeViewController`, you initialized and presented the `MFMessageComposeViewController`. You set the subject again using `setSubject:` and the body using `setBody:`. The body of a text message or iMessage cannot be HTML, so the `isHTML` argument is not present. The biggest difference is attaching the `bandImage` to the message. Instead of using a mime type string, you used the `kUTTypePNG` Universal Type Identifier constant.

You also implemented the `messageComposeViewControllerDidFinishwithResult:` method of the `MFMessageComposeViewControllerDelegate` protocol. In its implementation you dismiss the message `MFMessageComposeViewController` using the `dismissViewControllerAnimated:completion:` method and then check the `result` argument. If it is equal to the `MessageComposeResultFailed` constant, you show an error to users using a `UIAlertView`.

> **NOTE** The iOS simulator does not support text messaging or iMessages. You can use it to test your code and make sure you are using the `canSendText` method before attempting to present the `MFMessageComposeViewController`. You will need to use a physical device to test sending a text message or iMessage.

SIMPLIFYING SOCIAL NETWORK INTEGRATION

Apple began integrating social networking directly into iOS in iOS 5. They also gave developers access to this integration. Using the built-in integration was a big help to developers, because they no longer needed to learn the various APIs of different social networking services. Actually, you don't need to add any networking code. The integration is also great for users, because they can sign into those social networks in one place and have access to them in any app that includes the integration. Apple also gave developers a new view controller so that users would have a common experience in not only the Apple apps, but also in any third-party apps that implement it.

Introducing the Activity View Controller

The UIActivityViewController was first introduced in iOS 6. By using it, developers can give their users a common experience not only with social networking integration, but also with other activities, such as e-mailing, messaging, printing, and AirDrop to share between iOS devices. Adding it into your app is similar to the UIImagePickerController, MFMailComposeViewController, and MFMessageComposeViewController, but you don't need to add new frameworks to your project. The biggest benefit is no longer needing to know what capabilities are available on the device. You also don't need to know the Universal Type Identifiers for the data in your apps. Instead you simply pass in an array of objects you would like to share, and the system figures out what activities can be performed on them.

In the Bands app you can use the UIActivityController to replace the e-mail and message code you added previously in this chapter. You can also use it to add integration with social networking services.

TRY IT OUT Presenting the UIActivityViewController

1. Select the WBABandDetailsViewController.h file from the Project Navigator, and add the following method declaration to the interface:

   ```
   - (void)shareBandInfo;
   ```

2. Modify the WBAActivityButtonIndex enumeration with the following code:

   ```
   typedef enum {
   //    WBAActivityButtonIndexEmail,
   //    WBAActivityButtonIndexMessage,
       WBAActivityButtonIndexShare,
   } WBAActivityButtonIndex;
   ```

3. Select the WBABandDetailsViewController.m file from the Project Navigator.

4. Modify the activityButtonTouched: method with the following code:

   ```
   - (IBAction)activityButtonTouched:(id)sender
   {
       UIActionSheet *activityActionSheet = nil;
       /*
       if([MFMessageComposeViewController canSendText])
           activityActionSheet = [[UIActionSheet alloc] initWithTitle:nil
   delegate:self cancelButtonTitle:@"Cancel" destructiveButtonTitle:nil
   otherButtonTitles:@"Mail", @"Message", nil];
       else
           activityActionSheet = [[UIActionSheet alloc] initWithTitle:nil
   delegate:self cancelButtonTitle:@"Cancel" destructiveButtonTitle:nil
   otherButtonTitles:@"Mail", nil];
       */


       activityActionSheet = [[UIActionSheet alloc] initWithTitle:nil
   ```

```
delegate:self cancelButtonTitle:@"Cancel" destructiveButtonTitle:nil
otherButtonTitles:@"Share", nil];

    activityActionSheet.tag = WBAActionSheetTagActivity;
    [activityActionSheet showInView:self.view];
}
```

5. Modify the `actionSheet:clickedButtonAtIndex:` with the following code:

```
- (void)actionSheet:(UIActionSheet *)actionSheet
clickedButtonAtIndex:(NSInteger)buttonIndex
{
    if(actionSheet.tag == WBAActionSheetTagActivity)
    {
        /*
        if(buttonIndex == WBAActivityButtonIndexEmail)
        {
            [self emailBandInfo];
        }
        else if (buttonIndex !=actionSheet.cancelButtonIndex  &&
buttonIndex == messageActivityButtonIndex)
        {
            [self messageBandInfo];
        }
        */


        if(buttonIndex == shareActivityButtonIndex)
        {
            [self shareBandInfo];
        }
    }
    else if(actionSheet.tag == WBAActionSheetTagChooseImagePickerSource)
    {
        if(buttonIndex == WBAImagePickerSourceCamera)
        {
            [self presentCameraImagePicker];
        }
        else if (buttonIndex == WBAImagePickerSourcePhotoLibrary)
        {
            [self presentPhotoLibraryImagePicker];
        }
    }
    else if(actionSheet.tag == WBAActionSheetTagDeleteBandImage)
    {
        if(buttonIndex == actionSheet.destructiveButtonIndex)
        {
            self.bandObject.bandImage = nil;
            self.bandImageView.image = nil;
            self.tapToSetLabel.hidden = NO;
        }
    }
    else if (actionSheet.tag == WBAActionSheetTagDeleteBand)
    {
```

```
            if(actionSheet.destructiveButtonIndex == buttonIndex)
            {
                self.bandObject = nil;
                self.saveBand = NO;

                if(self.navigationController)
                    [self.navigationController popViewControllerAnimated:YES];
                else
                    [self dismissViewControllerAnimated:YES completion:nil];
            }
        }
    }
```

6. Add the following method to the implementation:

```
- (void)shareBandInfo
{
    NSArray *activityItems = [NSArray arrayWithObjects:
[self.bandObject stringForMessaging], self.bandObject.bandImage, nil];

    UIActivityViewController *activityViewController =
[[UIActivityViewController alloc]initWithActivityItems:activityItems
applicationActivities:nil];
    [activityViewController setValue:self.bandObject.name forKey:@"subject"];

    [self presentViewController:activityViewController
animated:YES completion:nil];
}
```

7. Run the app in the iPhone 4-inch simulator. When you tap the Share option, you now see the Activity View Controller, as shown in Figure 7-3.

8. Tap the Mail button. You should see the e-mail compose view with the subject and e-mail body set.

FIGURE 7-3

How It Works

The first thing you did was declare a new `shareBandInfo` method in the `WBABandDetailsViewController` interface. You then modified the `WBAActivityButtonIndex` enumeration commenting out the `WBAActivityButtonIndexEmail` and `WBAActivityButtonIndexMessage` constants while adding `WBAActivityButtonIndexShare`. The `UIActivityViewController` has options for both email and messaging, so you will no longer present those options separately in the `UIActionSheet`. With those buttons no longer being shown, you need to keep the `WBAActivityButtonIndex` enumeration order the same as the options you will be displaying.

In the implementation you changed the `activityButtonTouched:` method to show a `UIActionSheet` with just a single "Share" button. In the `actionSheet:didClickButtonAt Index:` method you commented out the code that checks for the `WBAActivityButtonIndexEmail` and `WBAActivityButtonIndexMessage` and replaced it with code to compare the `buttonIndex` with the `WBAActivityButtonIndexShare` constant. If true, the code calls the `shareBandInfo` method.

In the `shareBandInfo` method you created an `NSArray` with its first object being the `NSString` returned from the `stringForMessaging` method of the `bandObject` and its second being the `bandImage`. This is a great example of adding different objects to an `NSArray`. Because both the `NSString` class and `UIImage` class inherit from `NSObject`, they can both be added to the same `NSArray`.

In this implementation, you do not need to check whether the image is set, because the `UIActivityViewController` can figure it out for you. You initialize the `UIActivityViewController` using the `initWithActivityItems:applicationActivities:` method. For the `activityItems` argument you pass in the `NSArray` you created with the band information. You set the `applicationActivities` argument to nil. You could create your own supported activities in your app and pass them in using that argument for display in the `UIActivityViewController`, but the Bands app does not use this feature.

If the users select the Mail or Message options you still want the subject to be set. You do this by calling the `setValue:forKey:` method, with the value being the `name` property of the `bandObject` and the key being `subject`. Finally you present the `UIActivityViewController` using the `presentView Controller:animated:completion:` method.

The `UIActivityViewController` does not have a `UIActivityViewControllerDelegate`. It will dismiss any other `UIViewControllers` that may be shown depending on what option the user selects and return to your app when they have either completed the activity or canceled.

Learning About Twitter Integration

The first social networking service Apple integrated was Twitter with the release of iOS 5. Twitter is a microblogging service that enables its users to share text, links, and images to their timelines. They can also follow other users and see posts that they can reply to, favorite, or "retweet" on their own timelines.

Users can sign into their Twitter account or create a new one in the Settings app. The system then downloads the user's followers list and attempts to match e-mail addresses associated with Twitter users to e-mail addresses in the user's Contacts. If a match is found, the system adds the Twitter handle to the contact. The Twitter app integration enables apps only to post new messages on the user's timeline. To use all the features of the services, users need to download the Twitter app. The setup screen has a button to download the app, so users don't need to search the app store.

TRY IT OUT   Sending Messages to Twitter

1. Open the Settings app on the iPhone 4-inch simulator, and select Twitter.

2. Enter your Twitter credentials or create a new account.

3. Run the Bands app in the simulator. Now when you select the Share option, the `UIActivity ViewController` has Twitter as an option, as shown in Figure 7-4.

4. Selecting Twitter allows you to post the band info and band image to Twitter while staying in the Bands app, as shown in Figure 7-5.

FIGURE 7-4

FIGURE 7-5

How It Works

The first thing you did was to go into the Settings app and either entered your Twitter credentials or created a new account. Back in the Bands app, the UIActivityViewController now has a Twitter option, which, if selected, enables you to compose a new message and post it to Twitter without leaving the app.

Learning About Facebook Integration

Facebook is the most popular social networking service in the world. Its users can post messages, pictures, links, and videos to their walls as well as see what other users with whom they are friends with have posted. Users can also create events or RSVP to events posted by their friends or groups of which they are members.

Apple integrated Facebook in iOS 6. Users can sign in or create a new account in the Settings app, the same as with Twitter. When the user's account is added, the system downloads their friends and adds them to the Contacts app. It also downloads any events and adds them to the Calendar app. The in-app integration is more complex than with Twitter. Apps can request access to the user's Facebook profile with info such as the user's birthday, e-mail address, and other information the user has made public on Facebook. Apps can also request the users' list of Facebook friends. When an app attempts to access this information, the user is prompted and must explicitly grant access. Facebook has had privacy issues in the past, making some users wary of letting third-party apps access their profile and friends lists, so the Bands app will not request this information. Instead users can post band info only to their walls.

Sending Messages to Facebook

1. Go to the home screen in the iPhone 4-inch simulator.

2. Open the settings app and select Facebook.

3. Enter your Facebook account information or create a new account, and sign into Facebook.

4. Run the Bands app in the simulator. Now when you select the Share option, the `UIActivityViewController` has Facebook as an option.

5. Selecting Facebook allows you to post the band info and band picture to Facebook while staying in the Bands app, as shown in Figure 7-6.

How It Works

The integration with Facebook in the Bands app is almost identical to the Twitter integration. If users select the Facebook option in the `UIActivityViewController`, they can post the band info string and band image to their Facebook walls from within the Bands app. They also have can add their location and designate which friends on Facebook can see the post.

FIGURE 7-6

Learning About Flickr Integration

Flickr is a social networking service from Yahoo built around sharing pictures. Users post pictures to their photo streams, which can be public for everyone to see or visible only to their contacts. Contacts or other users can then comment on pictures.

Flickr integration was added with iOS 7. The user can connect to their Flickr account by signing in with their Yahoo account in the Settings app. They can then share Band images by selecting Flickr in the Activity View. As you see in the following Try It Out, the band image must be set for the Flickr option to be shown.

Sending a Picture to Flickr

1. Open the Settings app on the iPhone 4-inch simulator, and select Flickr.

2. Enter your Flickr credentials or create a new account.

3. Run the Bands app in the iPhone 4-inch simulator.

4. Select a Band that does not have a band image set. When you select the Share option, Flickr will NOT be an available option.

5. Select a Band that does have a band image set. When you select the Share option, Flickr will now be available.

How It Works

Flickr integration works the same as Facebook and Twitter integration. After the user connect the account in the Settings app, the `UIActivityViewController` will have the Flickr option if the `bandImage` property of the `bandObject` is set. They then can post Band images to their Flickr photo stream.

> **NOTE** *This chapter covered how to post a new message or status to the social networking services integrated into iOS using the* `UIActivityViewController`*. The iOS SDK also includes the* `SLRequest` *class, which can be used to send requests directly to social networking services. This approach is for more advanced iOS developers, so it is not covered in this book. You can learn more about* `SLRequest` *in the iOS Developer Library at* `https://developer.apple.com/library/iOs/documentation/Social/Reference/SLRequest_Class/`*.*

Limiting Sharing Options

Using the Activity View Controller does simplify your code, but it also presents users with many options for sharing. Some of those options may not make sense for your app or your audience. The `UIActivityViewController` has a `setExcludedActivityTypes:` method you can call with an `NSArray` of activity type constants you don't want presented. Table 7-1 lists the built-in activity type constants.

TABLE 7-1: Activity Types

ACTIVITY TYPE	DESCRIPTION
`UIActivityTypePostToFacebook`	Enables posting strings, pictures, videos, and URLs to the user's Facebook wall
`UIActivityTypePostToTwitter`	Enables posting strings, pictures, videos, and URLs to the user's Twitter timeline
`UIActivityTypePostToWeibo`	Enables posting strings, pictures, videos, and URLs to the Chinese microblogging site Weibo
`UIActivityTypeMessage`	Enables sending strings, pictures, videos, and URLs via text message or iMessage.
`UIActivityTypeMail`	Enables sending strings, pictures, and URLs via e-mail
`UIActivityTypePrint`	Enables printing images
`UIActivityTypeCopyToPasteboard`	Enables copying strings, images, and URLs to the pasteboard
`UIActivityTypeAssignToContact`	Enables assigning an image to a contact

UIActivityTypeSaveToCameraRoll	Enables saving an image or a video (using its URL) to the camera roll
UIActivityTypeAddToReadingList	Enables adding a URL to the reading list
UIActivityTypePostToFlickr	Enables posting an image to Flickr
UIActivityTypePostToVimeo	Enables posting a video to Vimeo
UIActivityTypePostToTencentWeibo	Enables posting strings, images, videos, and URLs to the Chinese microblogging site Weibo
UIActivityTypeAirDrop	Enables sharing strings, images, videos, and URLs via AirDrop

TRY IT OUT Removing the Assign to Contact Option

1. Select the WBABandDetailsViewController.m file from the Project Navigator.

2. Modify the shareBandInfo with the following code:

```
- (void)shareBandInfo
{
    NSArray *activityItems = [NSArray arrayWithObjects:
[self.bandObject stringForMessaging], self.bandObject.bandImage, nil];

    UIActivityViewController *activityViewController =
[[UIActivityViewController alloc]initWithActivityItems:activityItems
applicationActivities:nil];
    [activityViewController setValue:self.bandObject.name forKey:@"subject"];

    NSArray *excludedActivityOptions = [NSArray arrayWithObjects:
UIActivityTypeAssignToContact, nil];
    [activityViewController setExcludedActivityTypes:excludedActivityOptions];

    [self presentViewController:activityViewController
animated:YES completion:nil];
}
```

3. Run the app in the iPhone 4-inch simulator. When you select the Share option, you no longer see the Assign to Contact option in the UIActivityViewController.

How it Works

The code to remove an activity from the UIActivityViewController is pretty simple. You first create an NSArray with the UIActivityTypeAssignToContact constant. You can add as many constants from Table 7-1 as you would like in this NSArray. You then use the NSArray with the setExcluded ActivityTypes: method of the UIActivityViewController.

SUMMARY

Social networking can be a valuable feature to add to your apps. From simple e-mails to posting to Twitter and Facebook, it gives your users a way to tell their friends, family, and coworkers about your app. Apple has built integration with Facebook, Twitter, Flickr, and Vimeo directly into iOS and gives you a simple way to add them to your app using the `UIActivityViewController`. The Bands app now has the capability to share bands via e-mail or text message and Twitter, Facebook, and Flickr.

EXERCISES

1. How do you add a new framework to an Xcode project?

2. What framework needs to be added to a project in order to use the `MFMailComposeViewController`?

3. What additional framework needs to be added to a project to send text messages using the `MFMessageComposeViewController` and why?

4. What method should you call before showing the `MFMessageComposeViewController` and why?

5. What social networks are integrated with iOS?

6. Where does a user sign into their social networking accounts in iOS?

7. How can you keep users of the Bands app from sharing band images on Flickr using the `UIActivityViewController`?

➤ WHAT YOU LEARNED IN THIS CHAPTER

TOPIC	KEY CONCEPTS
Sending E-mails Within an App	The iOS SDK includes the MFMailComposeViewController and MFMailComposeViewControllerDelegate, which you can add to your app to give your users the ability to send e-mails. You can set the subject, set the e-mail body, and add attachments with just a few lines of code.
Sending Text Messages and iMessages with Images	Similar to the MFMailComposeViewController is the MFMessageComposeViewController and MFMessageComposeViewControllerDelegate, which you can add to your app to send text messages and iMessages. With the release of iOS 7 you can also add attachments to messages similar to e-mail.
Adding the Same Sharing Experience Found in Apple apps	Apps from Apple all have the same user experience to send emails or iMessages as well as using AirDrop, copying to the pasteboard, and printing. By using the UIActivityViewController you can add the same experience to your app.
Integrating with Social Networking Services	Apple has been integrating with a handful of social networking services starting with Twitter in iOS 5, then adding Facebook, Flickr, and Vimeo. Users can sign into their accounts in the Settings app giving any third-party app using the UIActivityViewController the ability to send messages and status updates to these services without needing to add any additional code.

Using Web Views

WHAT YOU LEARN IN THIS CHAPTER:

➤ Displaying web pages in an app

➤ Calling Core Foundation methods for efficient string manipulation

➤ Using toolbars and buttons to create a lightweight web browser

WROX.COM CODE DOWNLOADS FOR THIS CHAPTER

You can find the wrox.com code downloads for this chapter at www.wrox.com/go/
begiosprogramming on the Download Code tab. The code is in the chapter 08 download
and individually named according to the names throughout the chapter.

One of the first and biggest selling points of smartphones was the ability to surf the web.
Many refer to this as having the entire web in your pocket. Even before smartphones were the
norm, some flip phones also allowed you to search the web with your cellular connection.

iOS devices come with Apple's Mobile Safari web browser, but similar to sending e-mails
and posting to social networking, it's a better experience for users to view web pages without
leaving the app they're in. One of the feature requirements for the Bands app gives users the
ability to search the web for information about a particular band. As the developer you could
accomplish this by simply jumping the user out of the app and into Safari. Though easy to
do, it breaks the flow of the user in your app. A better approach is to allow the user to surf
the web within the app itself. In this chapter, you add a lightweight web browser to the bands
apps, allowing users to search the web for their bands without leaving the app.

LEARNING ABOUT WEB VIEWS

In the Bands app you want to give the user the ability to search the web for information about
a particular band. To do this you need a way to view web pages. UIKit has a user interface
object called UIWebView that gives you this ability.

15. Select the `WBABandDetailsViewController.m` class from the Project Navigator.

16. Modify the `activityButtonTouched:` method with the following code:

```objc
- (IBAction)activityButtonTouched:(id)sender
{
    UIActionSheet *activityActionSheet = nil;

    /*
    if([MFMessageComposeViewController canSendText])
    activityActionSheet = [[UIActionSheet alloc] initWithTitle:nil delegate:self
cancelButtonTitle:@"Cancel" destructiveButtonTitle:nil otherButtonTitles:@"Email",
@"Message", nil];
    else
    activityActionSheet = [[UIActionSheet alloc] initWithTitle:nil delegate:self
cancelButtonTitle:@"Cancel" destructiveButtonTitle:nil otherButtonTitles:@"Email",
nil];
    */

    activityActionSheet = [[UIActionSheet alloc] initWithTitle:nil delegate:self
cancelButtonTitle:@"Cancel" destructiveButtonTitle:nil otherButtonTitles:@"Share",
@"Search the Web", nil];

    activityActionSheet.tag = WBAActionSheetTagActivity;
    [activityActionSheet showInView:self.view];
}
```

17. Modify the `actionSheet:clickedButtonAtIndex:` with the following code:

```objc
- (void)actionSheet:(UIActionSheet *)actionSheet
    clickedButtonAtIndex:(NSInteger)buttonIndex
{
    if(actionSheet.tag == WBAActionSheetTagActivity)
    {
        /*
        if(buttonIndex == WBAActivityButtonIndexEmail)
        {
        [self emailBandInfo];
        }
        else if (buttonIndex == WBAActivityButtonIndexMessage)
        {
        [self messageBandInfo];
        }
        */

        if(buttonIndex == WBAActivityButtonIndexShare)
        {
            [self shareBandInfo];
        }
        else if (buttonIndex == WBAActivityButtonIndexWebSearch)
        {
            [self performSegueWithIdentifier:@"webViewSegue" sender:nil];
        }
    }
    else if(actionSheet.tag == WBAActionSheetTagChooseImagePickerSource)
    {
```

```
            if(buttonIndex == WBAImagePickerSourceCamera)
            {
                [self presentCameraImagePicker];
            }
            else if (buttonIndex == WBAImagePickerSourcePhotoLibrary)
            {
                [self presentPhotoLibraryImagePicker];
            }
        }
        else if(actionSheet.tag == WBAActionSheetTagDeleteBandImage)
        {
            if(buttonIndex == actionSheet.destructiveButtonIndex)
            {
                self.bandObject.bandImage = nil;
                self.bandImageView.image = nil;
                self.addPhotoLabel.hidden = NO;
            }
        }
        else if (actionSheet.tag == WBAActionSheetTagDeleteBand)
        {
            if(actionSheet.destructiveButtonIndex == buttonIndex)
            {
                self.bandObject = nil;
                self.saveBand = NO;

                if(self.navigationController)
                    [self.navigationController popViewControllerAnimated:YES];
                else
                    [self dismissViewControllerAnimated:YES completion:nil];
            }
        }
    }
}
```

18. Run the app in the iPhone 4-inch simulator. When you select the
Search Web option from the activities, you should see the new Web
View, as shown in Figure 8-3.

How It Works

The first thing you did was to create a new subclass of the
UIViewController and name it WBAWebViewController. You then added a
new UIWebView property named webView.

In the Storyboard, you added a new scene and set its identity to the
WBAWebViewController class. This is the new Web View scene. You then
created a manual segue from the Band Details scene to the Web View scene
and set the segue identifier to webViewSegue. You set the identifier of this
segue in order to initiate the segue in code.

FIGURE 8-3

The segue added a UINavigationItem to the Web View scene, giving you the ability to set its title.
Finally, in the Storyboard you added the UIWebView to the Web View scene and connected it to
the webView property in the WBAWebViewController class. You may have noticed that part of the

UIWebView lies underneath the UINavigationItem. The UIWebView can detect this and make sure that the tops of pages load underneath the UINavigationItem without you needing to add any extra code.

In the WBABandDetailsViewController class you added a new option to the UIActivitySheet shown from the activity UIBarButtonItem and named it Search the Web. In the actionSheet: clickedButtonAtIndex: method you added a check for the WBAActivityButtonIndexWebSearch button index. If found, the code initiates the segue between the Band Details scene and the Web View scene using the performSegueWithIdentifier:sender: method of the UIViewController class (remember that WBABandDetailsViewController is a subclass of UIViewController, so you can use self to call this method) with the webViewSegue identifier you set in the storyboard.

Loading a URL

The app can now show a UIWebView, but it's not interesting without a URL to load. To implement the search feature, you could load a site such as Google or Bing and have the user type the name of the band into the search box and go from there. A user-friendly approach is to build a URL that does the search right away without the user needing to type anything. The simplest search URL to build is from Yahoo. To search for a band, you simply add it to the end of the query string.

Loading the URL in a UIWebView is a little bit more involved. UIWebView does not have a method that takes a string and loads it as a URL. Instead, it has a loadRequest: method that takes an NSURLRequest. The NSURLRequest object is designed to handle any protocol; though for the Bands app, you use only HTTP. NSURLRequest, like the UIWebView, also does not have an initialization method that takes a simple string but instead takes an NSURL. The NSURL class enables you to manipulate the various aspects of a URL such as the host, port, and query string. It does have an initialization method that takes a string. The string needs to be well formed for NSURL to parse it. If it fails to parse, the initialization method returns nil.

In the bands app you create the Yahoo search URL as a string with the band name in the query string. This means you need to have the band name in the WBAWebViewController. To accomplish this, you need to implement the prepareForSegue:sender: method again, as you did in Chapter 5, "Using Table Views."

TRY IT OUT   Loading a URL

1. Select the WBAWebViewController.h file from the Project Navigator, and add the following property to the interface:

```
#import <UIKit/UIKit.h>

@interface WBAWebViewController : UIViewController

@property (nonatomic, weak) IBOutlet UIWebView *webView;
@property (nonatomic, strong) NSString *bandName;

@end
```

2. Select the WBAWebViewController.m file from the Project Navigator, and add the following viewDidAppear: method:

```
- (void)viewDidAppear:(BOOL)animated
{
    [super viewDidAppear:animated];

    NSString *yahooSearchString = [NSString
stringWithFormat:@"http://search.yahoo.com/search?p=%@", self.bandName];
    NSURL *yahooSearchUrl = [NSURL URLWithString:yahooSearchString];
    NSURLRequest *yahooSearchUrlRequest = [NSURLRequest
requestWithURL:yahooSearchUrl];

    [self.webView loadRequest:yahooSearchUrlRequest];
}
```

3. Select the WBABandDetailsViewController.m file from the Project Navigator.

4. Import the WBAWebViewController.h with the following code:

```
#import "WBAWebViewController.h"
```

5. Add the following prepareForSegue:sender: method:

```
-(void)prepareForSegue:(UIStoryboardSegue *)segue sender:(id)sender
{
    if([segue.destinationViewController class] == [WBAWebViewController class])
    {
        WBAWebViewController *webViewController = segue.destinationViewController;
        WBAWebViewController.bandName = self.bandObject.name;
    }
}
```

6. Run the app in the iPhone 4-inch simulator. When you select the
Search the Web option, the web view displays a Yahoo search using
the band name, as shown in Figure 8-4.

How It Works

First, you added a bandName property to the WBAWebViewController.
Then in the implementation you added the UIViewControllerDelegate
method viewWillAppear:. In that method you first create an NSString for
the Yahoo search URL. Using that NSString you initialized a new NSURL
instance, which you then used to initialize an NSURLRequest instance.
The last step you added was a call to the loadRequest: method of the
UIWebView using the NSURLRequest.

You also added the prepareForSegue:sender: method to the
WBABandDetailsViewController class. In its implementation you use the
class static method, which is part of the NSObject class. You can use this
method to test if one object is the same type as another or if one object is
an instance of a class. In this code you check to see if the destinationView
Controller is an instance of the WBAWebViewController class. If it is, you
set the bandName property of the WBAWebViewController to the name prop-
erty of the bandObject prior to the WBAWebViewController being pushed onto the navigation stack.

FIGURE 8-4

Loading a URL That Contains Special Characters

If you have a band with a space in its name, you can notice that only the first word is searched. This is because spaces are not allowed in URLs, along with a handful of other characters such as ampersands, question marks, and exclamation points. To have those characters in the query string, they need to be URL-encoded, which means replacing them with a percent character followed by the hexadecimal value for the character in ASCII.

String manipulation can be coded in a straightforward way, but it also requires a lot of CPU time. This can be both slow and power draining in a mobile app, which has limited CPU power and memory. Some languages are better at string manipulation than others. The C language is low level, which makes writing these types of methods faster and more efficient. Because it is also the base language of Objective-C, you can write C methods into apps.

Learning C is not an easy task. Writing complex string methods is even more difficult. Fortunately for iOS developers Apple has done the heavy lifting and made those methods available in the Core Foundation Framework. Core Foundation is written entirely in C but can be called from Objective-C. Core Foundation has a string method called CFURLCreateStringByAddingPercentEscapes that can scan a string for a set of characters and replace them with their percent character/hex value. You can use this method in the Bands app to properly encode the band name before adding it to the query string of the URL.

Calling the method is simple but Core Foundation uses different data types than Objective-C. For example, NSString in Core Foundation is CFStringRef. These data types are not ARC-compliant. ARC, as explained in Chapter 2, "Introduction to Objective-C," stands for Automatic Reference Counting. It moves the burden of memory management from the developer to the compiler. The Core Foundation and Objective-C objects can be used interchangeably, but they need to be bridged. Apple has provided a solution for this called toll-free bridging. Essentially it's a macro that transfers the ownership Core Foundation objects to ARC. In the Bands app, you call the CFBridgeRelease macro that transfers total control of the CFStringRef returned by the CFURLCreateStringByAddingPercentEscapes method back to an NSString controlled by ARC.

WHY USING THE NEW NSURLCOMPONENTS CLASS IS NOT ALWAYS THE BEST OPTION

iOS 7 includes a new class called NSURLComponents that you can use to build a properly encoded URL in most situations. As you set the various components of a URL, the class compares the characters and encodes any that are not part of the allowed characters. The reason you cannot use NSURLComponents with the band name is because ampersands are a valid character for the query string component of a URL and part of the URLQueryAllowedCharacterSet used to encode invalid characters. If there is a band with the name "this & that," the URL created with NSURLComponents would be **http://search .yahoo.com/search?p=this%20&%20that,** which is incorrect. The correct URL is http://search.yahoo.com/search?p=this%20%26%20that. Using the CFURLCreateStringByAddingPercentEscapes function will escape the band name properly.

TRY IT OUT   URL Encoding a String

1. Select the `WBAWebViewController.m` file from the Project Navigator.

2. Modify the `viewDidAppear:` method with the following code:

```
- (void)viewDidAppear:(BOOL)animated
{
    [super viewDidAppear:animated];

    NSString *urlEncodedBandName = (NSString *)
CFBridgingRelease(
CFURLCreateStringByAddingPercentEscapes(NULL,(CFStringRef)self.bandName, NULL,
(CFStringRef)@"!*'();:@&=+$,/?%#[]", kCFStringEncodingUTF8 ));
    NSString *yahooSearchString = [NSString
stringWithFormat:@"http://search.yahoo.com/search?p=%@", urlEncodedBandName];
    NSURL *yahooSearchUrl = [NSURL URLWithString:yahooSearchString];
    NSURLRequest *yahooSearchUrlRequest = [NSURLRequest
requestWithURL:yahooSearchUrl];

    [self.webView loadRequest:yahooSearchUrlRequest];

}
```

3. Run the app in the iPhone 4-inch simulator. Searching the web for a band with an ampersand or other special characters now works.

How It Works

Prior to adding the band name to the query string, the `bandName` is URL encoded using the Core Foundation method `CFURLCreateStringByAddingPercentEscapes`. For example, if the `bandName` is "this & that," the `urlEncodedBandName` is "this%20%26%20that" with the spaces being replaced with %20 and the ampersand replaced with %26.

The syntax for Core Foundation functions is C instead of Objective-C. This function takes five parameters. The first is the `allocator`, which you do not need so you pass in `NULL`. The second is the `originalString` to be fixed. The third is a `CFStringRef` with the characters to leave alone. If the `bandName` had characters already escaped, you would list them in this parameter. Because it doesn't, you can again pass in `NULL`. The fourth parameter is the list of characters that should be escaped. For this you pass in all the characters that are not valid in a query string or which are part of building a query string, such as ampersands and question marks. The last parameter is the character encoding. The code passes in the `kCFStringEncodingUTF8` constant because UTF8 is the correct encoding for URLs.

The code also uses casts to both cast the `CFStringRef` result back to an `NSString` as well as cast the `NSString` `bandName` and the `NSString` of characters to escape to `CFStringRefs`. The last thing this code does is use the toll-free bridging macro `CFBridgingRelease` to make the result compatible with ARC.

Showing User Feedback

When making a network connection and transferring data, it is important to let users know that this activity is taking place. iOS uses the Network Activity Indicator to give this feedback. The Network Activity Indicator is the tiny spinning icon in the status bar that you see when you surf around in Mobile Safari or check your e-mail in Mail. It's available in your apps through the shared `UIApplication` object. You need to show this indicator in the Bands app (or any app that makes any type of network connection, for that matter) while the search is performed and the page loads. If you don't, your app may be rejected by Apple.

For a `UIWebView` you need to implement three methods in the `UIWebViewDelegate` protocol to achieve this. As a web page loads, it does so with a series of requests. These requests happen asynchronously, so there can be any number of them loading at the same time. In your app, you want the Network Activity Indicator visible from the time the first request starts to when the last request finishes. The easiest way to keep track of this is to use a counter. When a request starts to load, the `webViewDidStartLoad:` method is called in the delegate. The `webViewDidFinishLoad:` method is called when a request finishes loading. Your code should increment and decrement the counter when these methods are invoked. When the count gets back to 0, your app knows that all the requests that have started have now completed, and the Network Activity Indicator can be hidden. Some requests may fail. When a request fails, the `webViewDidFinishLoad:` method is not called. If you don't handle these failures, the load count never gets back to 0, and the Network Activity Indicator remains visible indefinitely. To handle this you also need to implement the `webView:didFailLoadWithError:` method to decrement the load count.

TRY IT OUT Showing the Network Activity Indicator

1. Select the `WBAWebViewController.h` file from the Project Navigator.

2. Declare that the class implements the `UIWebViewDelegate` using the following code:

```
@interface WBAWebViewController : UIViewController <UIWebViewDelegate>

@property (nonatomic, weak) IBOutlet UIWebView *webView;
@property (nonatomic, strong) NSString *bandName;

@end
```

3. Add the following property and method declaration to the interface:

```
@interface WBAWebViewController : UIViewController <UIWebViewDelegate>

@property (nonatomic, weak) IBOutlet UIWebView *webView;
@property (nonatomic, strong) NSString *bandName;
@property (nonatomic, assign) int webViewLoadCount;

- (void)webViewLoadComplete;

@end
```

4. Select the `Main.storyboard` and connect the delegate of the `UIWebView` to the `WBAWebViewController`.

5. Select the `WBAWebViewController.m` file from the Project Navigator.

6. Modify the `viewDidLoad` method with the following code:

```
- (void)viewDidLoad
{
```

```
    [super viewDidLoad];
    self.webViewLoadCount = 0;
}
```

7. Add the following `UIWebViewDelegate` methods to the implementation:

```
- (void)webViewDidStartLoad:(UIWebView *)webView
{
    self.webViewLoadCount++;
    [UIApplication sharedApplication].networkActivityIndicatorVisible = YES;
}

- (void)webViewDidFinishLoad:(UIWebView *)webView
{
    self.webViewLoadCount--;

    if(self.webViewLoadCount == 0)
        [self webViewLoadComplete];
}

- (void)webView:(UIWebView *)webView didFailLoadWithError:(NSError *)error
{
    self.webViewLoadCount--;

    if(self.webViewLoadCount == 0)
        [self webViewLoadComplete];
}
```

8. Add the `webViewLoadComplete` method to the implementation:

```
- (void)webViewLoadComplete
{
    [UIApplication sharedApplication].networkActivityIndicatorVisible = NO;
}
```

9. Run the app in the iPhone 4-inch simulator. As the web page loads, you can now see the Network Activity Indicator visible in the status bar.

How It Works

In the `WBAWebViewController` interface file, you declared that it implements the `UIWebViewDelegate` protocol and then added a property named `webViewLoadCount` to keep track of the load count. You also declared the `webViewLoadComplete` method. Then in the Storyboard you connected the `UIWebView` delegate to the `WBAWebViewController`.

In the `WBAWebViewController` implementation you initialized the `webViewLoadCount` to zero in the `viewDidLoad` method. Next, you implemented three methods of the `UIWebViewDelegate` protocol. In the `webViewDidStartLoad:` method you incremented the `webViewLoadCount` and set the Network Activity Indicator to be visible using the `networkActivityIndicatorVisible` property of the `sharedApplication`. In the `webViewDidFinishLoad:` method you decremented the `webViewLoadCount` and checked to see if it's back to 0. If it is, you call the `webViewLoadComplete` method that sets the Network Activity Indicator back to being hidden. The `webView:didFailLoadWithError:` method does the same thing as the `webViewDidFinishLoad` method, making sure that the Network Activity Indicator is hidden when all the requests either finish or fail.

ADDING NAVIGATION

The Bands app can now search the web and show the results in the UIWebView. When users click a search result link, they can go to that page, but they have no way of getting back to the search results to look at another. Web browsers give you navigation buttons that enable you to go back to the previous page or go forward to a page you just visited. They typically have a backward navigation stack where the current page URL is added prior to loading the linked page. When a user goes back, the current URL is added to a forward navigation stack before being removed from the backward stack and reloaded. Though the UIWebView does not give you a user interface to navigate these stacks, it does keep track of them for you and gives you methods to know if they have items as well as methods to perform the navigation. To add navigation to the Bands app, you need to build your own user interface. You do that using a UIToolbar.

Creating a Toolbar

A UIToolbar is similar to the UINavigationItem you've been using in previous chapters. It takes the entire width of the screen and enables you to add UIBarButtonItems. Unlike the UINavigationItem, the UIBarButtonItems do not have a set place. By default they are left-aligned with no spacing between them. To get UIBarButtonItems arranged in a UIToolbar with proper spacing, you use either fixed space or flexible space UIBarButtonItems. These are special implementations of UIBarButtonItem that do not enable user interaction and appear as blank space. Fixed-space UIBarButtonItems have a set width you can set. Flexible-space UIBarButtonItems can expand to the right, taking as much space as they can before encountering another UIBarButtonItem. For example, if you have two regular UIBarButtonItems with a single flexible UIBarButtonItem in between them, you will have one button on the left of the toolbar and the other all the way on the right.

UIBarButtonItems in a UIToolbar work the same as they do in the UINavigationItem. You can connect them with IBOutlets in your code to do things such as setting whether they are enabled. You can also connect them to IBActions so that they actually do something when touched.

In the Bands app you can add a UIToolbar that enables the user to navigate forward and back as well as stop a page from loading or reload the page after it has been loaded. To start, you first get the UIToolbar and UIBarButtonItems added to the scene and connected to IBOutlets and IBActions.

TRY IT OUT Adding a Toolbar and Buttons

1. Select the WBAWebViewController.h file from the Project Navigator.

2. Add the following IBOutlets to the interface:

```
@property (nonatomic, weak) IBOutlet UIBarButtonItem *backButton;
@property (nonatomic, weak) IBOutlet UIBarButtonItem *stopButton;
@property (nonatomic, weak) IBOutlet UIBarButtonItem *refreshButton;
@property (nonatomic, weak) IBOutlet UIBarButtonItem *forwardButton;
```

3. Add the following IBActions to the interface:

```
- (IBAction)backButtonTouched:(id)sender;
- (IBAction)stopButtonTouched:(id)sender;
```

```
- (IBAction)refreshButtonTouched:(id)sender;
- (IBAction)forwardButtonTouched:(id)sender;
```

4. Select the `WBAWebViewController.m` file from the Project Navigator, and add the following methods to the implementation:

```
- (IBAction)backButtonTouched:(id)sender
{
    NSLog(@"backButtonTouched");
}

- (IBAction)stopButtonTouched:(id)sender
{
    NSLog(@"stopButtonTouched");
}

- (IBAction)refreshButtonTouched:(id)sender
{
    NSLog(@"refreshButtonTouched");
}

- (IBAction)forwardButtonTouched:(id)sender
{
    NSLog(@"forwardButtonTouched");
}
```

5. Select the `Main.storyboard` from the Project Navigator.

6. Drag a Toolbar from the Object library onto the bottom of the Web View scene.

7. Adjust the `UIWebView` so that the bottom aligns with the top of the `UIToolbar`, as shown in Figure 8-5.

8. Select the default `UIBarButtonItem` on the `UIToolbar`, and set its Identifier to Rewind in the Attribute Inspector.

9. Drag a new Bar Button Item from the Object library to the `UIToolbar` and set its Identifier to Stop in the Attribute Inspector.

10. Drag a new Bar Button Item from the Object library to the `UIToolbar` and set its Identifier to Refresh.

11. Drag one more Bar Button Item from the Object library to the `UIToolbar`, and set its Identifier to Fast Forward.

12. Drag a Flexible Space Bar Button Item from the Object library, and place it in between the Rewind and Stop buttons.

13. Drag another Flexible Space Bar Button Item from the Object library, and place it between the Stop and Refresh buttons.

14. Drag one more Flexible Space Bar Button Item from the Object library, and place it between the Refresh and Fast Forward buttons, as shown in Figure 8-6.

15. Connect the buttons with their appropriate `IBOutlets` and `IBActions`.

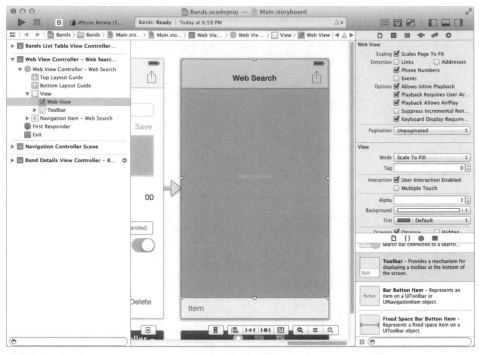

FIGURE 8-5

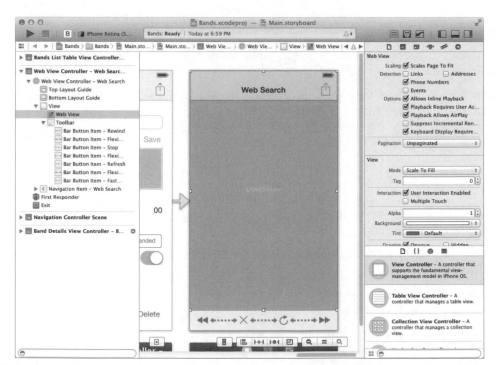

FIGURE 8-6

16. Run the app in the iPhone 4-inch simulator. You now see the
UIToolbar with the UIBarButtonItems equally spaced, as shown in
Figure 8-7.

How It Works

The first thing you did was to declare the IBOutlets for the four
UIBarButtonItems you will be adding to the UIToolbar in the
WBAWebViewController interface. Next, you declared the IBActions that
will be called when the UIBarButtonItems are tapped. In the implementation you added simple implementations of each IBAction that write which
one was called to the console.

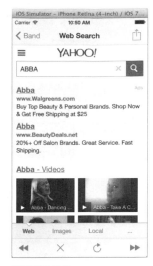

FIGURE 8-7

You did the work for this Try It Out in the Storyboard. First, you added
the actual UIToolbar to the Web View scene. Next, you adjusted the frame
of the UIWebView to align to the top of the UIToolbar. This differs from
the UINavigationItem. The UINavigationItem is designed to be semi-
transparent, so when users scroll the page, they see a blurred representation
under the UINavigationItem. UIToolbar is not designed to be transparent,
so any part of the UIWebView that lies underneath it will never be visible to
users. You may have noticed, though, that you did not need to add auto-layout constraints to either the
UIWebView or the UIToolbar to keep them anchored to the bottom of the UIView. Those constraints
are built in for you.

Next, you added the four UIBarButtonItems and set their identifiers to show an appropriate icon. You
then added the three flexible-space UIBarButtonItems so that all the UIBarButtonItems are spaced
equally across the UIToolbar. Finally, you connected the appropriate IBOutlets and IBActions to the
UIBarButtonItems.

With the UIToolbar user interface in place, you can now add the calls for navigation. The
UIBarButtonItems can add a little more user feedback so that users know when the page is
loading, when it's complete, and when they can navigate back and forth. To do this you disable
UIBarButtonItems depending on what state the UIWebView is in.

The back and forward UIBarButtonItems should be enabled only when there is a URL on their
respective stacks. The UIWebView has methods you can call to determine this. The canGoBack
method returns true if there's a URL on the back navigation stack. The canGoForward does the
same for the forward navigation stack. You can use the isLoading property of the UIWebView to
determine when the stop and reload UIBarButtonItems should be enabled. Stop should be enabled
only when the isLoading property is true. The reload button is enabled only when the isLoading
property is false.

UIWebView also gives you the goBack and goForward methods to load URLs off the navigation
stacks. There is also the stopLoading method that stops the current page that is loading. The
UIWebView has a request property that holds the initial NSURLRequest made to load the page.
Reloading simply loads the UIWebView using the current request.

TRY IT OUT Controlling the Web View

1. Select the `WBAWebViewController.h` file from the Project Navigator, and add the following method declaration:

```
- (void) setToolbarButtons;
```

2. Select the `WBAWebViewController.m` file from the Project Navigator.

3. Add the `setToolbarButtons` method to the implementation:

```
- (void) setToolbarButtons
{
    self.backButton.enabled = self.webView.canGoBack;
    self.forwardButton.enabled = self.webView.canGoForward;
    self.stopButton.enabled = self.webView.isLoading;
    self.refreshButton.enabled = !self.webView.isLoading;
}
```

4. Modify the `webViewDidStartLoad:` method with the following code:

```
- (void) webViewDidStartLoad: (UIWebView *) webView
{
    self.webViewLoadCount++;
    [UIApplication sharedApplication].networkActivityIndicatorVisible = YES;
    [self setToolbarButtons];
}
```

5. Modify the `webViewLoadComplete:` with the following code:

```
- (void) webViewLoadComplete
{
    [UIApplication sharedApplication].networkActivityIndicatorVisible = NO;
    [self setToolbarButtons];
}
```

6. Modify the `backButtonTouched:` method with the following code:

```
- (IBAction) backButtonTouched: (id) sender
{
    NSLog(@"backButtonTouched");
    [self.webView goBack];
}
```

7. Modify the `forwardButtonTouched:` method with the following code:

```
- (IBAction) forwardButtonTouched: (id) sender
{
    NSLog(@"forwardButtonTouched");
    [self.webView goForward];
}
```

8. Modify the `stopButtonTouched:` method with the following code:

```
- (IBAction) stopButtonTouched: (id) sender
{
    NSLog(@"stopButtonTouched");
```

```
    [self.webView stopLoading];
    self.webViewLoadCount = 0;
    [self webViewLoadComplete];


}
```

9. Modify the `refreshButtonTouched:` method with the following code:

```
- (IBAction)refreshButtonTouched:(id)sender
{
    NSLog(@"refreshButtonTouched");
    [self.webView loadRequest:self.webView.request];
}
```

10. Run the app in the iPhone 4-inch simulator. You can now navigate back and forth through the `UIWebView` navigation stacks as well as stop and reload web pages.

How It Works

In the `WBAWebViewController` interface you declared the `setToolbarButtons` method. In the implementation you implemented the method so that the back button is enabled when `canGoBack` returns true, the forward button when `canGoForward` returns true, the stop button when the `isLoading` property is true, and the reload button when the `isLoading` property is false. Next, you modified the `IBActions` to call their corresponding methods in `UIWebView`. In the `backButtonTouched:` and `forwardButtonTouched:` methods you call the `goBack` and `goForward` methods of the `UIWebView`. The `stopButtonTouched:` method first calls the `stopLoading` method of the `UIWebView`. Next it resets the `webViewLoadCount` to 0, then calls the `webViewLoadComplete` method to reset the `UIToolbar` and hide the Network Activity Indicator. The `reloadButtonTouched:` method calls the same `loadRequest:` method you call in the `viewDidAppear:`, using the `request` property of the `UIWebView`.

Opening Safari

`UIWebViews` are a nice addition to an app, but they do not give users all the functionality they have in Mobile Safari. Apple gives third-party developers access to some of its native apps using URL schemes and the `openURL` method in the shared `UIApplication`. Opening a URL in Mobile Safari requires only passing the URL into `openURL`. You can remember from early in this chapter, though, that the `UIWebView` can load many URL requests while loading the page. To get the main URL, you again use the `NSURLRequest` stored in the `request` property of the `UIWebView`. It has a property named `mainDocumentURL` that holds the URL for the main page.

To add this feature to the Bands app, you implement another Action `UIBarButtonItem` in the `UINavigationItem` as you did in the Band Details scene. When tapped, it shows a `UIActionSheet` with Open in Safari and Cancel as options. This approach makes users aware that they are about to leave the app and gives them an option to cancel.

➤ WHAT YOU LEARNED IN THIS CHAPTER

TOPIC	KEY CONCEPTS
UIWebView	The `UIWebView` is the `UIKit` object used to render HTML or to preview well-known file types such as PDFs and Word documents. They can load a web page using a network connection or display an HTML string or a file included with the app.
Core Foundation Framework	The Core Foundation Framework is a collection of functions written in C, which you can call from an Objective-C class. Because string manipulation is resource intensive, it is better to use Core Foundation Frameworks when performing complex tasks.
Network Activity Indicator	When an app is making a network connection and sending or downloading data, it needs to let the user know this activity is taking place. All iOS devices include a spinning icon in the status bar called the Network Activity Indicator. The Bands app needs to show the Network Activity Indicator while the `UIWebView` is loading a request.
UIToolbar	The `UIToolbar UIKit` object is how you implement a toolbar in an app. It has a set of `UIBarButtonItems` that act as both the visible buttons as well as the blank space separating buttons.
Open in Safari	The shared `UIApplication` has a method named `openURL` that you can use to launch built in Apple apps such as Mobile Safari. When used in combination with a `UIWebView`, you give users the ability to open the web page they are viewing in your app directly in Mobile Safari.

Exploring Maps and Local Search

The availability of maps and showing a user's location are very handy features of mobile devices. Apple's Maps app has been part of iOS since the launch of the iPhone. When the iOS SDK became public, Apple included its Map Kit framework for developers to build their own location-based apps, and they've been popular ever since.

Location-based search has become a popular feature in iOS apps as well. Urban Spoon was one of the first to use this type of location awareness by enabling you to view restaurants near your current location. Urban Spoon had spent a great deal of time building its database and search infrastructure to support its app and make it one of the most popular apps ever released.

Apple saw how popular location-based search had become. It partnered with the popular local search service Yelp and created new search classes and protocols that it released with iOS 6. With the new additions to Map Kit, developers can search and show local search results with just a few lines of code.

In this chapter you add the Find Local Record Stores feature to the Bands app. It displays a map with pins showing record stores around the user's current location.

LEARNING ABOUT MAP VIEWS

Adding an interactive map to an iOS app is done using the MKMapView. It is similar to the UIWebView you added in the previous chapter in that it's a standalone subview you can add to any other UIView. Though it's available in the Object library in Interface Builder, it does require adding the MapKit.framework to the project. The Bands project will compile just fine without the framework, but running the app causes a crash on launch. To start on the Find Record Store feature, you first add a new scene to the Bands app to present the MKMapView, as in the following Try It Out

TRY IT OUT Adding a Map View

1. Select the Project in the Project Navigator.

2. On the General tab in the Linked Frameworks and Libraries section, add the MapKit.framework as you did in Chapter 7, "Integrating Social Media."

3. From the Xcode menu, select File ⇨ New ⇨ File, and create a new UIViewController subclass named **WBAMapSearchViewController.**

4. Select the WBAMapSearchViewController.h file in the Project Navigator.

5. Add the MapKit.h file to the imports with the following code:

```
#import <UIKit/UIKit.h>
#import <MapKit/MapKit.h>

@interface WBAMapSearchViewController : UIViewController

@end
```

6. Add an IBOutlet for an MKMapView with the following code:

```
@interface WBAMapSearchViewController : UIViewController

@property (nonatomic, assign) IBOutlet MKMapView *mapView;

@end
```

7. Select the Main.storyboard from the Project Navigator.

8. Drag a new View Controller from the Object library onto the storyboard.

9. Select the new View Controller, and set its class in the Identity Inspector to the WBAMapSearchViewController class. This is now the Map Search scene.

10. Select the Band Details scene, and add a manual push segue from it to the new Map Search scene.

11. Select the new segue, and set its identifier to mapViewSegue in the Attributes Inspector.

12. Select the UINavigationItem of the Map Search scene, and set its title to Record Stores in the Attributes Inspector.

13. Drag a Map View from the Objects library onto the `WBAMapSearchViewController`.

14. Connect the `MKMapView` to the `mapView IBOutlet` in the `WBAMapSearchViewController`.

15. Select the `WBABandDetailsViewController.h` file from the Project Navigator.

16. Add a new value to the `WBAActivityButtonIndex` using the following code:

```
typedef enum {
//    WBAActivityButtonIndexEmail,
//    WBAActivityButtonIndexMessage,
    WBAActivityButtonIndexShare,
    WBAActivityButtonIndexWebSearch,
    WBAActivityButtonIndexFindLocalRecordStores,
} WBAActivityButtonIndex;
```

17. Select the `WBABandDetailsViewController.m` file from the Project Navigator and modify the `activityButtonTouched:` method with the following code:

```
- (IBAction)activityButtonTouched:(id)sender
{
    UIActionSheet *activityActionSheet = nil;

    activityActionSheet = [[UIActionSheet alloc] initWithTitle:nil delegate:self
    cancelButtonTitle:@"Cancel" destructiveButtonTitle:nil otherButtonTitles:
    @"Share", @"Search the Web", @"Find Local Record Stores", nil];

    activityActionSheet.tag = WBAActionSheetTagActivity;
    [activityActionSheet showInView:self.view];
}
```

18. Modify the `actionSheet:clickedButtonAtIndex:` method with the following code:

```
- (void)actionSheet:(UIActionSheet *)actionSheet
clickedButtonAtIndex:(NSInteger)buttonIndex
{
    if(actionSheet.tag == WBAActionSheetTagActivity)
    {
        if(buttonIndex == WBAActivityButtonIndexShare)
        {
            [self shareBandInfo];
        }
        else if (buttonIndex == WBAActivityButtonIndexWebSearch)
        {
            [self performSegueWithIdentifier:@"webViewSegue" sender:nil];
        }
        else if (buttonIndex == WBAActivityButtonIndexFindLocalRecordStores)
        {
            [self performSegueWithIdentifier:@"mapViewSegue" sender:nil];
        }
    }

    // the rest of this method is available in the sample code
}
```

19. Run the app in the iPhone 4-inch simulator. When you select the Search Map option, you now see the `MKMapView`, as shown in Figure 9-1.

FIGURE 9-1

How It Works

The first thing you did was to add the `MapKit.framework` to the project. Next you created a new `UIViewController` subclass called `WBAMapSearchViewController`. The class is quite simple with just an `IBOutlet` for an `MKMapView`, which requires importing the `MKMapKit.h` file.

In the Storyboard you added a new view controller and set its class to the new `WBAMapSearchViewController`. This is now the Map Search scene. You then created a new manual push segue to the Map Search scene from the Band Details scene. After that you added the `MKMapView` to the Map Search scene and set its `IBOutlet` to the `mapView` in the `WBAMapSearchViewController`.

In the `WBABandDetailsViewController` you added a new `WBAActivityButtonIndexFindLocalRecordStores` value to the `WBAActivityButtonIndex` enumeration. In the `actionSheet:clickedButtonAtIndex:` method you looked for the new `WBAActivityButtonIndexFindLocalRecordStores` value and called `performSegueWithIdentifier:sender:` method, using the `mapViewSeque` identifier to show the new Map Search scene.

Getting the User's Location

To perform a local search, you need to get the user's location. There are a few ways of doing this depending on the needs of the app, but all use the Location Service of the system. The Location Service is part of the `CoreLocation.framework` and uses hardware on the device to get an approximate location. For iPod touches and Wi-Fi-only iPads, the service can look up the location using the Wi-Fi hotspot to which the device is connected. iPads and iPhones that have a cellular connection can use the location of the cell tower. iPhones also have a GPS antenna for the most accurate location information.

> ### DESIGN YOUR APPS TO CONSERVE BATTERY POWER
>
> When adding location-aware features to an app, you need to keep battery life in mind. All these methods require the system to power on one of the antennas of the device. When an antenna is on, it consumes a good amount of battery power until the antenna gets powered back off. For location-aware apps you need to decide how accurate the location data needs to be and how often your app needs to be updated about changes.

Apps that need greater control over how accurate the location information is and how often it's delivered can use an instance of the CLLocationManager class in the Core Location framework and the CLLocationManagerDelegate. Using these you can set how accurate the location data needs to be and control how often the Location Service sends updates to the app. Developers using this method need to choose their settings wisely so that they can implement the feature they want while conserving as much battery life as possible.

Apps that use the MKMapView and need location data only when the device moves a significant distance can skip using the CLLocationManagerDelegate and instead use the MKMapViewDelegate. This method shifts the burden of conserving battery life back to the system. It still uses Core Location, but you as the developer don't need to worry about the details. This is the approach you take with the Bands app.

Location information also brings with it privacy concerns. Some apps in the past have passed the user's location on to other services without notifying the user. Because of this Apple added the Location Service to the privacy section of the Settings app. Users can turn off Location Services for either the entire device or per app. Some users may turn them off simply to boost their battery life. As the developer you need to keep this in mind. The CLLocationManager class has a static method called locationServicesEnabled that you can call to determine if Location Services are indeed available to your app. If they are not, you should at least tell the user why the location feature is not available. You do this in the following Try It Out using a UIAlertView.

For the Find Local Record Stores feature, showing the user's location on the map is useful only when it's zoomed in. As the developer, you can set the region of the map to show, as you see in the following Try It Out.

TRY IT OUT   Displaying the User's Current Location

1. Select the Project from the Project Navigator.

2. On the General tab in the Linked Frameworks and Libraries section, add the CoreLocation .framework.

3. Select the WBAMapSearchViewController.h file from the Project Navigator.

4. Declare that the class implements the MKMapViewDelegate and also add a property for the MKUserLocation using the following code:

```
@interface WBAMapSearchViewController : UIViewController <MKMapViewDelegate>

@property (nonatomic, assign) IBOutlet MKMapView *mapView;
@property (nonatomic, strong) MKUserLocation *userLocation;

@end
```

5. Select the WBAMapSearchViewController.m file from the Project Navigator.

6. Add the `viewDidAppear:` method of the `UIViewControllerDelegate` using the following code:

```
- (void)viewDidAppear:(BOOL)animated
{
    [super viewDidAppear:animated];
    if(![CLLocationManager locationServicesEnabled])
    {
        UIAlertView *noLocationServicesAlert = [[UIAlertView alloc]
initWithTitle:@"The Find Local Record Stores feature is not available"
message:@"Location Services are not enabled" delegate:nil
cancelButtonTitle:@"OK" otherButtonTitles:nil];
        [noLocationServicesAlert show];
    }
    else
    {
        self.mapView.showsUserLocation = YES;
    }
}
```

7. Add the `mapView:didUpdateUserLocation` method of the `MKMapViewDelegate` using the following code:

```
- (void)mapView:(MKMapView *)mapView
didUpdateUserLocation:(MKUserLocation *)userLocation
{
    self.userLocation = userLocation;

    MKCoordinateSpan coordinateSpan;
    coordinateSpan.latitudeDelta = 0.3f;
    coordinateSpan.longitudeDelta = 0.3f;

    MKCoordinateRegion regionToShow;
    regionToShow.center = userLocation.coordinate;
    regionToShow.span = coordinateSpan;

    [self.mapView setRegion:regionToShow animated:YES];
}
```

8. From the Xcode menu select Xcode ⇨ Open Developer Tool ⇨ iOS Simulator.

9. From the iOS Simulator menu, select Debug ⇨ Location ⇨ Apple.

10. Run the app in the iPhone 4-inch simulator. When you select the Find Local Record Stores option, you can now zoom into the San Francisco area with the user location annotation near Cupertino, as shown in Figure 9-2.

How It Works

The first thing you did was to declare that the `WBAMapSearchViewController` implements the `MKMapViewDelegate` protocol as well as add a property for the `MKUserLocation`. Locations are shown on an `MKMapView` using a class that implements the `MKAnnotation` protocol. It's a simple protocol that has three required properties. The `coordinate`

FIGURE 9-2

property is a `CLLocationCoordinate2d` struct that holds the latitude and longitude for the location. The `title` and `subtitle` properties are `NSStrings` that describe the location. The `MKUserLocation` is shown as a pulsing dot that automatically gets added to the map when the user's location is determined. You want to store the `MKUserLocation` in its own property so that your code knows that the location has been determined.

In the Storyboard you connected the delegate of the `MKMapView` to the `WBAMapSearchViewController`. In the `WBAMapSearchViewController` implementation you added the `viewDidAppear:animated:` method. It calls the `locationServicesEnable` static method of the `CLLocationManager` class to check if Location Services are enabled. If they are not, you show a `UIAlertView` to users letting them know that the feature is not available.

If they are available, you set the `showUserLocation` property of the `mapView` to `YES`. This tells the `MKMapView` to use Core Location to get the current location. When it determines the location, the `mapView:didUpdateUserLocation:` method of the `MKMapViewDelegate` is called.

In your implementation of the `mapView:didUpdateUserLocation:`, you first save the `MKUserLocation` in the `userLocation` property of the `WBAMapSearchViewController`. Next, you create an `MKCoordinateSpan` and an `MKCoordinateRegion`. The coordinate region determines the region of the map to show while the span determines how big of an area is visible. The latitude and longitude deltas are measured in degrees, with 1 degree equaling approximately 69 miles. In this implementation the map shows approximately 20 miles around the user's location.

Finally, you call the `setRegion:animated:` method of the `MKMapView` using the `MKCoordinateRegion` you created for the region parameter and pass `YES` for the animated parameter. With the animated parameter set to `YES` the user will see the `MKMapView` zoom in to their location.

> **NOTE** The iOS Simulator may reset its debug location setting back to None. If you run the app in the simulator and no location is found, check to make sure that the location debug setting is still set to Apple.

Changing the Map Type

If you have used Apple's Maps app, you have probably noticed the three different view types. Maps can be shown as the standard map with all the roads, highways, cities, and towns labeled, as a satellite view showing just satellite images, or as a hybrid with satellite images and all the labels. Some users may prefer the hybrid view when searching for record stores, so the Bands app you build gives them the option to change how the map displays.

TRY IT OUT Showing the Satellite and Hybrid Map Types

1. Select the `WBAMapSearchViewController.h` file from the Project Navigator.

2. Add a new enumeration named `WBAMapViewActionButtonIndex` using the following code:

```
typedef enum {
    WBAMapViewActionButtonIndexMapType,
```

3. Modify the `mapView:didUpdateUserLocation:` with the following code:

```
- (void)mapView:(MKMapView *)mapView
didUpdateUserLocation:(MKUserLocation *)userLocation
{
    self.userLocation = userLocation;

    MKCoordinateSpan coordinateSpan;
    coordinateSpan.latitudeDelta = 0.3f;
    coordinateSpan.longitudeDelta = 0.3f;

    MKCoordinateRegion regionToShow;
    regionToShow.center = userLocation.coordinate;
    regionToShow.span = coordinateSpan;

    [self.mapView setRegion:regionToShow animated:YES];
    [self searchForRecordStores];
}
```

4. Add the `searchForRecordStores` method to the implementation using the following code:

```
- (void)searchForRecordStores
{
    if(!self.userLocation)
        return;

    MKLocalSearchRequest *localSearchRequest = [[MKLocalSearchRequest alloc] init];
    localSearchRequest.naturalLanguageQuery = @"Record Store";
    localSearchRequest.region = self.mapView.region;

    MKLocalSearch *localSearch = [[MKLocalSearch alloc]
initWithRequest: localSearchRequest];

    [localSearch startWithCompletionHandler:nil];
}
```

How It Works

You first declared the `searchForRecordStores` method in the `WBAMapSearchViewController` interface. In the implementation of the `WBAMapSearchViewController` you modified the `mapView:didUpdateUserLocation:` to call the `searchForRecordStores` method when the user's location is determined.

The `searchForRecordStores` method is where the actual search is performed. The code first makes sure the `userLocation` property of the `WBAMapSearchViewController` is set. Without the `userLocation` set, the `MKMapView` is most likely showing the entire United States. You can perform a search of the entire United States, but it would not be very useful.

If the `userLocation` property is set, then the region of the `MKMapView` has been set to the area around the user's location. Next you initialized the `MKLocalSearchRequest` class instance. You set its `naturalLanguageQuery` property to "Record Store" and the `region` property to the `region` property of the `MKMapView`. This sets up the search to look for record stores within the visible region of the

MKMapView. Next you initialized the MKLocalSearch class instance using the MKLocalSearchRequest. Finally you called the startWithCompletionHandler: method of the MKLocalSearch class with a nil completion handler to send the request to Apple.

Unlike most of what you've coded up to this point, the MKLocalSearch class does not have a delegate protocol associated with it. Instead it uses a block passed into the startWithCompletionHandler: method.

Blocks, as you may recall from Chapter 2, "Introduction to Objective-C," are a way of passing a chunk of code into a method like any other parameter. The implementation of that method can then execute the code when it's appropriate. With the local search implementation you define an inline block as the completion handler to the startWithCompletionHandler: method. When the search is complete and the results have been retrieved, the block will be executed. The following Try It Out shows how this is implemented.

TRY IT OUT   Implementing a Completion Handler Using an Inline Block

1. Select the WBAMapSearchViewController.m file from the Project Navigator.

2. Modify the call to startWithCompletionHandler: in the searchForRecordStores method using the following code:

```
[localSearch startWithCompletionHandler:
^(MKLocalSearchResponse *response, NSError *error)
{
    if(error)
    {
        NSLog(@"An error occured while performing the local search");
    }
    else
    {
        NSLog(@"The local search found %d record stores", [response.mapItems count]);
    }
}];
```

3. Run the app in the iPhone 4-inch simulator. You will see the count from the local search result printed in the Xcode debugger console.

How It Works

The startWithCompletionHandler: method takes only one parameter, which is an inline block. You declare the start of the block with the ^ character. This block has two parameters: The first is an MKLocalSearchResponse object named response and the second is an NSError named error. You can think of the inline block as a method that gets called when the search completes. Instead of declaring a separate method and adding its implementation somewhere else in the file, you define the implementation inline. The implementation gets passed in the MKLocalSearchResponse and the NSError. In this Try It Out the code first checks to see if the NSError parameter is set. If it is, then the search results in an error. If the search was successful the NSError will be nil and the response parameter will have the search results stored in its mapItems property. This code writes the count of mapItems to the console.

COMPLETION HANDLERS AND THREADING

The MKLocalSearch completion handler allows for hiding the lower-level networking code that actually sends the request to Apple and receives the results. That lower-level networking may not be performed on the main thread, however.

Threads are a programming construct that enables multiple execution paths to be performed in parallel. The main thread in an app is almost always responsible for the user interface. When an app needs to perform a method that takes some time to complete, such as a networking call in this case, it's better to call it on a background thread to keep the user interface from freezing up while the task is performed. If the task results in the user interface needing an update, that update must be performed back on the main thread.

When using completion handlers you should assume that the code will not be executed on the main thread unless specifically stated in the Apple documentation. The documentation for the startSearchWithCompletionHandler: method of the MKLocalSearch class, found at https://developer.apple.com/library/ios/ documentation/MapKit/Reference/MKLocalSearch/Reference/Reference .html, includes the sentence "The provided completion handler is always executed on your app's main thread." This is very important, as you do not need to add your own code to make sure the completion handler is called on the main thread.

The Bands app can now perform a local search and get the results in the inline block. The next step is showing the record stores on the MKMapView. The actual search results are returned as MKMapItems. These items hold data about each record store found, including their name, a URL, and a phone number if available. To show them on the map, you need to create a class that implements the MKAnnotation protocol. For the Bands app you use an MKPointAnnotation, as demonstrated in the following Try It Out.

TRY IT OUT   Implementing Local Search

1. Select the WBAMapSearchViewController.h file from the Project Navigator.

2. Add the following property to the interface:

```
@property (nonatomic, strong) NSMutableArray *searchResultMapItems;
```

3. Select the WBAMapSearchViewController.m file from the Project Navigator.

4. Modify the viewDidLoad method with the following code:

```
- (void)viewDidLoad
{
    [super viewDidLoad];
    self.searchResultMapItems = [NSMutableArray array];
}
```

5. Modify the `searchForRecordStores` method to the implementation using the following code:

```objc
- (void)searchForRecordStores
{
    if(!self.userLocation)
        return;

    MKLocalSearchRequest *localSearchRequest = [[MKLocalSearchRequest alloc] init];
    localSearchRequest.naturalLanguageQuery = @"Record Store";
    localSearchRequest.region = self.mapView.region;

    MKLocalSearch *localSearch = [[MKLocalSearch alloc]
initWithRequest: localSearchRequest];

    [UIApplication sharedApplication].networkActivityIndicatorVisible = YES;

    [localSearch startWithCompletionHandler:
    ^(MKLocalSearchResponse *response, NSError *error)
    {
        [UIApplication sharedApplication].networkActivityIndicatorVisible = NO;

        if (error != nil)
        {
            UIAlertView *mapErrorAlert = [[UIAlertView alloc]
initWithTitle:@"Error" message:[error localizedDescription] delegate:nil
cancelButtonTitle:@"OK" otherButtonTitles:nil];

            [mapErrorAlert show];
        }
        else
        {
            NSMutableArray *searchAnnotations = [NSMutableArray array];
            for(MKMapItem *mapItem in response.mapItems)
            {
                if(![self.searchResultMapItems containsObject:mapItem])
                {
                    [self.searchResultMapItems addObject:mapItem];

                    MKPointAnnotation *point = [[MKPointAnnotation alloc] init];
                    point.coordinate = mapItem.placemark.coordinate;
                    point.title = mapItem.name;

                    [searchAnnotations addObject:point];
                }
            }
            [self.mapView addAnnotations:searchAnnotations];
        }
    }];
}
```

6. Run the app in the iPhone 4-inch simulator. When you select Find Record Stores, you see pins representing the search results for the record stores, as shown in Figure 9-4.

How It Works

In order to keep track of what record stores are found and added to the MKMapView you first declared an NSMutableArray property named searchResultMapItems in the WBAMapSearchViewController interface. You initialize it in the viewDidLoad method. The reason you do this in viewDidLoad and not in viewDidAppear:animated: is to make sure it is only initialized once. The viewDidAppear:animated: method will be called whenever the WBAWebSearchViewController becomes visible. This will be important in the Interacting with Annotations section on this chapter.

FIGURE 9-4

Next you modified the searchForRecordStores method. Before starting the local search you first set the Network Activity Indicator visible using the sharedApplication and networkActivityIndicatorVisible property. It is important to do this because the search is a network call. You then hide the Network Activity Indicator in the completion handler, because it gets invoked when the search has completed. Next the code looks at the error parameter, which when set means an error occurred during the search. The code now uses a UIAlertView to tell users what happened using the localizedDescription property of the NSError class.

If there is no error, you create an NSMutableArray that will hold all the new record store locations you will add to the MKMapView. You then use a for-loop to go through each MKMapItem returned in the mapItems property of the response parameter. You check to see if the MKMapItem is already in searchResultMapItems, which tells you if the search result has already been added to the MKMapView. If not, you add the MKMapItem to the searchResultMapItems.

To show the record stores on the MKMapView you need to use a class that implements the MKAnnotation protocol. The MKMapItem class has an MKPlacemark property named placemark that implements the MKAnnotation protocol. You could add the MKPlacemark to the MKMapView. It is displayed as a pin that shows the title in a callout when tapped by users. The title, however, is read-only and is set to the street address of the record store. The name of the record store is more useful, so instead you create an MKPointAnnotation.

The MKPointAnnotation also implements the MKAnnotation protocol and is also displayed as a pin. The title property, however, is not read-only. You set its coordinate property using coordinate from the MKPlacemark. You set its title to the name property of the MKMapItem, which is the actual name of the record store. Now when a user taps on the pin the callout will show the record store name. Finally you add all the new MKPointAnnotations to the MKMapView using the addAnnotations: method.

As the app is coded now, the local search is performed only when the user's location changes. If user is physically moving around, they see new results loaded. If they are staying still but panning around in the map, the search isn't triggered again, so no new search results display. To fix this you implement the mapView:regionDidChangeAnimated delegate method in the following Try It Out.

TRY IT OUT Updating Search Results After Panning

1. Select the WBAMapSearchViewController.m file from the Project Navigator.

2. Add the mapView:regionDidChangeAnimated method to the implementation with the following code:

```
- (void)mapView:(MKMapView *)mapView regionDidChangeAnimated:(BOOL)animated
{
    [self searchForRecordStores];
}
```

3. Modify the mapView:didUpdateUserLocation with the following code:

```
- (void)mapView:(MKMapView *)mapView
didUpdateUserLocation:(MKUserLocation *)userLocation
{
    self.userLocation = userLocation;

    MKCoordinateSpan coordinateSpan;
    coordinateSpan.latitudeDelta = 0.3f;
    coordinateSpan.longitudeDelta = 0.3f;

    MKCoordinateRegion regionToShow;
    regionToShow.center = userLocation.coordinate;
    regionToShow.span = coordinateSpan;

    [self.mapView setRegion:regionToShow animated:YES];
    //[self searchForRecordStores];
}
```

4. Run the app in the iPhone 4-inch simulator. As you pan around the map view or zoom in and out, you should see new pins added to the map.

How It Works

First, you implemented the mapView:regionDidChangeAnimated: delegate method of the MKMapViewDelegate protocol. This method gets called when users pan the MKMapView or zoom in and out. The implementation simply calls the searchForRecordStores method, which performs the local search again using the new region of the MKMapView. You then modified the mapView:didUpdateUserLocation: method to no longer call searchForRecordStores. Its implementation calls setRegion:animated: on the MKMapView, which triggers the mapView:regionDidChangeAnimated: delegate method. If you do not remove the call to searchForRecordStores, the local search will be performed twice.

Animating Annotations

Animations can add some polish to an app and help make the user interface more aesthetically pleasing. With map pin annotations, it's common to see the pins fall into place from the top of the screen rather than just showing them, as the Bands app now does. To animate the pins you need to change how you are adding them to the MKMapView.

You can recall from earlier in this chapter that all locations on a map are represented using a class that implements the MKAnnotation protocol. Both the MKUserLocation object used to show the user's location and the MKPointAnnotation objects you create to show the results of the record store search implement this protocol.

These annotations are represented visually on an MKMapView using an MKAnnotationView. Up to this point the MKMapView has used the default MKAnnotationView for both the user's location and record store locations. The default MKAnnotationView for the MKUserLocation annotation is the pulsing dot. This MKAnnotationView is private and not made available to you. The default MKAnnotationView for an MKPointAnnotation is an MKPinAnnotationView that you can use.

The MKPinAnnotationView has a property named animatesDrop that when set to true performs the drop animation. The default MKPinAnnotationView sets this property to false. In order to set it, you need to create and supply your own MKPinAnnotationView for the MKMapView to display. You do this using the mapView:viewForAnnotation: method of the MKMapViewDelegate protocol.

Before any annotation is displayed on an MKMapView it calls the mapView:viewForAnnotation: method of its delegate. If this method is not implemented or if it returns nil, the MKMapView uses the default MKAnnotationView for the annotation. This is important for the MKUserLocation annotation, because you want the default pulsing dot to be shown. For an MKPointAnnotation used for a record store location, you want to return your own MKPinAnnotationView with the animatesDrop property set to true.

Creating, adding, and deallocating subviews is expensive and can cause jittery animations when a user pans around an MKMapView. To combat this, the MKMapView attempts to reuse MKAnnotationViews that are already created and added to the MKMapView but are no longer visible. This is the same approach you learned about with UITableViewCells in Chapter 5, "Using Table Views." Before creating a new MKPinAnnotationView, you first try to dequeue one from the MKMapView using a reuse identifier. Only if none are available do you create a new one.

This approach may sound difficult, but the code to implement it is fairly straightforward, as you will see in the following Try It Out.

TRY IT OUT Animating Pin Drops

1. Select the WBAMapSearchViewController.m file from the Project Navigator.

2. Add the mapView:viewForAnnotation: method to the implementation using the following code:

```
- (MKAnnotationView *)mapView:(MKMapView *)mapView
viewForAnnotation:(id<MKAnnotation>)annotation
{
    if(annotation == self.userLocationAnnotation)
        return nil;

    MKPinAnnotationView *pinAnnotationView = (MKPinAnnotationView *)
[mapView dequeueReusableAnnotationViewWithIdentifier: @"pinAnnotiationView"];
    if (pinAnnotationView)
    {
        pinAnnotationView.annotation = annotation;
    }
```

```
        else
        {
            pinAnnotationView = [[MKPinAnnotationView alloc]
initWithAnnotation:annotation reuseIdentifier: @"pinAnnotiationView"];
            pinAnnotationView.canShowCallout = YES;
            pinAnnotationView.animatesDrop = YES;
        }

        return pinAnnotationView;
    }
```

3. Run the app in the iPhone 4-inch simulator. When results are retrieved, their pins will be animated onto the map.

How It Works

When the `mapView:viewForAnnotation:` method gets called you first check to see if the annotation being passed in is the `MKUserLocation` annotation. If it is you return `nil`, which tells the `MKMapView` to use the default pulsing dot.

If it is not, you can assume the annotation is an `MKPointAnnotation` for a record store location that needs an `MKPinAnnotationView`. Before creating a new `MKPinAnnotationView`, you attempt to reuse one by calling the `dequeueReusableAnnotationViewWithIdentifier:` method of the `MKMapView`. If an `MKPinAnnotationView` is available, you only need to associate it with the `MKPointAnnotation` by setting its `annotation` property using the `annotation` passed into `mapView:viewForAnnotation:` method. The other properties will remain set as they were when the `MKPinAnnotationView` was created.

If no reusable `MKPinAnnotationView` is found, you initialize a new one using the `initWithAnnotation: reuseIdentifier:` method. Next you set the `canShowCallout` property to `YES` so that the callout with the record store name is displayed when the pin is tapped. You also set the `animatesDrop` property to `YES` so that the drop animation is performed. Finally you return the `MKPinAnnotationView` to be displayed on the `MKMapView`.

Interacting with Annotations

One of the properties returned by the local search is a URL of the record store, if it is available. In the previous chapter, you learned how to display web pages, so to round out the record store search feature, you can also show the web page of record stores found.

When the callout of an `MKPinAnnotation` is shown, you can add accessory views to the left and right side. You can then implement the `mapView:annotationView:calloutAccessoryControl Tapped:` method of the `MKMapKitDelegate` protocol to know when the user taps the accessory. In the Bands app, you add an info button to the left side of the callout if the record store search result contains a URL. When the user taps the button, the app pushes the `WBAWebViewController` into view and displays that record store's web page.

TRY IT OUT Displaying Local Search Result Web Pages

1. Select the `Main.storyboard` from the Project Navigator.

2. Select the Map Search scene, and add a new manual push segue to the Web View scene as shown in Figure 9-5.

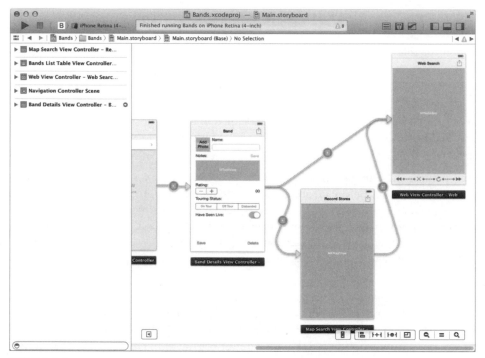

FIGURE 9-5

3. Select the new segue and set its identifier to `recordStoreWebSearchSegue` in the Attributes Inspector.

4. Select the `WBAWebViewController.h` file from the Project Navigator, and add the following property to the interface:

```
@property (nonatomic, strong) NSString *recordStoreUrlString;
```

5. Select the `WBAWebViewController.m` file from the Project Navigator, and modify the `viewDidAppear:` method with the following code:

```
- (void)viewDidAppear:(BOOL)animated
{
    [super viewDidAppear:animated];

    if(self.bandName)
    {
        NSString *urlEncodedBandName = (NSString *)
CFBridgingRelease(CFURLCreateStringByAddingPercentEscapes(NULL,
```

```
        (CFStringRef)self.bandName, NULL, (CFStringRef)@"!*'();:@&=+$,/?%#[]",
kCFStringEncodingUTF8 ));
            NSString *yahooSearchString = [NSString
stringWithFormat:@"http://search.yahoo.com/search?p=%@", urlEncodedBandName];
            NSURL *yahooSearchUrl = [NSURL URLWithString:yahooSearchString];
            NSURLRequest *yahooSearchUrlRequest =
[NSURLRequest requestWithURL:yahooSearchUrl];

            [self.webView loadRequest:yahooSearchUrlRequest];
    }
    else if (self.recordStoreUrlString)
    {
        NSURL *recordStoreUrl = [NSURL URLWithString:self.recordStoreUrlString];
        NSURLRequest *recordStoreUrlRequest =
[NSURLRequest requestWithURL:recordStoreUrl];

        [self.webView loadRequest:recordStoreUrlRequest];
    }
}
```

6. Select the `WBAMapSearchViewController.m` file from the Project Navigator.

7. Modify the inline block for the `startWithCompletionHandler:` in the `searchForRecordStores` method with the following code:

```
[localSearch startWithCompletionHandler:^(MKLocalSearchResponse *response,
    NSError *error)
    {
            [UIApplication sharedApplication].networkActivityIndicatorVisible = NO;

            if (error != nil)
            {
                UIAlertView *mapErrorAlert = [[UIAlertView alloc]
    initWithTitle:@"Error" message:[error localizedDescription]
    delegate:nil cancelButtonTitle:@"OK" otherButtonTitles:nil];
                [mapErrorAlert show];
            }
            else
            {
                NSMutableArray *searchAnnotations = [NSMutableArray array];
                for(MKMapItem *mapItem in response.mapItems)
                {
                    if(![self.searchResultMapItems containsObject:mapItem])
                    {
                        [self.searchResultMapItems addObject:mapItem];

                        MKPointAnnotation *point = [[MKPointAnnotation alloc] init];
                        point.coordinate = mapItem.placemark.coordinate;
                        point.title = mapItem.name;

                        if(mapItem.url)
                        {
                            point.subtitle = mapItem.url.absoluteString;
```

```
                              }

                              [searchAnnotations addObject:point];
                      }
                 }
                 [self.mapView addAnnotations:searchAnnotations];
          }
     }];
```

8. Modify the `mapView:viewForAnnotation:` method with the following code:

```
- (MKAnnotationView *)mapView:(MKMapView *)mapView
viewForAnnotation:(id<MKAnnotation>)annotation
{
    if(annotation == self.userLocationAnnotation)
        return nil;

    MKPinAnnotationView *pinAnnotationView = (MKPinAnnotationView *)
[mapView dequeueReusableAnnotationViewWithIdentifier: @"pinAnnotiationView"];
    if (pinAnnotationView)
    {
        pinAnnotationView.annotation = annotation;
    }
    else
    {
        pinAnnotationView = [[MKPinAnnotationView alloc]
initWithAnnotation:annotation reuseIdentifier: @"pinAnnotiationView"];
        pinAnnotationView.canShowCallout = YES;
        pinAnnotationView.animatesDrop = YES;
    }

    if(((MKPointAnnotation *)annotation).subtitle)
    {
        pinAnnotationView.leftCalloutAccessoryView =
[UIButton buttonWithType:UIButtonTypeDetailDisclosure];
    }
    else
    {
        pinAnnotationView.leftCalloutAccessoryView = nil;
    }

    return pinAnnotationView;
}
```

9. Add the `mapView:annotationView:calloutAccessoryControlTapped:` method of the `MKMapViewDelegate` using the following code:

```
- (void)mapView:(MKMapView *)mapView annotationView:(MKAnnotationView *)view
calloutAccessoryControlTapped:(UIControl *)control
{
    [self performSegueWithIdentifier:@"recordStoreWebSearchSegue" sender:view];
}
```

10. Add the `prepareForSegue:sender:` method to the implementation using the following code:

```
- (void)prepareForSegue:(UIStoryboardSegue *)segue sender:(id)sender
{
    MKAnnotationView *annotiationView = sender;
    MKPointAnnotation *pointAnnotation =
(MKPointAnnotation *)annotationView.annotation;
    WebViewController *webViewController =
(WebViewController *)segue.destinationViewController;
    webViewController.recordStoreUrlString = pointAnnotation.subtitle;
}
```

11. Run the app in the iPhone 4-inch simulator. When a local search result has a URL associated with it, you see the URL and the info button added to the callout, as shown in Figure 9-6. Tapping the info button loads the URL in the Web Search view.

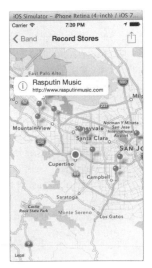

FIGURE 9-6

How It Works

The first thing you did was add a new manual segue from the Map Search scene to the Web View scene and set its identifier to `recordStoreWeb SearchSegue`. In the `WBAWebViewController` interface you declared a new `recordStoreUrlString` property. You then added code in the `viewDidAppear:animated:` method of the `WBAWebViewController` to create a new `NSURL` and `NSURLRequest` using the `recordStoreUrlString` and then asked the `webView` to load the new request.

In the `WBAMapSearchViewController`, you added code to the local search completion handler to look for a URL in the `MKMapItems` returned by the search. If one is found you set the `subtitle` property of the `MKPointAnnotation` using the URL string.

In the `mapView:viewForAnnotation:` method, you check to see if the annotation has its `subtitle` property set. If it does, you create a new `UIButton` with a button type of `UIButtonTypeDetailDisclosure` and set the `leftCalloutAccessoryView` of the `MKPinAnnotationView`. If it does not, you need to set the `leftCalloutAccessoryView` to `nil` in case the `MKPinAnnotationView` was reused.

Next you implemented the `mapView:annotationView:calloutAccessoryControlTapped:` method which calls `performSegueWithIdentifier:sender` using the `recordStoreWebSearchSegue` identifier. Finally, you added the `prepareForSegue:sender` method. It gets the `MKPinAnnotationView` as its sender. The `MKPinAnnotatoinView` has its `subtitle` property set to the URL string of the record store, which you then use to set the `recordStoreUrlString` of the `WBAWebViewController`.

SUMMARY

Local search is a powerful feature that can be used in many apps. Although location-based searches used to require your own backend service and low-level networking code, new versions of the iOS SDK make performing these searches much easier. With Apple Maps you can show users points of interest around them that relate to your app. In the Bands app, users can now search for record stores near their current locations as well as browse each store's web page while never needing to leave the app.

1. What framework is required to use an `MKMapView` in an app?

2. What framework is used to get the current location of an iOS device?

3. What delegate method of the `MKMapViewDelegate` protocol is called when a user's location is determined?

4. What are the two classes used to perform a local search?

5. What type of object is returned in local search results?

6. What character is used to denote the beginning of a block?

7. What subclass of `MKAnnotation` can you use to show a pin on an `MKMapView`?

8. What property of an `MKPinAnnotationView` do you set to animate the pin onto the `MKMapView`?

➤ WHAT YOU LEARNED IN THIS CHAPTER

TOPIC	KEY CONCEPTS
Map Kit	The MapKit.framework is used in iOS apps to display a map using an MKMapView. You can use this framework in conjunction with the CoreLocation.framework to get the current location of an iOS device.
Local Search	The iOS SDK includes two classes you can use to search for locations in a given region. The MKLocalSearchRequest class is used to build the request, while the MKLocalSearch class is used to send the request to Apple.
Completion Handlers	Some of the newer classes being added to the iOS SDK use completion handlers instead of delegates and protocols. A completion handler is an inline block of code that gets passed to a method like any other parameter. When the method completes, it will invoke the block of code. You use them to process the results returned from a local search.
Map Annotations	To mark locations on an MKMapView you use an instance of the MKAnnotation class. The MKPointAnnotation, which is the most common, shows a pin on the MKMapView. When users tap the pin it shows a callout with more information.

10

Getting Started with Web Services

WHAT YOU WILL LEARN IN THIS CHAPTER:

➤ Making simple networking calls

➤ Parsing JSON web service responses

➤ Streaming media from a URL using the Media Player

➤ Opening iTunes from within an application

WROX.COM CODE DOWNLOADS FOR THIS CHAPTER

You can find the wrox.com code downloads for this chapter at www.wrox.com/go/
begiosprogramming on the Download Code tab. The code is in the Chapter 10 download
and individually named according to the names throughout the chapter.

In the 1999, the phrase Web 2.0 was coined to describe the slew of new websites and services
being created. Websites in the past had been static and required new files to be uploaded to serv-
ers to change the content of the site. Web 2.0 sites use dynamic content with a back-end data
store to update content on the site without needing to update the files on the server. Blogging
sites are a simple example, whereas sites such as Facebook and Twitter are examples of more
complex services. Users can see new content on the site without having to even reload the page.
These sites typically use a set of API calls made using the Hyper Text Transfer Protocol, better
known as HTTP, to get new content. The set of API calls are known as web services.

Mobile apps have become an extension of these Web 2.0 sites. Using the same set of APIs,
mobile apps can move away from needing new builds and releases to update their content and
instead connect to these web services to get new data. This gives developers an endless amount
of new data they can add to their apps.

In this chapter you use the iTunes Search web service to add the Search for Tracks feature to
the Bands app.

LEARNING ABOUT WEB SERVICES

Web services enable two computers to exchange data over the web, typically using HTTP. Early web services used documented protocols that the data exchange conformed to. One of the first web service protocols was the Simple Object Access Protocol (SOAP), which was designed by Microsoft. SOAP uses the Extensible Markup Language (XML) to create messages that can be sent over HTTP. It was a popular choice of those developing software using Microsoft developer tools, because of its integration into those tools. Developers who were not using Microsoft tools found it to be overly complicated and hard to implement. As an alternative, developers began creating REST web services.

REST, which stands for Representational State Transfer, is a design pattern. Instead of creating a new protocol, REST web services build on documented aspects of HTTP. Because it's a design pattern and not a protocol, implementations of REST web services vary greatly, though the basic concept remains the same. In a REST web service the URL is used in conjunction with the four main HTTP verbs to perform basic tasks. The GET verb is used to request and retrieve data from the service, while the DELETE verb is used to delete data. The PUT and POST verbs both send data to a web service with PUT meaning to update data, while POST creates new data.

Exploring the iTunes Search API

The iTunes Search API (`www.apple.com/itunes/affiliates/resources/documentation/itunes-store-web-service-search-api.html`) is a REST API that does not require a username and password, making it a great tool to learn about web services. You can use the service to search iTunes for music, videos, books, and even other apps. In the Bands app you use it to search for tracks by band.

The search uses a well-formed URL and the HTTP GET verb to ask for data. This is the basic structure of the URL:

```
https://itunes.apple.com/search
```

You then add query parameters to the end of the URL the same way you built the Yahoo search URL in Chapter 8, "Using Web Views." In the Bands app you want to search for tracks only by artist. Table 10-1 describes the parameters and values you can use to build the search request.

TABLE 10-1: iTunes Search Parameters

PARAMETER KEY	VALUE	DESCRIPTION
media	music	Tells the service you would like to search for music only.
entity	musicTrack	Tells the service you would like to search for music tracks only and not music videos.
term	(band name)	The name of the band you would like to search for

Using these parameters and the band Rush as an example, the search URL would look like this:

```
https://itunes.apple.com/search?media=music&entity=musicTrack&attribute=artistTerm&
term=Rush
```

Using Safari on your desktop or laptop, you can enter that URL into the address bar and view the results, as shown in Figure 10-1.

FIGURE 10-1

Discussing JSON

The results from the iTunes Search API are returned in JavaScript Object Notation, or JSON. Originally designed for communicating between a web browser and server, it has become the most popular way of sending data in web services. It's a human-readable format that uses brackets and curly brackets to denote arrays and objects as well as key-value data with the key first, followed by a comma and then the data. Listing 10-1 shows a subset of the JSON returned by the iTunes Search API using the example URL in the previous section.

LISTING 10-1: JSON Results Sample

```json
{
  "resultCount":50,
  "results":
  [
    {
      "wrapperType":"track",
      "kind":"song",
      "artistId":50526,
      "collectionId":643419092,
      "trackId":643419201,
      "artistName":"Rush",
      "collectionName":"Moving Pictures (Remastered)",
      "trackName":"Tom Sawyer",
      "collectionCensoredName":"Moving Pictures (Remastered)",
      "trackCensoredName":"Tom Sawyer",
      "artistViewUrl":"https://itunes.apple.com/us/artist/rush/id50526?uo=4",
      "collectionViewUrl":"https://itunes.apple.com/us/album/
tom-sawyer/id643419092?i=643419201&uo=4",
      "trackViewUrl":"https://itunes.apple.com/us/album/
tom-sawyer/id643419092?i=643419201&uo=4",
      "previewUrl":"http://a1005.phobos.apple.com/us/r1000/061/Music2/
v4/4b/a1/aa/4ba1aa72-a6f5-4ac3-1b66-ca747aa490f8/
mzaf_4660742303953455851.aac.m4a",
      "artworkUrl30":"http://a2.mzstatic.com/us/r30/Music/
v4/17/ce/bc/17cebc97-e0cb-4774-8503-d7980e27f509/
UMG_cvrart_00602527893426_01_RGB72_1498x1498_12UMGIM19114.30x30-50.jpg",
      "artworkUrl60":"http://a1.mzstatic.com/us/r30/Music/
v4/17/ce/bc/17cebc97-e0cb-4774-8503-d7980e27f509/
UMG_cvrart_00602527893426_01_RGB72_1498x1498_12UMGIM19114.60x60-50.jpg",
      "artworkUrl100":"http://a3.mzstatic.com/us/r30/Music/
v4/17/ce/bc/17cebc97-e0cb-4774-8503-d7980e27f509/
UMG_cvrart_00602527893426_01_RGB72_1498x1498_12UMGIM19114.100x100-75.jpg",
      "collectionPrice":9.99,
      "trackPrice":1.29,
      "releaseDate":"2013-05-14T07:00:00Z",
      "collectionExplicitness":"notExplicit",
      "trackExplicitness":"notExplicit",
      "discCount":1,
      "discNumber":1,
      "trackCount":7,
      "trackNumber":1,
      "trackTimeMillis":276880,
      "country":"USA",
      "currency":"USD",
      "primaryGenreName":"Rock",
      "radioStationUrl":https://itunes.apple.com/us/station/idra.643419201
    }
  ]
}
```

The first data field in this sample is the `resultCount` whose value is 50. The next is an array of result objects. Only one is shown in the listing, although the full result set has 50 objects in the array. The result objects themselves have more than 30 fields, depending on what type of media it is. For the Bands app you can search for tracks. Table 10-2 lists the fields in the search results the Bands app will use.

TABLE 10-2: iTunes Search Result Keys

RESULT KEY	DESCRIPTION
collectionName	The name of the album or collection the track is part of
trackName	The name of the track
trackViewUrl	The URL of the track in the iTunes store
previewUrl	The URL to a preview of the track provided by Apple

Adding the Search View

To start the iTunes search feature, you first need to add a new scene to the Bands app to perform the search and display the results. In this scene you use a `UISearchBar` and `UITable` view. A `UISearchBar` is similar to a `UITextField` in the way it uses the software keyboard, which you learned about in Chapter 4, "Creating a User Input Form." When it becomes the first responder the keyboard is shown with a button labeled "Search." You then use the `UISearchBarDelegate` protocol to know when users tap the search button, as you will implement in the following Try It Out.

TRY IT OUT Using a Search Bar

1. From the Xcode menu select File ⇨ New ⇨ File and create a new subclass of the `UITableViewController` class named `WBAiTunesSearchViewController`.

2. Select the `WBAiTunesSearchViewController.h` file from the Project Navigator.

3. Declare the class implements the `UISearchBarDelegate` with the following code:

    ```
    @interface WBAiTunesSearchViewController : UITableViewController
    <UISearchBarDelegate>
    ```

4. Add an `IBOutlet` for a `UISearchBar` and a property for the band name using the following code:

    ```
    @property (nonatomic, assign) IBOutlet UISearchBar *searchBar;
    @property (nonatomic, strong) NSString *bandName;
    ```

5. Select the `WBAiTunesSearchViewController.m` file from the Project Navigator, and add the `viewWillAppear:` method using the following code:

    ```
    - (void)viewWillAppear:(BOOL)animated
    {
        [super viewWillAppear:animated];

        self.searchBar.text = self.bandName;
    }
    ```

6. Add the `searchBarSearchButtonClicked:` method of the `UISearchBarDelegate` using the following code:

```
- (void)searchBarSearchButtonClicked:(UISearchBar *)searchBar
{
    NSLog(@"Search Button Tapped");
}
```

7. Select the `Main.storyboard` from the Project Navigator.

8. Drag a new Table View Controller from the Object Library onto the Storyboard.

9. Select the new Table View Controller, and set its class to the `WBAiTunesSearchViewController` in the Identity Inspector. This is now the iTunes Search scene.

10. Create a new push segue from the Band Details scene to the iTunes Search scene, and set its identity to `iTunesSearchSegue` in the Attributes Inspector.

11. Select the `UINavigationItem` in the iTunes Search scene, and set its title to **iTunes Track Search**.

12. Drag a new Search Bar from the Object library, and add it to the top of the `UITableView` in the iTunes Search scene. You will know if it's a subview of the `UITableView` by looking at the Storyboard hierarchy, as shown in Figure 10-2.

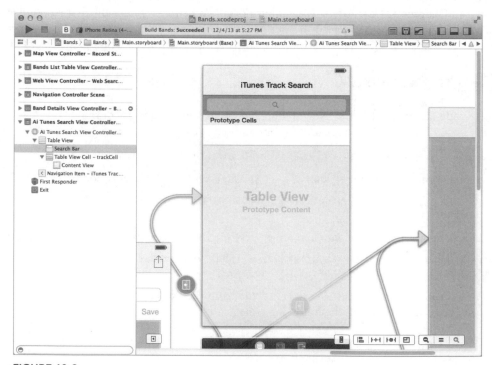

FIGURE 10-2

13. Connect the `UISearchBar` to the `IBOutlet` in the `WBAiTunesSearchViewController`.

14. Connect the delegate for the `UISearchBar` to the `WBAiTunesSearchViewController`.

15. Select the `WBABandDetailsViewController.h` file and add a new value to the `WBAActivityButtonIndex` enumeration using the following code:

```
typedef enum {
//    WBAActivityButtonIndexEmail,
//    WBAActivityButtonIndexMessage,
    WBAActivityButtonIndexShare,
    WBAActivityButtonIndexWebSearch,
    WBAActivityButtonIndexFindLocalRecordStores,
    WBAActivityButtonIndexSearchForTracks,
} WBAActivityButtonIndex;
```

16. Select the `WBABandDetailsViewController.m` file from the Project Navigator.

17. Add the `WBAiTunesSearchViewController.h` file to the imports using the following code:

```
#import "WBABandDetailsViewController.h"
#import <MessageUI/MFMailComposeViewController.h>
#import <MobileCoreServices/MobileCoreServices.h>
#import "WebViewController.h"
#import "WBAiTunesSearchViewController.h"
```

18. Modify the `activityButtonTouched:` method using the following code:

```
- (IBAction)activityButtonTouched:(id)sender
{
    UIActionSheet *activityActionSheet = nil;

    activityActionSheet = [[UIActionSheet alloc] initWithTitle:nil
delegate:self cancelButtonTitle:@"Cancel" destructiveButtonTitle:nil
otherButtonTitles:@"Share", @"Search the Web", @"Find Local Record Stores",
@"Search iTunes for Tracks", nil];

    activityActionSheet.tag = WBAActionSheetTagActivity;
    [activityActionSheet showInView:self.view];
}
```

19. Modify the `actionSheet:clickedButtonAtIndex:` method with the following code:

```
- (void)actionSheet:(UIActionSheet *)actionSheet
clickedButtonAtIndex:(NSInteger)buttonIndex
{
    if(actionSheet.tag == WBAActionSheetTagActivity)
    {
        if(buttonIndex == WBAActivityButtonIndexShare)
        {
            [self shareBandInfo];
        }
        else if (buttonIndex == WBAActivityButtonIndexWebSearch)
        {
            [self performSegueWithIdentifier:@"webViewSegue" sender:nil];
        }
        else if (buttonIndex == WBAActivityButtonIndexFindLocalRecordStores)
        {
```

```
            [self performSegueWithIdentifier:@"mapViewSegue" sender:nil];
        }
        else if (buttonIndex == WBAActivityButtonIndexSearchForTracks)
        {
            [self performSegueWithIdentifier:@"iTunesSearchSegue" sender:nil];
        }
    }

    // the rest of this method is available in the sample code
}
```

20. Modify the `prepareForSegue:sender:` method with the following code:

```
-(void)prepareForSegue:(UIStoryboardSegue *)segue sender:(id)sender
{
    if([segue.destinationViewController class] == [WebViewController class])
    {
        WebViewController *webViewController = segue.destinationViewController;
        webViewController.bandName = self.bandObject.name;
    }
    else if ([segue.destinationViewController class] ==
[WBAiTunesSearchViewController class])
    {
        WBAiTunesSearchViewController *WBAiTunesSearchViewController =
segue.destinationViewController;
        WBAiTunesSearchViewController.bandName = self.bandObject.name;
    }
}
```

21. Run the app in the iPhone 4-inch simulator. When you select the Search iTunes for Tracks option activity, you now see the iTunes Search scene with the `UISearchBar` containing the band name, as shown in Figure 10-3.

How It Works

The first thing you did was to create a new subclass of `UITableViewController` called `WBAiTunesSearchViewController`. In its interface, you declared that it implements the `UISearchBarDelegate` protocol and added an `IBOutlet` to a `UISearchBar` as well as a property for the band name to search for. In the implementation you added the `viewDidAppear:` method to set the `text` property of the `UISearchBar` using the `bandName` property.

In the `Main.storyboard` you added a new table view controller and set its class to the new `WBAiTunesSearchViewController`. This is now the iTunes Search scene. Because its parent class is `UITableViewController`, the `delegate` and `dataSource` of the `UITableView` and the `tableView` property are automatically connected.

FIGURE 10-3

Next, you created a manual push segue to the iTunes Search scene from the Band Details scene. With the segue added, the iTunes Search scene gets a `UINavigationItem` whose title you set to iTunes Track

Search. You then added a new UISearchBar to the scene, making sure to add it to the UITableView. This allows the UISearchBar to scroll off screen while the user looks at search results. Finally, you connected the UISearchBar and its delegate to the WBAiTunesSearchViewController.

In the WBABandDetailsViewController implementation, you added one more option to the UIAction Sheet, as you have done in previous chapters. You also updated the prepareForSegue:sender: method to set the bandName property of the WBAiTunesSearchViewController before the segue is performed. When selected this new option segues to the new iTunes Search scene.

INTRODUCING NSURLSESSION

The iOS SDK has a rich set of networking classes and protocols. Developers can control everything from caching and authentication to processing data as it is streamed in. This is great for applications that need that level of detail in their networking code, but it adds a lot of complexity for apps that need to make only simple network calls.

To address some of these complexities, Apple added the NSURLSession class and its companion classes and delegates to iOS 7. Using these classes developers can create different tasks that the system then handles, executing instead of having to implement all the lower-level details.

You can create three basic types of tasks. These tasks can then use either delegates to get the response and data or they can use completion handlers, as you did in the previous chapter.

➤ **Data task:** A data task is a simple http GET call that downloads data into memory.

➤ **Download task:** A download task is similar to a data task, except that the data is saved to a file on disk.

➤ **Upload task:** The third is an upload task that uploads a file from disk.

> **NOTE** For apps that require authentication, you need to implement the delegates that handle authentication challenges. This is beyond the scope of this book. To learn more about NSURLSession and its various delegates, refer to the URL Loading System Programming guide provided by Apple at https://developer.apple.com/library/ios/documentation/Cocoa/ Conceptual/URLLoadingSystem/URLLoadingSystem.html#//apple_ref/doc/ uid/10000165i.

Creating and Scheduling a Data Task

In the Bands app, the app needs to make a GET request then process the data that is returned. You will use an NSURLSessionDataTask to do this. The iTunes search API does not require a username and password, so there is no need to add any authentication capabilities. This means that you do not need to implement any delegates to handle authentication challenges. It also means that you can use the shared NSURLSession that uses the system defaults for its configuration. Because the results returned from the iTunes search API are relatively small, you also do not need to handle data as it's streamed from the network connection. Instead you can use a completion handler to process the data after it has been completely downloaded.

In Chapter 9 the documentation for MKLocalSearch explicitly stated the completion handler code would be executed on the main thread. This is not the case for NSURLSession. Since the code in the completion handler will be updating the user interface, you will need to code it in a way that ensures it is executed on the main thread. There are a handful of ways to do this. In the Bands app you will use Grand Central Dispatch.

Grand Central Dispatch, or GCD, was created by Apple and included in iOS 4. It was designed to remove much of the complexity of threading. The implementation of GCD still uses threads, but you as the developer no longer need to worry about them. Instead you *dispatch* blocks of code to different queues, which then schedule them to run on threads the system maintains. You use the dispatch_ async function to do this. This function takes two parameters. The first is the system queue to perform the block on and the second is the block itself. To get the main queue you use the dispatch_get_ main_queue function, which takes no parameters. Listing 10-2 shows a simple example of this syntax.

LISTING 10-2: Using dispatch_async

```
dispatch_async(dispatch_get_main_queue(),
^{
    NSLog(@"This will be scheduled and executed on the main thread");
});
```

The NSURLSession method you will use to call the iTunes search API is the dataTaskWithRequest: completionHandler: method. The request you pass in is an NSURLRequest, which you learned about in Chapter 8. You will build this request in the same manner as the Yahoo search request.

The block for the completion handler gets three parameters passed to it. The first is an NSData object that holds the data being returned from the request. The second is an NSURLResponse object, which holds the HTTP response. The last is an NSError object that will be set if the system encounters an error while performing the task. In the following Try It Out you will implement the call to the iTunes search API using the dataTaskWithRequest:completionHandler: method and print the response in the completion handler, using Grand Central Dispatch to make sure it executes on the main thread.

TRY IT OUT Calling the iTunes Search API

1. Select the WBAiTunesSearchViewController.h file from the Project Navigator.

2. Declare the following method in the interface:

   - (void)searchForTracks;

3. Select the WBAiTunesSearchViewController.m file from the Project Navigator.

4. Add the searchForTracks method using the following code:

   ```
   - (void)searchForTracks
   {
       [self.searchBar resignFirstResponder];
   ```

```objc
    NSString *bandName = self.searchBar.text;
    NSString *urlEncodedBandName = (NSString *)
CFBridgingRelease(CFURLCreateStringByAddingPercentEscapes(
NULL,(CFStringRef)bandName, NULL, (CFStringRef)@"!*'();:@&=+$,/?%#[]",
kCFStringEncodingUTF8 ));

    NSString *iTunesSearchUrlString = [NSString
stringWithFormat:@"https://itunes.apple.com/
search?media=music&entity=musicTrack&term=%@", urlEncodedBandName];
    NSURL *iTunesSearchUrl = [NSURL URLWithString:iTunesSearchUrlString];
    NSURLRequest *iTunesSearchUrlRequest = [NSURLRequest
requestWithURL:iTunesSearchUrl];

    NSURLSession *sharedUrlSession = [NSURLSession sharedSession];
    NSURLSessionDataTask *searchiTunesTask =
    [sharedUrlSession dataTaskWithRequest:iTunesSearchUrlRequest completionHandler:
     ^(NSData *data, NSURLResponse *response, NSError *error)
     {
         dispatch_async(dispatch_get_main_queue(),
         ^{
             [UIApplication sharedApplication].networkActivityIndicatorVisible
= NO;

             if(error)
             {
                 UIAlertView *searchAlertView = [[UIAlertView alloc]
initWithTitle:@"Error" message:error.localizedDescription delegate:nil
cancelButtonTitle:@"OK" otherButtonTitles:nil];
                 [searchAlertView show];
             }
             else
             {
                 NSString *resultString = [[NSString alloc] initWithData:data
encoding:NSUTF8StringEncoding];
                 NSLog(@"Search results: %@", resultString);
             }
         });
     }];

    [UIApplication sharedApplication].networkActivityIndicatorVisible = YES;
    [searchiTunesTask resume];
}
```

5. Modify the `viewWillAppear` method with the following code:

```objc
- (void)viewWillAppear:(BOOL)animated
{
    [super viewWillAppear:animated];

    self.searchBar.text = self.bandName;
    [self searchForTracks];
}
```

6. Modify the `searchBarSearchButtonClicked:` method of the `UISearchBarDelegate` using the following code:

```
- (void)searchBarSearchButtonClicked:(UISearchBar *)searchBar
{
    [self searchForTracks];
}
```

7. Run the app in the iPhone 4-inch simulator. When you select the Search iTunes for Tracks option, you see information about the search in the Xcode debug console, as shown in Figure 10-4.

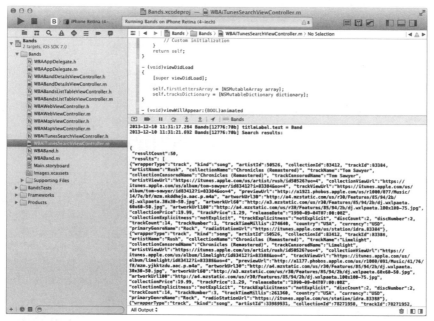

FIGURE 10-4

How It Works

In the interface of the `WBAiTunesSearchViewController`, you declared a new method called `searchForTracks`. In its implementation the first thing the code does is resign the `UISearchBar` as the first responder. This hides the keyboard if it is visible. Next, it gets the band name from the `UISearchBar` and URL encodes it using the same Core Foundation method you used in Chapter 8 to create the Yahoo search request. The code then builds the iTunes search URL string using the parameters discussed earlier in this chapter. Creating the `NSURL` and `NSURLRequest` are also the same as you implemented in Chapter 8.

Before creating the networking task, the code first gets the shared `NSURLSession` using the static `sharedSession` method of the `NSURLSession` class. You then use this instance to create a new `NSURLSessionDataTask` using the `NSURLRequest` and passing in a completion handler block.

The completion handler uses Grand Central Dispatch to make sure its code is executed on the main thread. It then hides the Network Activity Indicator and checks for any errors that may have occurred. If there is an error, the user is alerted; otherwise, the `NSData` returned from the data task is converted to an `NSString` using the `initWithData:encoding:` method and written to the debug console.

Creating the NSURLSessionDataTask does not start the request like the MKLocalSearch did. Instead you initiate the network request by calling the resume method of the NSURLSessionDataTask. The code does this after making the Network Activity Indicator visible.

Parsing JSON

A big advantage JSON has over XML in iOS is that it already conforms to data structures in Objective-C. Because all data in JSON is key-value formatted, NSDictionary is a natural match for mapping the data to Objective-C. The JSON returned from the iTunes Search API can be mapped to an NSDictionary with two keys: resultCount and results. The object stored for the resultCount key is an NSNumber with a value of 50. The object stored for the results key is an NSArray which contains NSDictionary objects that represent each track in the search results.

Parsing the actual data returned from the service may seem complicated, but fortunately Apple has already created a parser for you with the NSJSONSerialization class. It has a static method called JSONObjectWithData:options:error:, which returns the NSDictionary representing the JSON. The options tell the parser if you would like the data structures to be mutable. Since the Bands app won't be modifying the search results, you can pass 0 for the options. The method also takes an NSError parameter. It gets passed by reference which, as you learned in Chapter 2, "Introduction to Objective-C," means you are passing the address for an NSError object and not the object itself. If an error occurs while parsing, the parser will create an actual NSError object and set the address you passed in to point to it. The following Try It Out shows you how to use the NSJSONSerialization class to parse the results for the iTunes search.

TRY IT OUT Parsing iTunes Search Results

1. Select the WBAiTunesSearchViewController.m file from the Project Navigator.

2. Modify the completion handler for the NSURLSessionDataTask with the following code:

```
NSURLSessionDataTask *searchiTunesTask =
[sharedUrlSession dataTaskWithRequest:iTunesSearchUrlRequest completionHandler:
^(NSData *data, NSURLResponse *response, NSError *error)
{
    dispatch_async(dispatch_get_main_queue(),
    ^{
        [UIApplication sharedApplication].networkActivityIndicatorVisible = NO;

        if(error)
        {
            UIAlertView *searchAlertView = [[UIAlertView alloc]
initWithTitle:@"Error" message:error.localizedDescription delegate:nil
cancelButtonTitle:@"OK" otherButtonTitles:nil];

            [searchAlertView show];
        }
        else
        {
```

```
            NSString *resultString = [[NSString alloc] initWithData:data
encoding:NSUTF8StringEncoding];
            NSLog(@"Search results: %@", resultString);

        NSError *jsonParseError = nil;
            NSDictionary *jsonDictionary = [NSJSONSerialization
JSONObjectWithData:data options:0 error:&jsonParseError];

            if(jsonParseError)
            {
                UIAlertView *jsonParseErrorAlert = [[UIAlertView alloc]
initWithTitle:@"Error" message:jsonParseError.localizedDescription delegate:nil
cancelButtonTitle:@"OK" otherButtonTitles:nil];

                [jsonParseErrorAlert show];
            }
            else
            {
                for(NSString *key in jsonDictionary.keyEnumerator)
                {
                    NSLog(@"First level key: %@", key);
                }
            }
        }
    });
}];
```

3. Run the app in the iPhone 4-inch simulator. When searching for tracks you now see more information in the Xcode console, as shown in Figure 10-5.

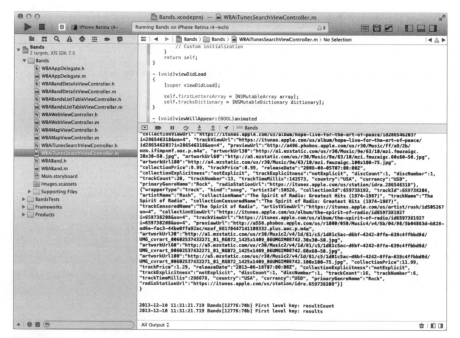

FIGURE 10-5

How It Works

If the data task returns successfully, the code now attempts to parse the data using the NSJSONSerialization class. The code first creates a pointer to an NSError and sets its value to nil, meaning it doesn't point to anything. It then passes the data from the NSURLSessionDataTask, 0 for the options (meaning it's OK to use immutable data structures) and the NSError pointer to the JSONObjectWithData:options:error: method. When the parse completes, the code checks to see if the NSError pointer was set to an actual NSError object. If so, an error has occurred during the parsing and the user is alerted. Otherwise, it prints the first-level keys of the dictionary—resultCount and results—to the debug console.

DISPLAYING SEARCH RESULTS

The last part of the iTunes Track Search feature is to display all the tracks in alphabetical order then give the user the ability to preview the track or to view the track in iTunes. The data source for the UITableView uses the same approach you implemented to display the bands. First, you need to create an object to hold the properties of each track returned from the search. You can then create the same first letters NSMutableArray to create the table index and a tracks NSMutableDictionary to hold the track objects for each of the results.

TRY IT OUT   Creating the Data Source

1. Select the Main.storyboard from the Project Navigator.

2. Select the prototype cell in the iTunes Search view.

3. Set its style to subtitle in the Attributes Inspector.

4. Set its reuse identifier to **trackCell** in the Attributes Inspector.

5. From the Xcode menu select File ⇨ New ⇨ File, and create a new subclass of NSObject called WBATrack.

6. Select the WBATrack.h file, and add properties for the track name, collection name, track preview URL, and iTunes URL using the following code:

```
@interface WBATrack : NSObject

@property (nonatomic, strong) NSString *trackName;
@property (nonatomic, strong) NSString *collectionName;
@property (nonatomic, strong) NSString *previewUrlString;
@property (nonatomic, strong) NSString *iTunesUrlString;

@end
```

7. Select the WBATrack.m file, and add the compare method using the following code:

```
- (NSComparisonResult)compare:(WBATrack *)otherObject
{
    return [self.trackName compare:otherObject.trackName];
}
```

8. Select the `WBAiTunesSearchViewController.h` file from the Project Manager.

9. Add properties for the tracks `NSMutableDictionary` and first letters `NSMutableArray` using the following code:

```
@property (nonatomic, strong) NSMutableArray *firstLettersArray;
@property (nonatomic, strong) NSMutableDictionary *tracksDictionary;
```

10. Select the `WBAiTunesSearchViewController.m` file from the Project Manager.

11. Import the `WBATrack.h` class using the following code:

```
#import "WBAiTunesSearchViewController.h"
#import "WBATrack.h"
```

12. Modify the `viewDidLoad` method with the following code:

```
- (void)viewDidLoad
{
    [super viewDidLoad];

    self.firstLettersArray = [NSMutableArray array];
    self.tracksDictionary = [NSMutableDictionary dictionary];
}
```

13. In the completion handler for the `NSURLSessionDataTask` add the following code to the `else` statement after the JSON has been successfully parsed:

```
for(NSString *key in jsonDictionary.keyEnumerator)
{
    NSLog(@"First level key: %@", key);
}

[self.firstLettersArray removeAllObjects];
[self.tracksDictionary removeAllObjects];

NSArray *searchResultsArray = [jsonDictionary objectForKey:@"results"];
for(NSDictionary *trackInfoDictionary in searchResultsArray)
{
    WBATrack *track = [[WBATrack alloc] init];
    track.trackName = [trackInfoDictionary objectForKey:@"trackName"];
    track.collectionName = [trackInfoDictionary objectForKey:@"collectionName"];
    track.previewUrlString = [trackInfoDictionary objectForKey:@"previewUrl"];
    track.iTunesUrlString = [trackInfoDictionary objectForKey:@"trackViewUrl"];

    NSString *trackFirstLetter = [track.trackName substringToIndex:1];
    NSMutableArray *tracksWithFirstLetter = [self.tracksDictionary
objectForKey:trackFirstLetter];

    if(!tracksWithFirstLetter)
    {
        tracksWithFirstLetter = [NSMutableArray array];
        [self.firstLettersArray addObject:trackFirstLetter];
    }

    [tracksWithFirstLetter addObject:track];
    [tracksWithFirstLetter sortUsingSelector:@selector(compare:)];
```

```
        [self.tracksDictionary setObject:tracksWithFirstLetter forKey:trackFirstLetter];
    }

    [self.firstLettersArray sortUsingSelector:@selector(compare:)];
    [self.tableView reloadData];
```

14. Modify the `numberOfSectionsInTableView:` method with the following code:

```
- (NSInteger)numberOfSectionsInTableView:(UITableView *)tableView
{
    return self.firstLettersArray.count;
}
```

15. Modify the `tableView:numberOfRowsInSection:` method with the following code:

```
- (NSInteger)tableView:(UITableView *)tableView
numberOfRowsInSection:(NSInteger)section
{
    NSString *firstLetter = [self.firstLettersArray objectAtIndex:section];
    NSArray *tracksWithFirstLetter =
      [self.tracksDictionary objectForKey:firstLetter];
    return tracksWithFirstLetter.count;
}
```

16. Modify the `tableView:cellForRowAtIndexPath:` method with the following code:

```
- (UITableViewCell *)tableView:(UITableView *)tableView
cellForRowAtIndexPath:(NSIndexPath)indexPath
{
    static NSString *CellIdentifier = @"trackCell";
    UITableViewCell *cell =
      [tableView dequeueReusableCellWithIdentifier:CellIdentifier
      forIndexPath:indexPath];

    NSString *firstLetter = [self.firstLettersArray objectAtIndex:indexPath.section];
    NSArray *tracksWithFirstLetter = [self.tracksDictionary objectForKey:firstLetter];
    WBATrack *track = [tracksWithFirstLetter objectAtIndex:indexPath.row];

    cell.textLabel.text = track.trackName;
    cell.detailTextLabel.text = track.collectionName;

    return cell;
}
```

17. Add the `tableView:titleForHeaderInSection:` method using the following code:

```
- (NSString *)tableView:(UITableView *)tableView
titleForHeaderInSection:(NSInteger)section
{
    return [self.firstLettersArray objectAtIndex:section];
}
```

18. Add the `sectionIndexTitlesForTableView:` method using the following code:

```
- (NSArray *)sectionIndexTitlesForTableView:(UITableView *)tableView
{
    return self.firstLettersArray;
}
```

19. Add the `tableView:sectionForSectionIndexTitle:atIndex` method using the following code:

```
- (int)tableView:(UITableView *)tableView sectionForSectionIndexTitle:
(NSString *)title atIndex:(NSInteger)index
{
    return [self.firstLettersArray indexOfObject:title];
}
```

20. Run the app in the iPhone 4-inch simulator. Searching for tracks now shows results in the Table view, as shown in Figure 10-6.

How It Works

The first thing you did was change the type of the prototype cell in the Storyboard to the subtitle type. This way you can display both the name of the track and the album or collection it is on in the same cell. You also set the reuse identifier of the cell.

FIGURE 10-6

Next, you created a new `WBATrack` object with four properties for the track name, collection name, iTunes URL string, and preview URL string. To sort the tracks by name, you also override the `compare:` method to use the track names as the comparison property.

In the `WBAiTunesSearchViewController` interface you declared the `firstLettersArray` and the `tracksDictionary`. These are analogous to `firstLettersArray` and `bandsDictionary` you implemented in Chapter 5, "Using Table Views." In the implementation you initialize the array and dictionary when the view appears.

The main focus of the Try It Out is processing the results of the search and creating the data source for the `UITableView`. Once the JSON result has been successfully parsed, you first clear all the objects in the `firstLettersArray` and the `tracksDictionary`. This is so users do not see mixed results if they type their own search term into the `UISearchBar`. Next you get the `NSArray` of search results from the `jsonDictionary` using the `results` key. This `NSArray` contains `NSDictionary` objects for each track returned from the search. The keys for a track `NSDictionary` correspond to the keys in the JSON response (refer to Table 10-2). The code uses a `for` loop to iterate through each track `NSDictionary`, creating `WBATrack` objects for each and then using them to repopulate the `firstLettersArray` and the `tracksDictionary`.

The rest of the Try It Out implements the `UITableViewDataSource` protocol methods. The code is the same pattern you implemented in Chapter 5 for the bands `UITableView` using the `firstLettersArray` as an index into the `tracksDictionary`. The only notable difference is in the `tableView:cellForRowAt IndexPath:` method. Because you set the type of the prototype cell to subtitle, the `detailsTextLabel` will be visible in the cell. You set its `text` property to the `collectionName` property of the `WBATrack`.

Previewing Tracks

The iTunes Search API includes a preview URL in the results. This URL points to a media file with a preview of the track that can be streamed using the `MPMoviePlayerViewController`. This is a special view controller similar to the `UIImagePickerController` and `MFMailComposeViewController` you have implemented in previous chapters. It does require the `MediaPlayer.framework` to be added to the project. You can then import the `MediaPlayer.h` file to access the `MPMoviePlayerViewController` and the `presentMoviePlayerViewControllerAnimated:` method it adds to the `UIViewController` class. When created and presented, the movie player handles all the network connections to stream the track preview from iTunes.

To give the user the option to preview a track, your code needs to know when the user has selected a track in the `UITableView`. You can use the `tableView:didSelectRowAtIndexPath:` method of the `UITableViewDelegate` protocol for this. When the user selects a track, this method is called. You can then show the track options using a `UIActionSheet`, as you will implement in the following Try It Out.

TRY IT OUT Using the Media Player

1. Select the Project from the Project Manager, and add the `MediaPlayer.framework` to the linked libraries and frameworks.

2. Select the `WBAiTunesSearchViewController.h` file.

3. Declare that the class implements the `UIActionSheetDelegate` using the following code:

```
@interface WBAiTunesSearchViewController : UITableViewController
<UISearchBarDelegate, UIActionSheetDelegate>
```

4. Create a new enumeration named `WBATrackOptionButtonIndex` using the following code:

```
typedef enum {
    WBATrackOptionButtonIndexPreview,
} WBATrackOptionButtonIndex;
```

5. Select the `WBAiTunesSearchViewController.m` file from the Project Manager.

6. Add the `MediaPlayer.h` file to the imports using the following code:

```
#import "WBAiTunesSearchViewController.h"
#import "WBATrack.h"
#import <MediaPlayer/MediaPlayer.h>
```

7. Add the `tableView:didSelectRowAtIndexPath:` method to the implementation using the following code:

```
- (void)tableView:(UITableView *)tableView
didSelectRowAtIndexPath:(NSIndexPath *)indexPath
{
    UIActionSheet *trackActionSheet = [[UIActionSheet alloc] initWithTitle:nil
delegate:self cancelButtonTitle:@"Cancel" destructiveButtonTitle:nil
otherButtonTitles:@"Preview Track", nil];

    [trackActionSheet showInView:self.view];
}
```

8. Add the `actionSheet:clickedButtonAtIndex:` method using the following code:

```
- (void)actionSheet:(UIActionSheet *)actionSheet
clickedButtonAtIndex:(NSInteger)buttonIndex
{
    NSIndexPath *selectedIndexPath = self.tableView.indexPathForSelectedRow;
```

```
    NSString *trackFirstLetter = [self.firstLettersArray
objectAtIndex:selectedIndexPath.section];

    NSArray *tracksWithFirstLetter = [self.tracksDictionary
objectForKey:trackFirstLetter];

    WBATrack *trackObject = [tracksWithFirstLetter
objectAtIndex:selectedIndexPath.row];

    if(buttonIndex == WBATrackOptionButtonIndexPreview)
    {
        NSURL *trackPreviewURL = [NSURL URLWithString:trackObject.previewUrlString];
        MPMoviePlayerViewController *moviePlayerViewController =
[[MPMoviePlayerViewController alloc] initWithContentURL:trackPreviewURL];

        [self presentMoviePlayerViewControllerAnimated:moviePlayerViewController];
    }
    else if (buttonIndex == WBATrackOptionButtonIndexOpenIniTunes)
    {
        NSURL *iTunesURL = [NSURL URLWithString:trackObject.iTunesUrlString];
        [[UIApplication sharedApplication] openURL:iTunesURL];
    }
}
```

9. Run the app in the iPhone 4-inch simulator. Selecting a search result now previews the track in the application using the Media Player, as shown in Figure 10-7.

How It Works

The first thing you did was to add the MediaPlayer.framework to the project. Next you declare that the WBAiTunesSearchViewController implements the UIActionSheetDelegate. You also added a new enumeration named WBATrackOptionButtonIndex, which maps to the options that will be shown in the UIActionSheet.

In the implementation you added the MediaPlayer.h file to the imports so you can access the MPMoviePlayerViewController. You then added the tableView:didSelectRowAtIndexPath: method that creates a new UIActionSheet with Preview Track as the only option.

Finally, you added the actionSheet:didClickButtonAtIndex: method. It first gets the WBATrack object correlating to the NSIndexPath of the currently selected row in the UITableView. If the preview button is clicked, it creates a new NSURL using the trackPreviewUrl property of the WBATrack object. It then creates a new instance of the MPMoviePlayerViewController using the initWithContentURL: method and the NSURL. The MPMoviePlayerViewController is then presented using the presentMoviePlayerViewControllerAnimated method.

FIGURE 10-7

Showing Tracks in iTunes

The last part of the Search iTunes for Tracks feature is opening iTunes to the track so that the user can purchase it. You do this the same way you opened Safari in Chapter 8. The system knows to pass URLs pointing to `http://itunes.apple.com` to the iTunes app, so all you need to do in code is call the `openURL` method of the shared application.

TRY IT OUT   Opening iTunes

1. Select the `WBAiTunesSearchViewController.h` file and add another value to the `WBATrackOptionButtonIndex` enumeration using the following code:

```
typedef enum {
    WBATrackOptionButtonIndexPreview,
    WBATrackOptionButtonIndexOpenIniTunes,
} WBATrackOptionButtonIndex;
```

2. Select the `WBAiTunesSearchViewController.m` file from the Project Navigator.

3. Modify the `tableView:didSelectRowAtIndexPath:` method with the following code:

```
- (void)tableView:(UITableView *)tableView
didSelectRowAtIndexPath:(NSIndexPath *)indexPath
{
    UIActionSheet *trackActionSheet = [[UIActionSheet alloc] initWithTitle:nil
delegate:self cancelButtonTitle:@"Cancel" destructiveButtonTitle:nil
otherButtonTitles:@"Preview Track", @"Open in iTunes", nil];

    [trackActionSheet showInView:self.view];
}
```

4. Modify the `actionSheet:clickedButtonAtIndex:` method with the following code:

```
- (void)actionSheet:(UIActionSheet *)actionSheet
clickedButtonAtIndex:(NSInteger)buttonIndex
{
    NSIndexPath *selectedIndexPath = self.tableView.indexPathForSelectedRow;
    NSString *trackFirstLetter = [self.firstLettersArray
objectAtIndex:selectedIndexPath.section];

    NSArray *tracksWithFirstLetter = [self.tracksDictionary
objectForKey:trackFirstLetter];

    WBATrack *trackObject = [tracksWithFirstLetter
objectAtIndex:selectedIndexPath.row];

    if(buttonIndex == WBATrackOptionButtonIndexPreview)
    {
        NSURL *trackPreviewURL = [NSURL URLWithString:trackObject.previewUrlString];
        MPMoviePlayerViewController *moviePlayerViewController =
[[MPMoviePlayerViewController alloc] initWithContentURL:trackPreviewURL];
        [self presentMoviePlayerViewControllerAnimated:moviePlayerViewController];
    }
    else if (buttonIndex == WBATrackOptionButtonIndexOpenIniTunes)
    {
```

```
        NSURL *iTunesURL = [NSURL URLWithString:trackObject.iTunesUrlString];
        [[UIApplication sharedApplication] openURL:iTunesURL];
    }
}
```

5. Run the app on an iOS test device. Selecting Open in iTunes now opens iTunes and scrolls to the track.

How It Works

First, you added the `WBATrackOptionButtonIndexOpenIniTunes` value to the
`WBATrackOptionButtonIndex` enumeration, which maps to the option in the `UIActionSheet`. Next,
you added the option to the `UIActionSheet` that is displayed when the user selects a track. Finally, in
the `actionSheet:clickedButtonAtIndex:` method you created a new `NSURL` using the `iTunesUrl`
`String` property of the `WBATrack` object and passed it into the `openURL` method of the shared
`UIApplication`.

> **NOTE** The iOS simulator does not include the iTunes app. If you try the Open
> in iTunes option for a track in the simulator, it will attempt to open the URL in
> Safari. This results in a Cannot Open Page error. This is not an error with your
> code, but a limitation of the iOS Simulator. To test the Open in iTunes option
> you need to use a physical device.

SUMMARY

Web services add a whole new dynamic to mobile apps. They can be used to build all kinds of new
and interesting features for your users. To lower the barrier for developers, Apple has put a lot of
effort into its networking classes and protocols to make simple tasks easy while still providing the
flexibility for developers to get to the lower-level details. In this chapter you implemented the Search
iTunes for Tracks feature of the Bands app. It uses an `NSURLSessionDataTask` to query the iTunes
Search API. The results are passed back using a completion handler that parses the JSON response
and displays the results in a `UITableView`. When users select a track, they are given the option to
either preview the track using the `MPMoviePlayerViewController` or view them in iTunes.

EXERCISES

1. What are the three types of `NSURLSession` tasks?

2. What is the name of the technology Apple introduced in iOS 4 to reduce the complexity of
   threading for developers?

3. What class and method can you use to parse JSON into Objective-C objects?

4. What framework is required to use the `MPMoviePlayerViewController`?

➤ **WHAT YOU LEARNED IN THIS CHAPTER**

TOPIC	KEY CONCEPTS
Web Services	Using applications that connect to web services to add dynamic features
Networking	Making network connections using `NSURLSession` to reduce the complexity of an application so that simple tasks can be performed with just a few lines of code
JSON Parsing	Using JSON, the most popular format for passing data between web services, which structure maps nicely with Objective-C data objects, making it easy to work within iOS applications
iTunes Search API	Using the iTunes Search API to query for different media types on sale in the iTunes store, as well as providing ways to preview them or open them in iTunes for purchase

11

Creating a Universal App

WHAT YOU WILL LEARN IN THIS CHAPTER:

➤ Creating an iPad Storyboard

➤ Supporting Rotation Using Auto Layout

➤ Implementing Popovers

WROX.COM CODE DOWNLOADS FOR THIS CHAPTER

You can find the wrox.com code downloads for this chapter at www.wrox.com/go/
begiosprogramming on the Download Code tab. The code is in the chapter 11 download
and individually named according to the names throughout the chapter.

The Bands app you have created so far is designed to run on an iPhone or an iPod Touch.
You can also run the app on an iPad using the iPads compatibility mode. Compatibility
mode displays the app on an iPad as though it is running on an iPhone, even using the
same dimensions. You can use the 2x button in compatibility mode to double the size of
the app so that it uses the full screen, but apps tend to look pixilated when doing this,
deteriorating the user experience. iPad users typically choose to run apps that were
designed for iPad. Developers have the option to create a separate iPad app or they can
create a universal app.

The guts of a typical iOS app will be the same no matter what device they run on. Therefore,
universal apps can share much of the code between their iPhone and iPad implementations.
The big difference is the user interface. Universal apps are a single build that contains user
interfaces and code for both iPhone/iPod touch and iPads. iPads are obviously bigger and thus
have more screen real estate. Designers can use that space to create a user interface that is
much different from their iPhone design.

The Bands app, as discussed in Chapter 1, "Building a Real-World iOS App: Bands," is not
meant to be an example of a well-designed user interface. Instead it is meant to be a tool

to teach you how you code an iOS app. The last part of that is learning how to create an iPad implementation. The user interface you will implement for iPad is almost identical to the iPhone version. There are user interactions that need to be changed to comply with Apple's Human Interface Guidelines. The other major difference is it will support rotation. To start, you need a new Storyboard with new scenes designed for iPad.

TRANSITIONING TO A UNIVERSAL APP

The first step in creating a universal app is to transition from an iPhone project to a universal project. This can be done in the project settings with just a few clicks. The other aspect is creating a new user interface for iPad. Instead of adding to the iPhone Storyboard, you need to create a new Storyboard designed for iPad. This is all straightforward, as you see in the next Try It Out.

TRY IT OUT   Adding an iPad Storyboard

1. From the Xcode menu select File ➪ New ➪ File.

2. Select the User Interface section on the left side of the dialog, select Storyboard, and click next.

3. On the next screen, select iPad as the Device Family.

4. Name the new Storyboard `Main-iPad`, and save it in the `Base.lproj` directory with the `Main .storyboard` file.

5. Select the `Main-iPad.storyboard` from the Project Navigator if it's not already selected.

6. Drag a new Navigation Controller from the Object library onto the new Storyboard.

7. Select the Project from the Project Navigator.

8. In the Deployment Info section, change the Devices setting to Universal.

9. Select Don't Copy in the dialog that appears after.

10. Under the Devices setting you now see iPhone and iPad. Select iPad.

11. Change the Main Interface to the `Main-iPad .storyboard`.

12. Check all the Device Orientation options.

13. Run the app in the iPad simulator. You now see an empty `UITableView`, as shown in Figure 11-1.

FIGURE 11-1

How It Works

The first thing you did was to create a new Storyboard targeted for iPad. When new view controllers are added to this storyboard, they will be the size of the iPad screen, as you saw after creating the Navigation Controller scene. You then changed the project to be a universal project. This gives you deployment settings for both iPhone and iPad. In those settings you can set which Storyboard is used when running on an iPad and which is used when running on an iPhone. You also have device orientation settings for both iPhone and iPad. iPad apps typically support rotation, so you need to design the iPad interface for the Bands app this way. Running the Bands app on the iPad simulator now uses the new Storyboard and iPad version instead of the iPhone version.

A large majority of the code you wrote for the Bands app on iPhone can also be used on an iPad. The major difference for the Bands app is how some things are presented on an iPad as opposed to an iPhone. Because the code is mostly the same, the best way to add an iPad implementation is to subclass the iPhone code and override only the parts that need to change. By subclassing, the code you have already written will still be executed. This keeps the amount of code in the project to a minimum. It also means that bug fixes will typically need to be made only in the original file.

TRY IT OUT Subclassing for iPad

1. From the Xcode menu select File ➪ New ➪ File.

2. Select the Cocoa Touch section on the left side of the dialog, select Objective-C class, and click Next.

3. Name the new class `WBABandsListTableViewController_iPad` and set the Subclass of selection to the `WBABandsListTableViewController` class.

4. Select the `WBABandsListTableViewController_iPad.m` file from the Project Navigator.

5. Override the `addBandTouched:` method using the following code:

```
- (IBAction)addBandTouched:(id)sender
{
    NSLog(@"addBandTouched iPad File");
}
```

6. Select the `Main-iPad.storyboard` file from the Project Navigator.

7. Select the Table View and set its Class to the `WBABandsListTableViewController_iPad` in the Identity Inspector. This Bands List scene is now the same as the Bands List scene in the iPhone Storyboard.

8. Select the `UINavigationItem` and set its title to **Bands** in the Attributes Inspector.

9. Select the Prototype Cell and set its Style to Basic and its Identifier to **Cell**.

10. Drag a `UIBarButtonItem` to the left side of the `UINavigationItem`.

11. Set the Identifier of the `UIBarButtonItem` to Add; then connect it to the `addBandTouched:` IBAction.

12. Run the app in the iPad simulator. You now see the Bands list, as shown in Figure 11-2. Tapping the add button prints to the Xcode debug console.

FIGURE 11-2

How It Works

When creating new Objective-C classes in Xcode, you can set its parent class. In previous chapters you have used classes created by Apple. In this Try It Out you created a new class that is a subclass of the WBABandsListTableViewController class you created in Chapter 5, "Using Table Views." By subclassing the new class has all the public properties and methods, including IBOutlets and IBActions, declared in the parent class as well as any protocols you declared in the parent class. You then set the class of the UITableView in the iPad Storyboard to use the iPad class. When the app runs on an iPad, it first looks for methods implemented in the iPad class. Methods that are not overridden use the methods implemented in the parent class instead. For the new iPad UITableView to work with the original class, you needed to set the cell type and reuse identifier. Finally, you added an override for the addBandTouched: method that for now simply writes to the debug console. When running the code in the iPad simulator, the UITableView appears as it does on an iPhone with all the UITableViewDelegate and UITableViewDataSource methods working but with the Add UIBarButtonItem now executing the overridden method instead of the original method.

> **NOTE** When creating the new file you may have noticed the Target for iPad check box. This is for projects that use Mac OS X Interface Builder files, better known as XIB files. Because the Bands app is built using Storyboards instead of XIB files, this check box has no affect. If you were using XIB files and checked the "With XIB for User Interface" box, the XIB would be sized for an iPad.

The next step to creating the universal app is to create the Band Details scene for iPad. The scene will be laid out the same as for iPhone, just a little bigger. Some of the interactions need to be changed for the iPad. You do this in the Learning About Popovers section of this chapter, but to keep the app from crashing while testing, you can override the methods in this Try It Out.

TRY IT OUT Adding the Band Info View

1. From the Xcode menu select File ➪ New ➪ File and create a new subclass of the WBABandDetailsViewController named WBABandDetailsViewController_iPad.

2. Select the WBABandDetailsViewController_iPad.m file from the Project Navigator.

3. Override the `activityButtonTouched:` method using the following code:

```
- (IBAction)activityButtonTouched:(id)sender
{
    NSLog(@"activityButtonTouched iPad File");
}
```

4. Override the `deleteButtonTouched:` method using the following code:

```
- (IBAction)deleteButtonTouched:(id)sender
{
    NSLog(@"deleteButtonTouched iPad File");
}
```

5. Select the `Main-iPad.storyboard` from the Project Navigator.

6. Drag a new View Controller onto the storyboard, and set its Class to the `WBABandDetailsViewController_iPad` class in Identity Inspector. This is now the Band Details scene, same as in the iPhone Storyboard.

7. Set the Storyboard ID to `bandDetails_iPad` in the Identity Inspector.

8. Re-create the Band Details scene as you did in Chapter 4, "Creating a User Input Form," without adding the Save and Delete buttons.

9. Drag a new `UIToolbar` to the bottom of the view, and add the Save and Delete buttons as `UIBarButtonItems` separated using a flexible space `UIBarButtonItem`. The view should look like Figure 11-3 when you finish.

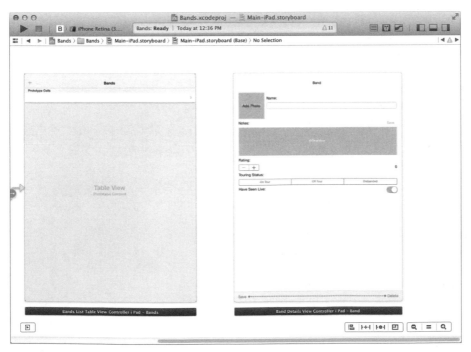

FIGURE 11-3

10. Create the segue from the prototype cell in the Bands List scene to the Band Details scene, as you did in Chapter 4.

11. Set the title in the `UINavigationItem` to **Band** in the Band Details scene.

12. Add the activity `UIBarButtonItem` to the `UINavigationItem`.

13. Connect all the `IBOutlets`, `IBActions`, and delegates between the Band Details scene and the `WBABandDetailsViewController_iPad`.

14. Select the `WBABandsListTableViewController_iPad.m` file from the Project Navigator.

15. Import the `WBABandDetailsViewController_iPad.h` file using the following code:

```
#import "WBABandDetailsViewController_iPad.h"
```

16. Modify the `addBandTouched:` method using the following code:

```
- (IBAction)addBandTouched:(id)sender
{
    NSLog(@"addBandTouched iPad File");

    UIStoryboard *iPadStoryBoard =
[UIStoryboard storyboardWithName:@"Main-iPad" bundle:nil];
    self.bandInfoViewController = (WBABandDetailsViewController_iPad *)
[iPadStoryBoard instantiateViewControllerWithIdentifier:@"bandInfo_iPad"];

    [self presentViewController:self.bandInfoViewController
animated:YES completion:nil];
}
```

17. Run the app in the iPad simulator. You can now use the Band Details scene, as shown in Figure 11-4.

How It Works

First, you created a new subclass of the `WBABandDetailsViewController` class as you did in the previous Try It Out. In the iPad implementation you added override methods for the `activityButtonTouched:` and the `deleteButtonTouched:` methods. Right now these methods write only to the debug console. Next, you created the Band Details scene in the storyboard, set its class to the new `WBABandDetailsViewController_iPad` class, and set its Storyboard ID. You then recreated the user interface of the Band Details scene using the bigger dimensions of the iPad. The reason you used a `UIToolbar` instead of standalone `UIButtons` for Save and Delete will become clear in the Learning About Popovers section of this chapter. Because the `WBABandDetailsViewController_iPad` class is a subclass of `WBABandDetailsViewController`, all the `IBOutlets`, `IBActions`, and protocol declarations are available in Interface Builder to connect to without needing to add any additional code to the `WBABandDetailsViewController_iPad` class.

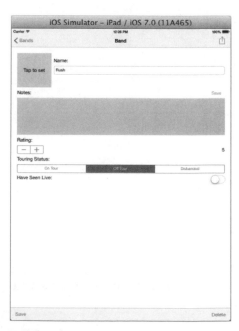

FIGURE 11-4

In the `WBABandsListTableViewController_iPad` implementation, you first imported the `WBABandDetailsViewController_iPad.h` file. Next you modified the `addBandTouched:` method to get an instance of `UIStoryboard`, using the new iPad Storyboard identifier in order to present the correct iPad Band Details scene instead of the iPhone version.

Supporting Rotation Using Auto Layout

If you run the app in the iPad simulator at this point and rotate to landscape, you can see that parts of the user interface of the Band Details scene are out of place. To support rotation you need to add auto layout constraints so that everything adjusts to the new screen size. You first learned about auto layout constraints in Chapter 3, "Starting a New App." Though auto layout constraints can be complex, you need to know about only three of them to support rotation in the Band Details scene.

The first is the Leading Space to Container constraint. You use this to set a static amount of space between the user interface object and the left edge of the screen. When the device is rotated and the screen size changes, the object continues to be that distance. The second is the Trailing Space to Container constraint that does the same except to the right side of the screen. The other is the Bottom Space to Bottom Layout Guideline. This sets the static space between an object and the bottom of the screen.

TRY IT OUT   Using Auto Layout for Rotation

1. Select the `Main-iPad.storyboard` from the Project Navigator.

2. Select the `nameTextField`, and Control-drag to the left edge of the `UIView`. When you release the mouse, select a Leading Space to Container auto layout constraint from the dialog.

3. Add Leading Space to Container auto layout constraints to the `notesTextField`, `touringStatusSegmentedController`, and the bottom `UIToolbar`.

4. Select the `nameTextField`, Control-drag to the right edge of the `UIView`, and add a Trailing Space to Container auto layout constraint.

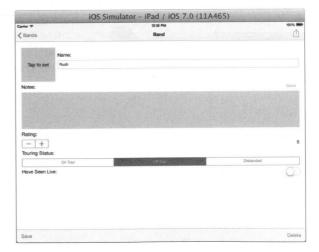

FIGURE 11-5

5. Add Trailing Space to Container auto layout constraints to the `saveNotesButton`, `notesTextView`, `ratingsValueLabel`, `touringStatusSegmentedController`, `haveSeenLiveSwitch`, and the bottom `UIToolbar`.

6. Select the bottom `UIToolbar`, Control-drag to the bottom of the `UIView`, and add a Bottom Space to Bottom Layout Guide auto layout constraint.

7. Run the app in the iPad simulator. Rotating to landscape now displays the user interface correctly, as shown in Figure 11-5.

How It Works

What you did here was make sure the various user interface objects of the Band Details scene adjust their size when the app is rotated to landscape. The Leading Space to Container layout constraint keeps the same amount of space between the left edge of the screen and the user interface object. The Trailing Space to Container layout constraint does the same but to the right edge of the view. The `UIToolbar` also requires a Bottom Space to Bottom Layout Guide to keep it anchored to the bottom of the `UIView`. Now when the iPad is rotated, those user interface objects grow and shrink while keeping those distances the same.

LEARNING ABOUT POPOVERS

The bigger screen of an iPad brings with it new user interaction challenges. iPhone apps, as you have implemented in previous chapters, show scenes that encompass the entire screen. They also show user options that do not display over the entire height of the screen but do stretch the entire width. Because the iPhone screen is smaller, these transitions are comfortable to the user. These types of transitions can be rather jarring on an iPad, leading to a less-than-optimal user experience.

With the release of the iPad, Apple added a new user interface paradigm to the iOS SDK called the `UIPopover`. A *UIPopover* is a type of `UIView` that appears to float over the `UIView` from which it is displayed. They take up only a small portion of the screen while leaving the rest of the `UIView` displayed. They also have an arrow pointing back to the part of the `UIView` the user tapped. This gives users a better user experience because they can concentrate just on the portion of the screen with which they are interacting, yet still keep context of where they are at in the app. To keep apps consistent, Apple's Human Interface Guidelines require that developers use popovers in iPad apps, so you need to implement them where necessary in the Bands app.

Presenting Action Sheets in Popovers

The first change you need to make is to present the `UIActionSheet` in a `UIPopover`. In iPhone apps, `UIActionSheets` stretch the entire width of the screen and animate from the bottom up. In iPad apps `UIActionSheets` are shown in a `UIPopover` with the arrow pointing back to the button or other user interface object the user tapped. To display a `UIActionSheet` in a `UIPopover`, you need to modify the code so that the system knows where the arrow should point. The first `UIActionSheet` you implement is the Delete Band confirmation. By modifying the Band Details scene to use a `UIBarButtonItem` for the Delete and Save buttons, you can now use the `showFromBarButtonItem:animated:` method of the `UIActionSheet` class to present the `UIActionSheet` in a `UIPopover`.

One major difference with a `UIActionSheet` displayed in a `UIPopover` is that it no longer shows the Cancel button even if you pass in a title for it in the `initWithTitle:delegate:cancelButton Title:destructiveButtonTitle:otherButtonTitle:` method. Instead users can "cancel" by tapping anywhere outside the `UIPopover`. This is expected behavior.

TRY IT OUT Presenting Action Sheets in Popovers

1. Select the `WBABandDetailsViewController_iPad.h` file from the Project Navigator.

2. Add new `IBOutlet` for the delete `UIBarButtonItem` using the following code:

   ```
   @property (nonatomic, weak) IBOutlet UIBarButtonItem *deleteBarButtonItem;
   ```

3. Add a property for a `UIActionSheet` using the following code:

   ```
   @property (nonatomic, strong) UIActionSheet *actionSheet;
   ```

4. Select the `WBABandDetailsViewController_iPad.m` file from the Project Navigator.

5. Modify the `deleteButtonTouched:` method using the following code:

   ```
   - (void)deleteButtonTouched:(id)sender
   {
       NSLog(@"deleteButtonTouched iPad File");

       if(self.actionSheet)
           return;

       self.actionSheet = [[UIActionSheet alloc] initWithTitle:nil delegate:self
   cancelButtonTitle:@"Cancel" destructiveButtonTitle:@"Delete Band"
   otherButtonTitles:nil];
       self.actionSheet.tag = WBAActionSheetTagDeleteBand;

       [self.actionSheet showFromBarButtonItem:self.deleteBarButtonItem animated:YES];
   }
   ```

6. Override the `actionSheet:clickedButtonAtIndex:` method using the following code:

   ```
   - (void)actionSheet:(UIActionSheet *)actionSheet
   clickedButtonAtIndex:(NSInteger)buttonIndex
   {
       self.actionSheet = nil;
       [super actionSheet:actionSheet clickedButtonAtIndex:buttonIndex];
   }
   ```

7. Select the `Main-iPad.storyboard` from the Project Navigator, and connect the Delete button to the `deleteBarButtonItem` `IBOutlet`.

8. Run the app in the iPad simulator. Tapping the Delete button now shows the `UIActionSheet` in a `UIPopover` from the Delete `UIBarButtonItem`, as shown in Figure 11-6.

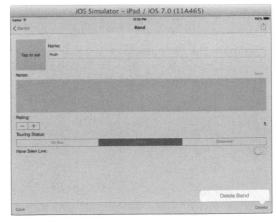

FIGURE 11-6

How It Works

The first thing you did was to add an IBOutlet for the delete UIBarButtonItem as well as a new property for a UIActionSheet to the WBABandDetailsViewController_iPad interface. In its implementation you then modified the deleteButtonTouched: method to first look and see if the UIActionSheet property is set. You need this check to prevent showing the delete UIActionSheet multiple times. In the iPhone version of the Bands app the delete UIButton is covered when the UIActionSheet is displayed. This is not the case in the iPad version of the Bands app, so users can continue to tap the delete UIBarButtonItem. This check makes sure your code does not create and show another UIActionSheet should that happen.

The code then creates and presents the UIActionSheet using the showFromBarButtonItem:animated: method. By passing in the deleteBarButtonItem, the UIActionSheet will be displayed in a UIPopover with the arrow pointing back to the deleteBarButtonItem.

You also needed to override the actionSheet:clickedButtonAtIndex: method in order to set the activitySheet property back to nil. Without this override the user would never see another UIActionSheet if they cancel the one shown by tapping outside the UIPopover or if they select an option. Instead of duplicating the code to handle whichever option was selected, you can call the actionSheet:clickedButtonAtIndex: method on super, which will execute the code you have written in the WBABandDetailsViewController parent class.

Using the UIPopoverController

UIActionSheets are not the only user interfaces to be shown in a UIPopover. According to Apple's Human Interface Guidelines, other things must use a UIPopover when used in an iPad interface. One of those is the UIImagePickerController.

In Chapter 6, "Integrating the Camera and Photo Library in iOS Apps," you implemented the UIImagePickerController by presenting it over the entire scene. This still works in the iPad implementation, but it could get your app rejected when submitted to Apple. Instead you need to display the UIImagePickerController in a UIPopover by using a UIPopoverController.

The UIPopoverController class can show any subclass of UIViewController. When you present the UIPopover, you need to tell it both where its arrow should point to as well as what direction the arrow should be pointing. You tell the UIPopover what to point to by either displaying it from a UIBarButtonItem or from a CGRect on the screen. A CGRect, as you can recall from Chapter 2, "Introduction to Objective-C," is a common struct containing a CGPoint and a CGSize (refer to Listing 2-4). It's a way of denoting a rectangle by its origin point, width, and height. All user interface objects have a frame that is a CGRect, which you can use when displaying a UIPopover.

You tell a UIPopover which direction its arrow should point by using a value of the UIPopoverArrowDirection enumeration. Table 11-1 describes these values. When designing an iPad apps user interface, you may want to specifically tell the system which direction the arrow should point. The Bands app iPad design does not require this, so you can use the UIPopoverArrowDirectionAny constant, as you will see in the following Try It Out.

TABLE 11-1: Popover Arrow Constants

CONSTANT	DESCRIPTION
UIPopoverArrowDirectionUp	An arrow that points up with the content shown underneath
UIPopoverArrowDirectionDown	An arrow that points down with the content shown above
UIPopoverArrowDirectionLeft	An arrow that points left with the content shown on the right
UIPopoverArrowDirectionRight	An arrow that points right with the content shown on the left
UIPopoverArrowDirectionAny	The system determines which arrow direction should be used based on the frame or button the popover is displayed from.
UIPopoverArrowDirectionUnknown	There arrow direction is not known. Used when getting the popoverArrowDirection property of the UIPopoverController when the popover is not presented.

TRY IT OUT Using a Popover Controller

1. Select the WBABandDetailsViewController_iPad.h file from the Project Navigator, and add a new property for a UIPopoverController using the following code:

```
@property (nonatomic, strong) UIPopoverController *popover;
```

2. Select the WBABandDetailsViewController_iPad.m file from the Project Navigator.

3. Override the bandImageViewTapDetected method using the following code:

```
- (void)bandImageViewTapDetected
{
    if([UIImagePickerController
isSourceTypeAvailable:UIImagePickerControllerSourceTypeCamera])
    {
        UIActionSheet *chooseCameraActionSheet = [[UIActionSheet alloc]
initWithTitle:nil delegate:self cancelButtonTitle:@"Cancel"
destructiveButtonTitle:nil otherButtonTitles:@"Take with Camera",
@"Choose from Photo Library", nil];
        chooseCameraActionSheet.tag = WBAActionSheetTagChooseImagePickerSource;

        [chooseCameraActionSheet showFromRect:self.bandImageView.frame
inView:self.view animated:YES];
    }
    else if([UIImagePickerController
isSourceTypeAvailable:UIImagePickerControllerSourceTypePhotoLibrary])
```

```
    {
        [self presentPhotoLibraryImagePicker];
    }
    else
    {
        UIAlertView *photoLibraryErrorAlert = [[UIAlertView alloc]
initWithTitle:@"Error" message:@"There are no photo libraries available"
delegate:nil cancelButtonTitle:@"OK" otherButtonTitles:nil];
        [photoLibraryErrorAlert show];
    }
}
```

4. Override the `bandImageSwipeDetected` method using the following code:

```
- (void)bandImageViewSwipeDetected
{
    if(self.actionSheet)
        return;

    self.actionSheet = [[UIActionSheet alloc] initWithTitle:nil delegate:self
cancelButtonTitle:@"Cancel" destructiveButtonTitle:@"Delete Band Image"
otherButtonTitles:nil];
    self.actionSheet.tag = WBAActionSheetTagDeleteBandImage;
    [self.actionSheet showFromRect:self.bandImageView.frame inView:self.view
animated:YES];
}
```

5. Override the `presentPhotoLibraryImagePicker` method using the following code:

```
- (void)presentPhotoLibraryImagePicker
{
    UIImagePickerController *imagePickerController =
[[UIImagePickerController alloc] init];
    imagePickerController.sourceType =
UIImagePickerControllerSourceTypePhotoLibrary;
    imagePickerController.delegate = self;
    imagePickerController.allowsEditing = YES;

    self.popover = [[UIPopoverController alloc]
 initWithContentViewController:imagePickerController];
    [self.popover presentPopoverFromRect:self.bandImageView.frame inView:self.view
permittedArrowDirections:UIPopoverArrowDirectionAny animated:YES];
}
```

6. Override the `imagePicker:didFinishPickingMediaWithInfo:` method using the following code:

```
- (void)imagePickerController:(UIImagePickerController *)picker
didFinishPickingMediaWithInfo:(NSDictionary *)info
{
    [super imagePickerController:picker didFinishPickingMediaWithInfo:info];
    [self.popover dismissPopoverAnimated:YES];
    self.popover = nil;
}
```

7. Add the `imagePickerControllerDidCancel:` method using the following code:

```
- (void)imagePickerControllerDidCancel:(UIImagePickerController *)picker
{
    [self.popover dismissPopoverAnimated:YES];
    self.popover = nil;
}
```

8. Run the app in the iPad simulator. The image picker is now shown in a popover, as shown in Figure 11-7.

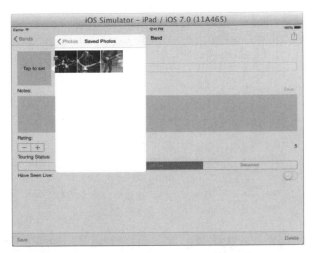

How It Works

When tapping the band image on a device with both a camera and a photo library, you need to ask users which one they would like to use. In Chapter 6 you did this using a `UIActionSheet`. For the iPad version you need to show the `UIActionSheet` in a `UIPopover` pointing to the `UIImageView`. By overriding the `bandImageViewTapped` method, you can present the `UIActionSheet` by using the `frame` property of the `UIImageView`. The `bandImageSwipeDetected` method also needs to present the `UIActionSheet` in a `UIPopover`, so you override it as well.

FIGURE 11-7

Next, you override the `presentPhotoLibraryImagePicker` to present the `UIImagePickerController` using a `UIPopoverController`. You do this by first initializing the `UIPopoverController` using the `initWithContentViewController:` method and passing in the `UIImagePickerController`. You present the `UIPopover` using the `presentPopoverFromRect:inView:permittedArrowDirections:animated:` method. For the `CGRect` you pass in the `frame` property of the `UIImageView`. For the `view` parameter you use the `view` property of the `WBABandDetailsViewController_iPad`. Because you don't care what direction the arrow points, you used the `UIPopoverArrowDirectionAny` constant. For a better user experience you set the animated property to `YES` so that the `UIPopover` animates into view instead of appearing instantly.

After the user picks an image, your code needs to dismiss the `UIPopover`. You do this by overriding the `imagePicker:didFinishPickingMediaWithInfo:` method. Because this is an overridden method, you can still execute the code in the parent class by calling the `imagePicker:didFinishPickingMediaWith Info:` method on `super`. After the parent classes code is executed, it returns to the code in the subclass where you dismiss the `UIPopover` by calling `dismissPopoverAnimated:`, again passing `YES` for the animated parameter so that the `UIPopover` animates out of view instead of disappearing immediately.

In the iPhone version you needed to dismiss the `UIImagePickerController` if the user taps the Cancel button. In the iPad version you need to dismiss the `UIPopover`, so you need to override the `imagePickerControllerDidCancel:` method and call `dismissPopoverAnimated:` there as well.

Another view controller that should be shown in a UIPopover is the UIActivityViewController. You do this the same way as the UIImagePickerController; by first initializing the UIActivityViewController and then initializing the UIPopoverController using the initWithContentViewController: method.

In the Bands app you have an activity UIBarButton for the Band Details scene. When tapped in the iPhone version, you show a UIActionSheet with the activity options. In the iPad app you need to display the UIActionSheet in a UIPopover pointing to the activity UIBarButtonItem. You do this by using the showFromBarButtonItem:animated: method. If the user selects the share option, you also want the UIActivityViewController in the UIPopoverController to point to the activity UIBarButtonItem. You do this by using the presentPopoverFromBarButtonItem:permittedArrowDirections:animated: method. Again, you can use the UIPopoverArrowDirectionAny constant, though you could use the UIPopoverArrowDirectionUp constant, because that's the only direction the arrow can point.

UIPopoverController also has a delegate that can tell your code when important things happen with the UIPopover. If users tap outside of the UIPopover, it's the same as if they had tapped a Cancel button. When this happens, it's up to your code to actually dismiss the UIPopover. You do this by implementing the popoverControllerDidDismissPopover method of the UIPopoverControllerDelegate.

TRY IT OUT Showing the UIActivityViewController in a Popover

1. Select the WBABandDetailsViewController_iPad.h file from the Project Navigator.

2. Declare, the class implements the UIPopoverControllerDelegate using the following code:

```
@interface WBABandDetailsViewController_iPad : WBABandDetailsViewController
<UIPopoverControllerDelegate>
```

3. Add a new IBOutlet for the activity UIBarButtonItem using the following code:

```
@property (nonatomic, weak) IBOutlet UIBarButtonItem *activityBarButtonItem;
```

4. Select the Main-iPad.storyboard from the Project Navigator, and connect the activity UIBarButtonItem to the new IBOutlet.

5. Select the WBABandDetailsViewController_iPad.m file from the Project Navigator.

6. Modify the activityButtonTouched: method using the following code:

```
- (void)activityButtonTouched:(id)sender
{
    NSLog(@"activityButtonTouched iPad File");

    if(self.actionSheet)
        return;

    self.actionSheet = [[UIActionSheet alloc] initWithTitle:nil delegate:self
 cancelButtonTitle:@"Cancel" destructiveButtonTitle:nil
otherButtonTitles:@"Share", nil];
    self.actionSheet.tag = WBAActionSheetTagActivity;
    [self.actionSheet showFromBarButtonItem:self.activityBarButtonItem
animated:YES];
}
```

7. Override the `shareBandInfo` method using the following code:

```
- (void)shareBandInfo
{
    NSArray *activityItems = [NSArray arrayWithObjects:[self.bandObject
stringForMessaging], self.bandObject.bandImage, nil];

    UIActivityViewController *activityViewController =
[[UIActivityViewController alloc]initWithActivityItems:activityItems
applicationActivities:nil];
    [activityViewController setValue:self.bandObject.name forKey:@"subject"];

    NSArray *excludedActivityOptions =
[NSArray arrayWithObjects:UIActivityTypeAssignToContact, nil];
    [activityViewController setExcludedActivityTypes:excludedActivityOptions];

    self.popover = [[UIPopoverController alloc]
initWithContentViewController:activityViewController];
    self.popover.delegate = self;
    [self.popover presentPopoverFromBarButtonItem:self.activityBarButtonItem
 permittedArrowDirections:UIPopoverArrowDirectionAny animated:YES];
}
```

8. Add the `popoverControllerDidDismissPopover` method using the following code:

```
- (void)popoverControllerDidDismissPopover:(UIPopoverController *)popoverController
{
    [self.popover dismissPopoverAnimated:YES];
    self.popover = nil;
}
```

9. Run the app in the iPad simulator. The `UIActivityViewController` is now displayed in a popover, as shown in Figure 11-8.

How It Works

You first declare that the `WBABandDetailsViewController_ iPad` class implements the `UIPopoverControllerDelegate`. Next, you added an `IBOutlet` for the activity `UIBarButtonItem` so that you can use it when presenting the `UIActionSheet` as well as the `UIActivityViewController` popover.

In the implementation you override the `activityButtonTouched:` method to show the `UIActionSheet` from the activity `UIBarButtonItem`. You allow only the Share option at this point, because the other scenes have not been added to the iPad implementation.

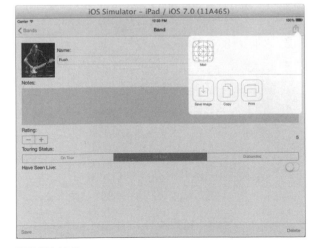

FIGURE 11-8

You then override the `shareBandInfo` method. Creating the `UIActivityViewController` is the same as in the iPhone implementation. You then create and display it using the `UIPopoverController` displayed from the activity `UIBarButtonItem`. You also set its delegate to `self`, so your code is notified when the user taps outside the `UIPopover` while it is shown. Finally, you implemented the `popoverControllerDidDismissPopover:` method to dismiss the `UIPopover` if the user taps anywhere outside the `UIPopover`.

FINISHING THE IPAD IMPLEMENTATION

You now have all the tools you need to complete the iPad version of the Bands app. The remainder of this chapter will walk you through adding the remaining three scenes to the iPad Storyboard.

The next scene to add to the iPad Storyboard is the Web View scene. This scene shows the Open in Safari option in a `UIActionSheet`, which will need to be displayed in a `UIPopover` from the activity `UIBarButtonItem`. You will use the same approach for this that you implemented in the Band Details scene. The `prepareForSegue:sender:` method needs to be overridden to use the new iPad class for the Web View scene.

The user interface will almost be identical to the iPhone version except for one difference. In the iPad version the `UIWebView` needs to be displayed between the `UINavigationItem` and the `UIToolbar`. This is because the page will not adjust to display under the `UINavigationItem` like it does in the iPhone version. You will also learn a new technique for adding auto layout constraints in the following Try It Out.

TRY IT OUT   Adding the Web Search Scene for the iPad

1. From the Xcode menu select File ➪ New ➪ File, and create a subclass of the `WBAWebViewController` called `WBAWebViewController_iPad`.

2. Select the `WBAWebViewController_iPad.h` file from the Project Navigator.

3. Add an `IBOutlet` for the action `UIBarButtonItem` using the following code:

```
@property (nonatomic, weak) IBOutlet UIBarButtonItem *actionBarButtonItem;
```

4. Add a property for a `UIActionSheet` using the following code:

```
@property (nonatomic, strong) UIActionSheet *actionSheet;
```

5. Select the `WBAWebViewController_iPad.m` file and override the `webViewActionButtonTouched:` method using the following code:

```
- (IBAction)webViewActionButtonTouched:(id)sender
{
    self.actionSheet = [[UIActionSheet alloc] initWithTitle:nil delegate:self
cancelButtonTitle:@"Cancel" destructiveButtonTitle:nil
otherButtonTitles:@"Open in Safari", nil];
    [self.actionSheet showFromBarButtonItem:self.actionBarButtonItem animated:YES];
}
```

6. Override the `actionSheet:clickedButtonAtIndex:` method with the following code:

```
- (void)actionSheet:(UIActionSheet *)actionSheet
clickedButtonAtIndex:(NSInteger)buttonIndex
{
    self.actionSheet = nil;
    [super actionSheet:actionSheet clickedButtonAtIndex:buttonIndex];
}
```

7. Select the `WBABandDetailsViewController_iPad.m` file from the Project Navigator.

8. Import the `WBAWebViewController_iPad.h` file using the following code:

```
#import "WBAWebViewController_iPad.h"
```

9. Add the `prepareForSegue:sender:` method using the following code:

```
-(void)prepareForSegue:(UIStoryboardSegue *)segue sender:(id)sender
{
    if([segue.destinationViewController class] == [WBAWebViewController_iPad class])
    {
        WBAWebViewController_iPad *webViewController =
segue.destinationViewController;
        webViewController.bandName = self.bandObject.name;
    }
}
```

10. Modify the `activityButtonTouched:` method using the following code:

```
- (void)activityButtonTouched:(id)sender
{
    NSLog(@"activityButtonTouched iPad File");

    if(self.actionSheet)
        return;

    self.actionSheet = [[UIActionSheet alloc] initWithTitle:nil delegate:self
cancelButtonTitle:@"Cancel" destructiveButtonTitle:nil
otherButtonTitles:@"Share", @"Search the Web", nil];
    self.actionSheet.tag = WBAActionSheetTagActivity;
    [self.actionSheet showFromBarButtonItem:self.activityBarButtonItem
animated:YES];
}
```

11. Select the `Main-iPad.storyboard` from the Project Navigator.

12. Drag a new View Controller onto the Storyboard, and set its class to the `WBAWebViewController_iPad` class in the Identity Inspector. This is the iPad version of the Web View scene.

13. Create a push segue named **webViewSegue** from the Band Details scene to the Web View scene.

14. Create the Web View scene user interface as you did in Chapter 8, "Using Web Views," by adding the `UIWebView` along with the `UIToolbar` and `UIBarButtonItems` for navigation.

15. Adjust the `UIWebView` so that it sits between the `UINavigationItem` and the `UIToolbar`.

16. Select the `UIWebView` and then click the Pin auto layout button. In the dialog, select the lines at the top of the dialog for all four sides of the `UIWebView`. This will change the lines from dashed to solid as shown in Figure 11-9.

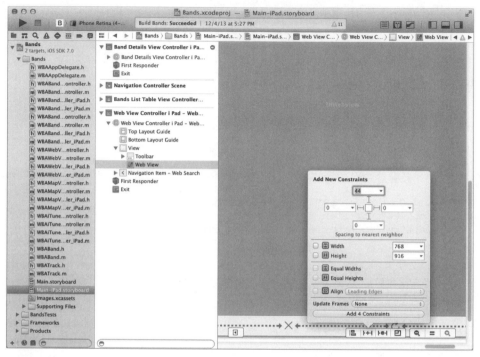

FIGURE 11-9

FIGURE 11-10

17. Select the `UIToolbar`, click the Pin auto layout button, select the lines for the left, right, and bottom. Then, click the Add 3 Constraints button.

18. Connect the `IBOutlets`, `IBActions`, and delegate to the `WBAWebViewController_iPad`.

19. Run the app in the iPad simulator. The Search the Web feature now works, as shown in Figure 11-10.

How It Works

The first step in creating the iPad version of the Web Search scene is creating a new `WBAWebViewController_iPad` class as a subclass of the `WBAWebViewController` you implemented in Chapter 8, "Using Web Views." The iPad implementation needs to show the `UIActionSheet` in a `UIPopover`. You implemented this in the iPad Web View scene the same as the activity options in the Band Details scene. In the `WBAWebViewController_iPad` you added an `IBOutlet` for the activity `UIBarButtonItem` as well as a property for the `UIActionSheet`. You then override the `webViewActionButtonTouched:` method to perform the same check on the `UIActionSheet` property to prevent multiple `UIPopovers` before creating and displaying the `UIActionSheet` in a `UIPopover` from the activity `UIBarButtonItem`. You also added an override of the `actionSheet:clickedButtonAtIndex:` method to set the `UIActionSheet` property back to `nil` so that it can be displayed again. In the `WBABandDetailsViewController_iPad` implementation you added an override for the `prepareForSegue:sender:` method to check for the `WBAWebSearchViewController_iPad` class. Without this override the iPhone implementation that checks for the `WBAWebSearchViewController` class to set the `bandName` would be called. This would fail, because it's a different class in the iPad implementation, so the `bandName` would not be set.

You re-created the user interface for the Web View scene the same as it appears in the iPhone version. To support rotation you added the auto layout constraints using the Pin auto layout constraint dialog. Instead of needing to Control-drag to the various sides of the `UIView`, you can use this dialog to quickly add all the constraints you need by simply clicking the sides you want the constraints to be added to.

The next scene to add is the Map Search scene. This scene needs the same implementation of the `UIActionSheet` in a `UIPopover` as well as auto layout constraints to support rotation. The following Try It Out is close to identical to the previous Try It Out.

TRY IT OUT **Adding the Find Local Record Store Feature for iPad**

1. From the Xcode menu select File ⇨ New ⇨ File, and create a new subclass of the `WBAMapViewController` called `WBAMapViewController_iPad`.

2. Select the `WBAMapViewController_iPad.h` file from the Project Navigator.

3. Add an `IBOutlet` for the action bar button item using the following code:

```
@property (nonatomic, weak) IBOutlet UIBarButtonItem *actionBarButtonItem;
```

4. Add a property for an action sheet using the following code:

```
@property (nonatomic, strong) UIActionSheet *actionSheet;
```

5. Select the `WBAMapViewController_iPad.m` file from the Project Navigator, and override the `actionButtonTouched:` method using the following code:

```
- (IBAction)actionButtonTouched:(id)sender
{
    if(self.actionSheet)
        return;

    self.actionSheet = [[UIActionSheet alloc] initWithTitle:nil delegate:self
cancelButtonTitle:@"Cancel" destructiveButtonTitle:nil
otherButtonTitles:@"Map View", @"Satellite View", @"Hybrid View", nil];
    [self.actionSheet showFromBarButtonItem:self.actionBarButtonItem animated:YES];
}
```

6. Override the `actionSheet:clickedButtonAtIndex:` method with the following code:

```
- (void)actionSheet:(UIActionSheet *)actionSheet
clickedButtonAtIndex:(NSInteger)buttonIndex
{
    self.actionSheet = nil;
    [super actionSheet:actionSheet clickedButtonAtIndex:buttonIndex];
}
```

7. Select the `WBABandDetailsViewController_iPad.m` file from the Project Navigator, and modify the `activityButtonTouched:` method using the following code:

```
- (void)activityButtonTouched:(id)sender
{
    NSLog(@"activityButtonTouched iPad File");

    if(self.actionSheet)
        return;

    self.actionSheet = [[UIActionSheet alloc] initWithTitle:nil delegate:self
cancelButtonTitle:@"Cancel" destructiveButtonTitle:nil
otherButtonTitles:@"Share", @"Search the Web",
@"Find Local Record Stores", nil];
    self.actionSheet.tag = WBAActionSheetTagActivity;
    [self.actionSheet showFromBarButtonItem:self.activityBarButtonItem
animated:YES];
}
```

8. Select the `Main-iPad.storyboard` from the Project Navigator.

9. Drag a new View Controller onto the storyboard, and set its class to the `WBAMapViewController_iPad` class in the Identity Inspector. This is now the iPad version of the Map Search scene.

10. Create a push segue named **mapViewSegue** from the Band Details scene to the Map View scene.

11. Create a push segue named **recordStoreWebSearchSegue** from the Map View scene to the Web View scene.

12. Create the Map View scene user interface as you did in Chapter 9 , "Exploring Maps and Local Search."

13. Connect the `IBOutlets`, `IBActions`, and delegates to the `WBAMapViewController_iPad` class.

14. Select the `MKMapView`, click the Pin auto layout button, select the lines for all four sides of the `MKMapView`, then click the Add 4 Constraints button.

15. Run the app in the iPad simulator. The Find Local Record Stores feature now works, as shown in Figure 11-11.

How It Works

This Try It Out follows the same pattern you implemented in both the Band Details scene and the Web View scene. The `UIActionSheet` to change the map type needs to be shown in a `UIPopover` from the activity `UIBarButtonItem`. You added properties for the `UIActionSheet` and `UIBarButtonItem` to achieve this. In the `actionButtonTouched:` implementation you again check if a `UIActionSheet` is already being displayed before creating and displaying a new one from the `UIBarButtonItem`. You also override the `actionSheet:clickedButtonAtIndex:` to set the `UIActionSheet` back to `nil`.

FIGURE 11-11

The only user interface object that needs auto layout constraints to support rotation is the `MKMapView`. You added the four constraints using the Pin auto layout constraint dialog.

The last feature you need to add to the iPad implementation is the Search iTunes for Tracks feature. In the iPhone implementation you show a `UIActionSheet` with the Preview and Open in iTunes options. In the iPad implementation you need to show this in a `UIPopover` that points to the selected row in the `UITableView`. You do this by overriding the `tableView:didSelectRowAt IndexPath:` method and then using the `rectForRowAtIndexPath:` method of the `UITableView` class to get the `CGRect` of the selected row that the `UIPopover` should point to. Because the user cannot tap the `UITableView` multiple times and continue to have the `UIActionSheet` displayed, you do not need to check if one is visible before displaying it. This means you do not need a property for the `UIActionSheet` as you have implemented in the other scenes. The `WBABandDetailsViewController_iPad` needs its `prepareForSegue:sender:` method updated again in order to set the `bandName`, same as you implemented for the iPad version of the Web View scene.

For the user interface, the `UITableView` already has the auto layout constraints it needs to support rotation, so you do not need to add any in the following Try It Out.

TRY IT OUT Adding the iTunes Search Feature for an iPad

1. From the Xcode menu select File ⇨ New ⇨ File, and create a new subclass of the `WBAiTunesSearchViewController` called `WBAiTunesSearchViewController_iPad`.

2. Select the `WBAiTunesSearchViewController_iPad.m` file from the Project Navigator.

3. Override the `tableView:didSelectRowAtIndexPath:` method using the following code:

```
- (void)tableView:(UITableView *)tableView
didSelectRowAtIndexPath:(NSIndexPath *)indexPath
{
```

```
    UIActionSheet *actionSheet = [[UIActionSheet alloc] initWithTitle:nil
delegate:self cancelButtonTitle:@"Cancel" destructiveButtonTitle:nil
otherButtonTitles:@"Preview Track", @"Open in iTunes", nil];
    CGRect selectedRowRect = [self.tableView rectForRowAtIndexPath:indexPath];
    [actionSheet showFromRect:selectedRowRect inView:self.view animated:YES];
}
```

4. Select the `Main-iPad.storyboard` from the Project Navigator.

5. Drag a new Table View Controller onto the Storyboard, and set its class to the `WBAiTunesSearchViewController_iPad` class in the Identity Inspector. This is now the iPad version of the iTunes Search scene.

6. Create a push segue named **iTunesSearchSegue** from the Band Details scene to the iTunes Search scene.

7. Select the prototype cell; then set its style to **Subtitle** and its reuse identifier to **trackCell**.

8. Add a `UISearchBar` to the top of the `UITableView` as you did in the previous chapter.

9. Connect the `IBOutlet` and delegate of the search bar to the `WBAiTunesSearchViewController_iPad`.

10. Select the `WBABandDetailsViewController_iPad.m` file from the Project Navigator.

11. Import the `WBAiTunesSearchViewController_iPad.h` file using the following code:

```
#import "WBAiTunesSearchViewController_iPad.h"
```

12. Modify the `prepareForSegue:sender:` method using the following code:

```
-(void)prepareForSegue:(UIStoryboardSegue *)segue sender:(id)sender
{
    if([segue.destinationViewController class] == [WebViewController_iPad class])
    {
        WebViewController_iPad *webViewController =
segue.destinationViewController;
        webViewController.bandName = self.bandObject.name;
    }
    else if ([segue.destinationViewController class] ==
[WBAiTunesSearchViewController_iPad class])
    {
        WBAiTunesSearchViewController_iPad *iTunesSearchViewController =
segue.destinationViewController;
        iTunesSearchViewController.bandName = self.bandObject.name;
    }
}
```

13. Modify the `activityButtonTouched:` method using the following code:

```
- (void)activityButtonTouched:(id)sender
{
    NSLog(@"activityButtonTouched iPad File");

    if(self.actionSheet)
        return;

    self.actionSheet = [[UIActionSheet alloc] initWithTitle:nil delegate:self
cancelButtonTitle:@"Cancel" destructiveButtonTitle:nil
```

```
otherButtonTitles:@"Share", @"Search the Web", @"Find Local Record Stores",
@"Search iTunes for Tracks", nil];
    self.actionSheet.tag = WBAActionSheetTagActivity;
    [self.actionSheet showFromBarButtonItem:self.activityBarButtonItem
animated:YES];
}
```

14. Run the app in the iPad simulator. The iTunes Track Search feature is now available, as shown in Figure 11-12.

How It Works

For the iPad implementation you override `table View:didSelectRowAtIndexPath:` to call the `rectForRowAtIndexPath:` method of the `UITableView` to get the `CGRect` of the selected row. You then use the `CGRect` of the row to present the `UIActionSheet` in a `UIPopover` using the `showFromRect:inView:` method of the `UIActionSheet`.

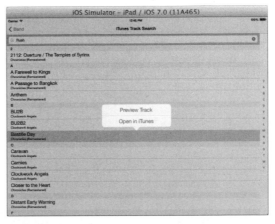

FIGURE 11-12

Next, you created the iPad scene and re-created the segues and cell identifiers so that the iPhone code continues to work. You then modified the `prepareForSegue:sender:` method to look for the `WBAiTunesSearchViewController_iPad` class to set the `bandName`. Finally you added the option back to the Band Details activity options.

SUMMARY

Creating a universal app can increase your user base by giving iPad users an app designed for their device. Your project and code do not need to change dramatically to do this. By adding a new Storyboard designed for the iPad and subclassing your iPhone implementation code, you can add support for the iPad and its design patterns quickly and efficiently.

EXERCISES

1. What is the name of the auto layout constraint that keeps a static amount of space between a user interface object and the right edge of the screen?

2. What method of the `UIActionSheet` class presents the action sheet in a `UIPopover` pointing to a `UIBarButtonItem` in a toolbar?

3. How can your code know when a user taps outside of a `UIPopover` presented from a `UIPopoverController`?

➤ WHAT YOU LEARNED IN THIS CHAPTER

TOPIC	KEY CONCEPTS
Universal Apps	Apps can be written as a single project designed to appear differently, depending on if it's running on an iPhone or an iPad.
Popovers	The iOS SDK includes a user interface paradigm for iPads that displays a user prompt or another view hovering over the main content of the app.
Auto Layout	When an iOS device is rotated, the screen size changes. The iOS SDK includes the concept of auto layout constraints that set the rules for how the user interface should adjust when the user rotates their device.

12

Deploying Your iOS App

WHAT YOU WILL LEARN IN THIS CHAPTER:

➤ Registering beta devices

➤ Creating and deploying ad hoc builds

➤ Using iTunes Connect

➤ Submitting to the Apple App Store

You have now created a universal iOS application. The next step is to send the app to beta testers and ultimately submit it to Apple for release in the App Store. Both of these processes are complex and highly specific to the application you are developing. They involve using Xcode and the iOS Developer portal as well as using the iTunes Connect portal, so you need to be a registered iOS developer. The iOS Developer program costs $99/year. You can enroll in the iOS Developer program by executing the following steps:

1. Going to `http://developer.apple.com/register`.

2. Signing in with an existing Apple ID or creating a new one.

3. Selecting either an individual developer account or a company account (you can change an individual account to a company account at any time by contacting Apple and providing additional information).

4. Entering all the information required and completing the purchase with a valid credit card (you must use a valid credit card to enroll. There are no other payment options).

This chapter walks you only through the steps you would follow to create beta versions of an iOS app as well as the steps you would follow to submit the app to Apple. It is based loosely on the Bands app you created in this book, but the details will be up to you when you create your own app and are ready to test and deploy. Technically, you can use this chapter to create a beta version of the Bands app, but you cannot release the Bands app you have built throughout this book to the App Store. Doing so would be stealing the intellectual property of this book as well as a violation of copyright.

Beta testing iOS applications is extremely important. Testing only in the simulator or on your own device is not enough. The simulator does not mimic all the system software and processes that are always running on an actual device. Similarly, when you run a debug version of an app on a device, it disables some of the processes the system uses to terminate apps that have gone afoul.

> **WARNING** *This is mentioned again for emphasis: Do not submit an app to be sold in the App Store without doing beta testing on actual devices.*

Also many legacy devices do not have the same capabilities as more modern devices. Older devices have much less memory available. If your app uses too much memory or does not properly handle its allocation, the system will force your application to exit. Older devices also have older processors. If your application has complex animations, they may be choppy on older devices. If your application uses table views like the Bands app and does not create or reuse the cells fast enough, the scrolling will not be smooth.

It is always a good idea to see how others use your application. You may find that parts of your app that seem simple to you are difficult for others. You may also find that some users never find features or even touch gestures you think are obvious. These can lead to bad ratings and reviews, which ultimately means fewer purchases and downloads.

When you are happy with your app and have found all the bugs and usability issues, it's time to submit it to Apple for release in the App Store. Apple reviews all apps before they are released. Even though you may think there are no other issues, your app could still be rejected. The two most common reasons for rejection are crashes and bugs, which is why beta testing is so important before submitting to Apple for approval.

If your app is rejected the first time you submit it, don't panic. It is a common thing. Just read the rejection reasons carefully and make the appropriate changes. If you don't understand a reason, you can contact Apple for more details. After all the issues are fixed and your app is accepted, you can smile and know you are now a published iOS app developer. Then you can start planning your next version!

DEPLOYING THE APP TO BETA TESTERS

Beta or developer preview releases of an iOS app are called ad hoc builds. The process for creating an ad hoc build is more involved for iOS apps than for other platforms you may have developed for. Any device on which you would like your ad hoc build to run must be registered with Apple to use Apple's digital rights management system (popularly referred to as DRM). Ad hoc builds include a provisioning profile that contains all the devices on which the app is allowed to run. They are also signed with a digital certificate that must also be registered with Apple. It may sound complicated;

that's because it is. In the early versions of the iOS SDK and developer portal you needed to follow many detailed steps to get it right. As the SDK and portal have matured, there have been significant improvements to the different processes. When you get everything right a couple times, it almost becomes second nature.

Registering Beta Devices

The first step to deploying an ad hoc version of your app is to invite beta testers and ask for the Universally Unique Identifier (UUID) of their device or devices. Every iOS device has a UUID that is unique to it out of all devices ever created. When you invite beta testers, you need to tell them how they can get the UUID of their device so that you can register them with Apple and include them in your app's ad hoc provisioning profile.

TRY IT OUT   Getting an iOS Device's Universally Unique ID

1. Open iTunes on either a Mac or a PC.

2. Connect the device to the computer.

3. Select the device from the iTunes menu bar.

4. In the device information, click the Serial Number label to reveal the Identifier, as shown in Figure 12-1.

FIGURE 12-1

5. Right-click the Identifier to copy to the pasteboard.

How It Works

iTunes is used to manage iOS devices for all users. Included in that is the ability to get the UUID of the device. Because the UUID is not something the casual user needs to see, it's hidden until revealed using the Control-click procedure. The UUID is long and can be difficult to transcribe, so Apple added the right-click option to copy it to the pasteboard where it can be pasted into an e-mail and sent to a developer.

When you have a beta tester's UUID, you need to register it with Apple in the iOS Dev Center. You are allowed to register only 100 devices. Though you can disable a device, you can delete them only once a year when your developer membership is renewed. With that in mind, you should be judicious in whom you invite to beta test your apps. Having a beta tester who constantly upgrades or exchanges devices may not be the best choice because the old device IDs still count against your device limit for that year. Also be wary of beta testers who never give you any feedback.

TRY IT OUT Registering Test Devices

1. Go to the iOS Dev Center in the web browser of your choice using the following URL: `https://developer.apple.com/devcenter/ios/`

2. Sign in using your iOS Developer Program username and password.

3. Click the Certificates, Identifiers & Profiles link on the right side of the page.

4. On the next page, click the Devices link in the iOS Apps section, as shown in Figure 12-2.

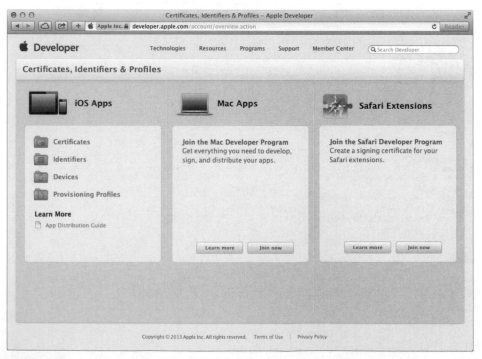

FIGURE 12-2

5. On the next page, click the + button to bring up the Registering a New Device or Multiple Devices page, as shown in Figure 12-3.

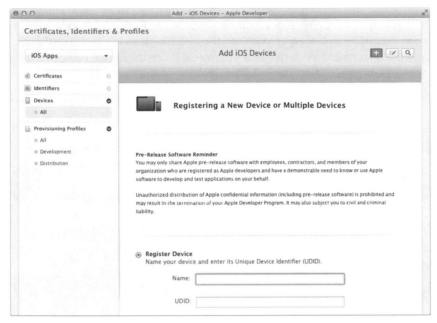

Registering a New Device or Multiple Devices

FIGURE 12-3

6. Select the Register Device radio button and enter a name for the device along with the UUID. Click Continue at the bottom of the page.

7. Review the information. If everything is correct, click the Submit button.

How It Works

The iOS Dev Center is where you manage all your devices and ultimately generate your provisioning profiles. Registering device IDs makes them eligible to be included in a provisioning profile. Be sure the UUID is correct. After it's registered it counts against your device limit even if it's incorrect. You can disable a UUID once it is registered, but it will still count against your 100 device IDs per year. When you renew your developer account after one year, you will be able to delete any disabled devices.

Generating Digital Certificates

When you build your ad hoc app, it needs to be signed with a digital certificate. Signing software with digital certificates has been around for a long time. They are used to create a chain of trust, so users know that the software they are installing was indeed created by the company or developer who created the software and that it has not been altered. When the app is signed, it creates a digital hash using the binary that can then be calculated and checked when being installed. If the hash does not match what is included in the signing information, the software is considered dangerous. It may contain malicious code added after the developer genuinely created the app.

To protect users from installing malicious software on iOS devices, all apps must be signed. The certificate information is specified in the provisioning profile and must match a certificate you have installed on your development machine. Because the provisioning profile is generated in the iOS Dev Center, you need to register there. The Mac operating system enables you to generate certificates and import them into Keychain. In the past you would need to use the Keychain Access app on your Mac to generate the certificate and then upload it to the iOS Dev Center. To make this process easier, Apple has included a feature in Xcode that can generate the certificate for you, install it on your development machine, and upload it to the iOS Dev Center.

> **NOTE** *There are two types of certificates used while developing and deploying an iOS app. The development certificate, created in Chapter 3, "Starting a New App," is used only to run an app on a device from Xcode. A deployment certificate, discussed in this chapter, is used to deploy an app either as an ad hoc or through the App Store.*

TRY IT OUT Creating a Distribution Certificate

1. From the Xcode menu select Xcode ⇨ Preferences.

2. Select the Accounts tab at the top of the dialog, as shown in Figure 12-4.

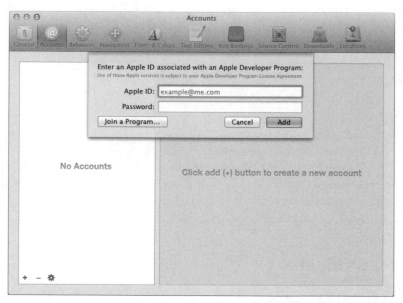

FIGURE 12-4

3. Enter your iOS Dev Center username and password.

4. Click the Details button at the bottom of the view.

5. In the next dialog your Signing Certificates are listed in the top part of the dialog, and your Provisioning Profiles are listed underneath, as shown in Figure 12-5.

FIGURE 12-5

6. Click the + button under the Signing Certificates and select iOS Distribution. You see a prompt when the certificate has been created and submitted to Apple.

How It Works

When you click the Details button, Xcode logs into the iOS Dev Center and downloads your existing Certificates and Provisioning Profiles. When you click the + button and iOS Distribution option, first Xcode generates a new certificate on your development machine. It then installs the certificate in the development machine's Keychain and then uploads it to the iOS Dev Center, making it available to your ad hoc provisioning profile.

> **NOTE** When the certificate is generated, it should also be imported into your development machine's Keychain. You can verify this by opening the Keychain Access app (Applications ⇨ Utilities ⇨ Keychain Access) and looking for a certificate that starts with iPhone Distribution followed by either your team name or your developer name.

Creating an App ID and Ad Hoc Provisioning Profile

The last piece of information that gets included in the provisioning profile is the App ID. There are two types of App IDs. An explicit App ID is used to identify a single app, while a wildcard App ID is used for sets of apps. An App ID is made up of two parts:

➤ The Apple-generated ID for your development account or development team.

➤ The bundle ID of the app.

The Bands app is not included in a set with other apps, so it would use an explicit App ID. The following Try It Out walks you through creating an explicit App ID you can use if you want to try and generate an ad hoc build of the Bands app.

TRY IT OUT Registering an App ID

1. In the iOS Dev Center, click the App IDs link on the left side of the Certificates, Identities & Profiles page.

2. Click the + button toward the top right of the page to bring up the Register iOS App ID page, as shown in Figure 12-6.

FIGURE 12-6

3. Set the Name of the new App ID.

4. Select the Team ID for the App ID Prefix.

5. Select the Explicit App ID radio button and set the Bundle ID using the recommended reverse-domain name style with the name of the app at the end (**com.wrox.Bands,** for example). Be sure to use the correct capitalization.

6. Click the Continue button at the bottom of the page.

7. Verify all the information is correct; then click the Submit button at the bottom of the page.

How It Works

The first part of the App ID is the team ID generated by Apple. You select it from the drop-down selection in the iOS Dev Center. The second part is the bundle ID. For the Bands app it's the bundle ID you used when you first created the project in Chapter 3, "Creating a New App."

The iOS Dev Center now has all the information it needs to create the ad hoc provisioning profile. You can create and manage your provisioning profiles in the iOS Dev Center. Xcode has some capabilities to manage them as well but its best to use the iOS Dev Center.

TRY IT OUT Creating and Downloading an Ad Hoc Distribution Provisioning Profile

1. In the iOS Dev Center, click the Provisioning Profiles link on the left side of the Certificates, Identities & Profiles page.

2. Click the + button toward the top right of the page to bring up the Add iOS Provisioning Profile page, as shown in Figure 12-7.

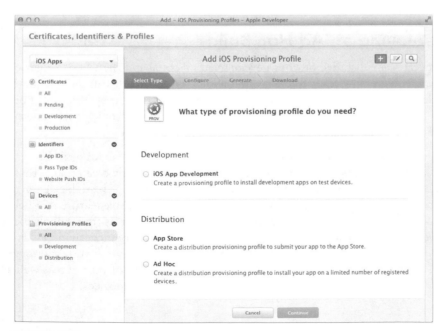

FIGURE 12-7

3. Select the Ad Hoc radio button toward the bottom of the page, and click Continue.

4. On the Select App ID page, select the App ID you created in the previous Try It Out.

5. On the Select certificates page, select the radio button next to the distribution certificate you created earlier in this chapter. Then click Continue.

6. On the Select devices page, select the devices you would like to test on; then click Continue.

7. On the Generate page give your new profile a name (**Bands Ad Hoc**, for example) and click Generate.

8. On the Download page, click the Download button to download the new provisioning profile.

9. With Xcode open, drag the downloaded file and drop it onto the Xcode icon in the Dock.

How It Works

There are three pieces of information in an ad hoc provisioning profile. The first step in the process is selecting which App ID should be included. Next is information about the certificate that will be used to sign the app when it's built in Xcode. The last is the list of UUIDs of devices the app will be allowed to run on. After the provisioning profile is generated, you can download and install it in Xcode so that it's available when you're building your ad hoc beta release.

> **NOTE** You can also download the new provisioning profile by going to Xcode ⇨ Preferences ⇨ Accounts ⇨ Details as you did when generating the signing certificate.

Signing and Deploying an Ad Hoc Build

With the deployment certificate installed on your development machine and the ad hoc provisioning profile added to Xcode, you are now ready to create your ad hoc build. Xcode can build a binary in debug mode that includes all the debug symbols, or in release, which strips the symbols. Stripping the symbols not only makes it much harder for someone to reverse-engineer your binary (as well as shrink the size of the binary), but it also makes crash logs unreadable.

When your app is running on a device and crashes, it creates a crash log. Crash logs can be invaluable when tracking down bugs. When you build a release binary, Xcode creates a file that maps the debug symbols to the binary. You can use this file to make crash logs readable again. Because these files are important to you as the developer, Xcode has an Archive feature that helps you not only keep track of release builds you send to beta testers, but also saves the symbols file so any crash logs you receive you can read. Archives can be managed in the Organizer window. From the Organizer you can also create and save the iPhone Application file (.ipa) that you send to your beta testers to install on their device. The .ipa file includes both the binary of your app as well as the ad hoc provisioning profile needed to successfully install the app on test devices.

TRY IT OUT Creating an Ad Hoc .ipa File

1. In Xcode select the Project from the Project Navigator.

2. Select the Info tab from the top of the screen.

3. In the Custom iOS Target Properties section locate the Bundle identifier key, and then set its value to the App ID you registered in the iOS Dev Center, as shown in Figure 12-8.

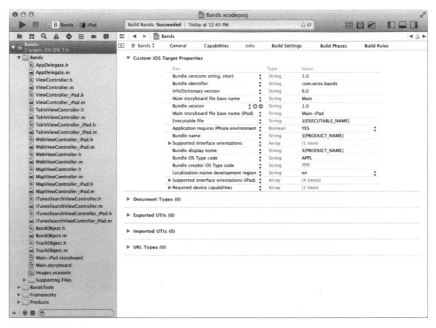

FIGURE 12-8

4. Select the Build Settings tab from the top of the screen.

5. Scroll down to the Code Signing section and locate the Provisioning Profile setting then expand it, as shown in Figure 12-9.

6. Click the None setting next to Release, and select the ad hoc provisioning profile you created in the previous section.

7. Change the scheme next to the Play button to iOS Device or any of the devices you have connected to the development machine.

8. From the Xcode menu select Product ➪ Archive.

9. When the build is complete, the Organizer opens with the new archive listed, as shown in Figure 12-10.

10. Select the new archive and click the Distribute button on the top right of the dialog.

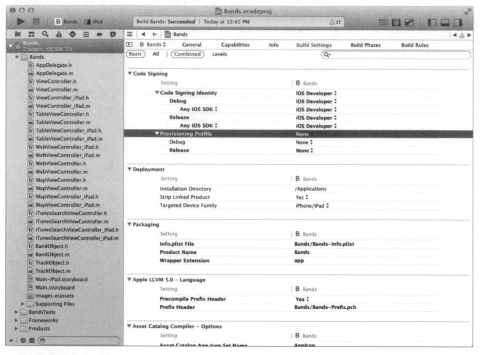

FIGURE 12-9

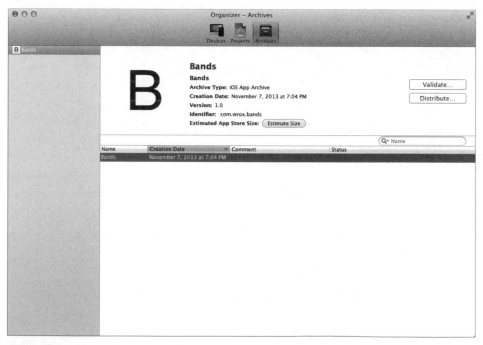

FIGURE 12-10

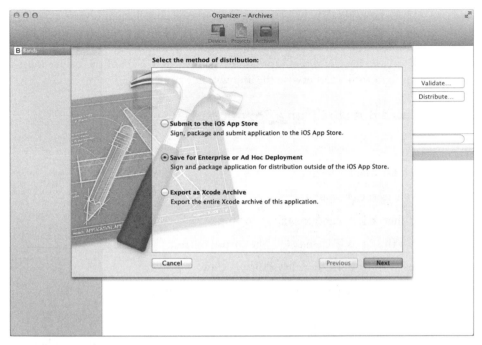

FIGURE 12-11

11. Select the Save for Enterprise or Ad Hoc Deployment radio button, as shown in Figure 12-11; then click Next.

12. On the next screen, verify the Provisioning Profile is correctly set to the ad hoc profile you created in the previous section. Then click the Export button.

13. Save the new `Bands.ipa` file to your desktop. You can now send this file to your beta testers.

How It Works

The first thing you did was set the bundle ID to match the bundle ID in the App ID you registered in the iOS Dev Center. That bundle ID is included in the provisioning profile and must match or else you cannot create the binary. You then changed the build settings, telling Xcode which provisioning profile should be used when creating a release binary. Keep in mind that the signing certificate used to generate the provisioning profile must also be installed in your development machine's Keychain. You then create the archive. This builds the binary and signs it using the signing certificate. After the binary is built, the archive is created and is shown in the Organizer window. From there you can distribute the app by creating the actual iPhone Application (`.ipa`) file.

> **NOTE** If the Archive option is disabled in the Xcode menu, be sure you have changed the scheme to be iOS Device or that of a connected device. If it is set to any of the iOS simulator settings, the Archive option will be disabled.

When you send the ad hoc .ipa file to your beta testers, you need to tell them how to install it. They will again use iTunes. The iTunes library includes all the apps a user has purchased through the App Store. Ad hoc builds will also be added to that library. When an app is in the library, it can be synced and installed on any device; though for ad hoc builds, the UUID of the device must be included in the provisioning profile. Otherwise the app will not run.

TRY IT OUT   Installing a Beta Build on a Provisioned Device

1. Open iTunes.

2. Double-click the .ipa file to add the app to iTunes.

3. Connect the test device to the computer.

4. Select the device and then select the Apps tab at the top of the screen.

5. Find the ad hoc app in the Apps list, and click the Install button.

6. Click the Apply button on the bottom right of the window.

7. After iTunes has completed syncing the device, the app will be installed.

How It Works

The iTunes library contains all the apps the user has bought from the App Store and any ad hoc apps. Ad hoc apps are added simply by double-clicking the .ipa file. When an app is in the library, it can by synced and installed on any device managed by iTunes.

SUBMITTING THE APP TO APPLE

You now have built an iOS application, tested it not only on your own device and in the simulator but also with beta testers, and worked out all the bugs and issues. It's now time to release it to the rest of the world through Apple's App Store.

Creating an App Store release is similar to creating an ad hoc release. Instead of using an ad hoc provisioning profile, you will need to create and use an app store provisioning profile. App store provisioning profiles do not contain a list of UUIDs. Instead the App Store handles the DRM that allows the app to run only on devices for users who have purchased the app. But before your users can buy your app, it needs to be in the App Store. You manage your app in the App Store through iTunes Connect.

Exploring iTunes Connect

iTunes Connect is the portal everyone uses to manage their creations in iTunes and the App Store. This includes musicians and recording labels as well as books, audio books, and, of course, app developers. When you purchase your iOS Developer Membership, you have access to iTunes Connect. In the portal you can not only manage your apps but also agree to Apple's contracts, see your sales reports, and manage your bank information so you can get paid. You will need to accept all the required contracts before you can submit. You will also need to add your banking and tax information. This chapter won't detail those steps, but keep in mind they are required.

Before you can submit an app to the App Store for approval, it needs to be added through iTunes Connect. This is where you set the price and availability of the app as well as the description, copyright information, and screen shots users see when browsing the App Store.

TRY IT OUT Adding an App to iTunes Connect

1. Go to iTunes Connect in the web browser of your choice using the following URL: `https://itunesconnect.apple.com`.

2. Sign in using your developer program username and password.

3. On the landing page, click the Manager Your Apps link, as shown in Figure 12-12.

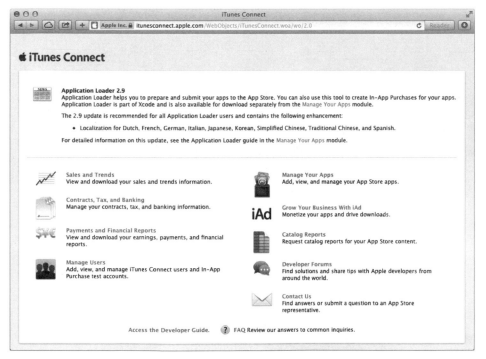

FIGURE 12-12

4. On the Manage Your Apps page, click the Add New App button on the top left to start the process.

5. In the App Information page, as shown in Figure 12-13, enter the name of the app, assign it a SKU number of your choosing, and select the appropriate Bundle ID.

6. On the next page shown in Figure 12-14, select when you want the app to become available as well as the pricing information.

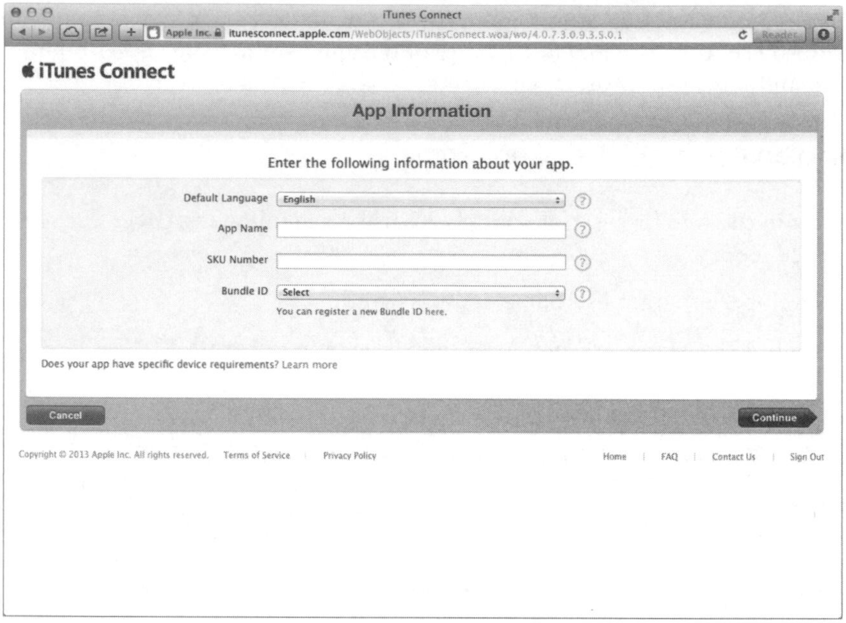

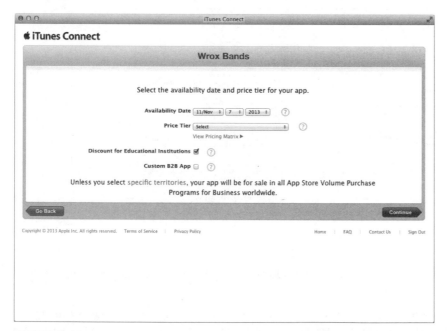

FIGURE 12-13

FIGURE 12-14

7. On the next page, as shown in Figure 12-15, you need to fill out all the fields that are not labeled as Optional and click Save. You are required to upload a Large App Icon that is 1024×1024 in size as well as at least one screen shot for all devices the app supports.

8. Your app is now in the Prepare for Upload stage. Click the View Details button.

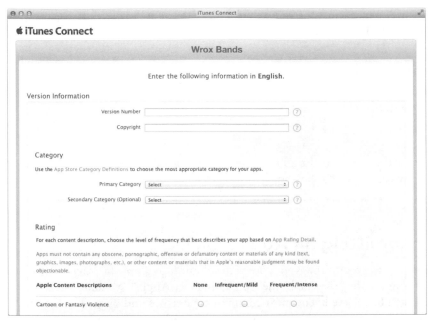

FIGURE 12-15

9. On the details page, click the Ready to Upload Binary button.

10. On the Cryptography page make the appropriate selection referring to cryptography in the app, and click the Save button. You can now upload your binary after it's created.

How It Works

You manage your apps in the App Store through iTunes Connect. When you are ready to submit a new app, or when you are ready to submit an update, you log in to iTunes Connect and set not only all the information Apple needs to display your app in the App Store, but also information reviewers may need to approve your app for sale.

Creating an App Store Provisioning Profile

Similar to the ad hoc build, your App Store build needs a special provisioning profile. Creating it is practically the same process as well. The only difference is you don't need to select which devices will be allowed to run the app.

TRY IT OUT Creating and Downloading an App Store Provisioning Profile

1. In the iOS Dev Center, click the Provisioning Profiles link on the left side of the Certificates, Identities & Profiles page. Then click the + button toward the top right of the page.

2. Select the App Store radio button, and click Continue.

3. On the Select App ID page, select the appropriate App ID, and click Continue.

4. On the Select certificates page, select the radio button next to the iOS Distribution certificate you created and used with the ad hoc provisioning profile earlier in this chapter, and click Continue.

5. On the Generate page, name the profile appropriately, and click Generate.

6. After the certificate is generated, click the download button and add the new Provisioning Profile to Xcode as you did with the ad hoc profile.

How It Works

This process is almost identical to creating the ad hoc provisioning profile. The only difference is the step where you select the devices on which the app is allowed to run.

Validating and Submitting an App

The final step to getting your app into the App Store is to submit it to Apple for review. The review process ensures that all apps for sale in the App Store meet Apple's standards. There are many reasons your app can be rejected. The most common are crashes and bugs. This is why the beta testing process is so important. To help you understand the other reasons your app could be rejected, Apple provides a detailed review guidelines document located at `https://developer.apple.com/appstore/resources/approval/guidelines.html`. You should familiarize yourself with this document prior to submitting an app for approval.

Having an app rejected can be frustrating. The review process can take up to two weeks to complete, so getting rejected and having to resubmit can delay the release of your app considerably. To help both developers and reviewers, Apple first runs a series of checks to make sure your app meets the minimum requirements for submission. These checks are made as soon as your binary is uploaded; however, you can run the same checks from the Xcode organizer using the Validate feature. The list of checks that are performed is not documented, but common mistakes such as using the wrong provisioning profile or signing certificate will be caught by these checks. It is worth your time to run the validate feature in Xcode prior to uploading your binary to catch those issues quickly.

Creating your App Store build is exactly the same as building the ad hoc build. Because the App Store is a release binary, it will also have the debug symbols stripped, so keeping the archive is important to read any crash logs. You can then use the Organizer to upload the binary to Apple for review.

TRY IT OUT Building and Submitting to the App Store

1. In Xcode, select the Project from the Project Navigator.

2. Select the Build Settings tab from the top of the screen.

3. Change the Provisioning Profile for Release to the App Store Provisioning Profile you created.

4. From the Xcode menu select Product ⇨ Archive.

5. When the app is done building and the Organizer window displays, click the Validate button.

6. Enter your developer program username and password in the dialog, and click Next.

7. On the next screen verify or select the appropriate app as well as the appropriate App Store Provisioning Profile. Then click Validate.

8. If any issues were found, fix them and repeat steps 1 through 7 until there are no issues found.

9. From the Organizer window, click the Distribute button.

10. In the dialog, select the Submit to the iOS App Store option, and click Next.

11. Enter your developer program username and password in the dialog, and click Next.

12. On the final screen, verify or select the appropriate app as well as the appropriate App Store Provisioning Profile; then click Submit. If no issues are found, your binary will be uploaded, processed, and queued for review.

How It Works

Before you create your App Store build, you need to change the provisioning profile used to sign the app. After you do that, follow the same steps to archive the build as you did with the ad hoc build. You can then validate the app to make sure everything is correct. When it is, you can submit the app to Apple for review. It should be noted that simply getting the app uploaded does not mean it will be queued for review. There is some additional processing that happens after the app is uploaded. If there are any issues, you will receive an e-mail telling you what needs to be fixed. If the review process finds any issues, you will also receive an e-mail with issues that need to be fixed. After the app has passed all reviews, it will be added to the App Store and ready for sale.

SUMMARY

Creating an iOS application is great, but getting it into the hands of your users is the ultimate goal. Before you start selling your app, you need to make sure you have fixed all the bugs and usability issues. To beta test your app, you need to gather your beta testers' device IDs and register them with Apple. From there you can create an ad hoc build and have your beta testers install it on their devices and send you feedback. When you are ready, you submit your app to Apple for its final review. If all goes well, your app will be approved and ready for sale in the App Store!

EXERCISES

1. What is the common name for beta or developer preview builds?

2. What is the difference between a debug build and a release build?

3. What are the three pieces of information you need to add to the iOS Dev Center to create a provisioning profile for your beta build?

4. What is the name of the portal used to manage your apps in the App Store?

➤ WHAT YOU LEARNED IN THIS CHAPTER

TOPIC	KEY CONCEPTS
Creating Ad Hoc Builds	Creating an ad hoc build when your app is ready for beta testers
Using iTunes Connect	Developers, musicians, and authors managing the things they sell in iTunes and the App Store through the iTunes Connect Portal
Submitting an App for App Store Approval	Apple must approve all apps in the App Store. Before your app is available for sale, it must be submitted and reviewed.

Answers to Exercises

At the end of each chapter, there were some exercises to help you determine if you understood the material in that chapter correctly. Here are the answers to those questions.

CHAPTER 1 ANSWERS

1. You need to keep in mind how your app's name will look when displayed on the home screen of an iPhone or iPad. Typically, you have approximately 12 characters before the name is abbreviated.

2. You need to scope your app to keep it useful without adding too many features that users may find confusing. You don't want a feature list that would take years to implement.

3. If you app duplicate features that are in Apple apps, your app may be rejected when submitted for the App Store. It is best to avoid almost any overlap.

CHAPTER 2 ANSWERS

1. Smalltalk.

2. The interface or header file with a `.h` file extension and the implementation file with a `.m` file extension.

3. The `NSObject` class.

4. The following code defines the `ChapterExercise` class with a single method named `writeAnswer`, which takes no arguments and returns nothing:

```
@interface ChapterExercise : NSObject

- (void)writeAnswer;

@end
```

5. You would use this code to instantiate the ChapterExercise class:

    ```
    ChapterExercise *anInstance = [[ChapterExercise alloc] init];
    ```

6. The retain keyword increments the reference count, whereas the release keyword decrements it.

7. ARC stands for Automatic Reference Counting.

8. The strong keyword indicates the class owns the instance of the object, and it will not be deallocated as long as the strong reference is in place.

9. Overloading an operator is not permitted in Objective-C as it is in Java and C#.

10. To compare to NSString instances, you use the isEqualToString: method.

11. An instance of an NSArray cannot be modified after it's created, whereas an NSMutableArray can be.

12. MVC stands for Model-View-Controller.

13. The following code shows how you declare the ChapterExercise class implements the ChapterExerciseDelegate protocol:

    ```
    @interface ChapterExercise : NSObject <ChapterExerciseDelegate>
    ```

14. The NSError class.

CHAPTER 3 ANSWERS

1. The pane on the left side of Xcode is the Navigator pane.

2. The Cocoa framework used to create an iOS applications user interface is the UIKit framework.

3. Application settings are stored in a plist file.

4. The Xcode feature you use to make sure your user interface is displayed correctly on all devices is Auto Layout.

5. The name of the inspector used to change user interface object attributes in Interface Builder is the Property Inspector.

6. To change the color of text:

    1. In the Project Navigator select Main.storyboard.

    2. In Interface Builder, select the Band label.

    3. In the Attributes Inspector, use the Color selector, and choose Light Gray Color.

7. To add the bottom label and set its auto layout constraint:

    1. In the Project Navigator, select `Main.storyboard`.

    2. Drag a new label onto the scene.

    3. In the attributes inspector, set its text to **Bottom**.

    4. Drag the label to the bottom of the scene until the bottom guideline appears.

    5. Drag the label to the middle of the scene until the center guideline appears.

    6. Select the label; then Control-drag to the bottom of the view.

    7. Release the mouse button; then select the Bottom Space to Bottom Layout constraint.

8. To change the version number in the settings:

    1. In the Project Navigator, select the project.

    2. In the editor, select the General tab and bring up the info property editor.

    3. In the Identity section, set the Version to 1.1.

CHAPTER 4 ANSWERS

1. `IBOutlet` is the keyword you use to connect a `UIKit` property in a class to a `UIKit` object in Interface Builder.

2. `IBAction` is the keyword you use to connect an event of a `UIKit` object in Interface Builder to a method in a class.

3. Being the first responder means the user interface object is the first to handle events caused by user interaction.

4. The `NSCoding` protocol is implemented to allow a class to be used with the `NSKeyedArchiver` class.

CHAPTER 5 ANSWERS

1. The `UITableViewDataSource` tells the table how many sections and rows are in the table, and what the section headers and indexes are, along with configuring the `UITableViewCells`. The `UITableViewDelegate` manages the editing of the `UITableView`.

2. Basic, Right Detail, Left Detail, and Subtitle.

3. To modify the `UITableViewCell` to a right detail style and show the band rating as the `detailTextLabel`:

    1. Open the `Main.storyboard`.

    2. Select the prototype cell and change its style to Right Detail.

3. Open the `WBABandsListTableViewController.m` file and modify the `tableView:cellForRowAtIndexPath:` with the following code:

```
- (UITableViewCell *)tableView:(UITableView *)tableView
cellForRowAtIndexPath:(NSIndexPath *)indexPath
{
    static NSString *CellIdentifier = @"Cell";
    UITableViewCell *cell = [tableView
dequeueReusableCellWithIdentifier:CellIdentifier forIndexPath:indexPath];

    NSString *firstLetter = [self.firstLettersArray
objectAtIndex:indexPath.section];
    NSMutableArray *bandsForLetter = [self.bandsDictionary
objectForKey:firstLetter];
    WBABand *bandObject = [bandsForLetter objectAtIndex:indexPath.row];

    // Configure the cell...
    cell.textLabel.text = bandObject.name;
    cell.detailTextLabel.text = [NSString stringWithFormat:@"%d",
bandObject.rating];

    return cell;
}
```

4. You can show a `UIViewController` that animates up from the bottom on the screen using the `presentViewController:animated:completion:method`.

5. The `UIKit` item added to the top of a view when using a `UINavigationController` is the `UINavigationItem`.

6. The push segue is used to transition between the Bands List scene and the Band Details scene.

CHAPTER 6 ANSWERS

1. Set the `numberOfTouchesRequired` to 2.

2. `UIImagePickerControllerSourceTypeCamera`, `UIImagePickerControllerSourceTypePhotoLibrary`, and `UIImagePickerControllerSourceTypeSavedPhotoAlbum`.

3. The system throws an exception that causes your app to crash.

4. The `tag` property.

CHAPTER 7 ANSWERS

1. To add a new framework to a project:

    1. Select the Project from the Project Navigator.

    2. Select the General settings editor.

3. In the Linked Frameworks and Libraries section click the + button and select the desired framework from the dialog.

2. The `MFMailComposeViewController` requires the `MessageUI.framework` to be added to the project.

3. The `MFMessageComposeViewController` requires the `MobileCoreServices.framework` to be added to the project in order to use the Universal Type constants when attaching images or other media types to a text message or iMessage.

4. You need to call the `canSendText` method to verify the device can send text messages or iMessages. If you do not and try presenting the `MFMessageComposeViewController`, the app will crash.

5. The social networking services integrated in iOS are Twitter, Facebook, Flickr, and Vimeo, as well as Weibo in Asia.

6. Users sign into their social networking accounts in the Settings app.

7. To prevent the Bands app from sharing the band picture on Flickr using the `UIActivityViewController`:

1. Create an `NSArray` that includes the `UIActivityTypePostToFlickr` constant.

2. Call the `setExcludedActivityTypes:` method of the `UIActivityViewController` and pass in the `NSArray`.

CHAPTER 8 ANSWERS

1. You can trigger a manually created segue by first setting the identifier of the segue in Interface Builder and then calling the `performSegueWithIdentifier:sender` method of `UIViewController` using that identifier.

2. The Core Foundation framework.

3. You can set the Network Activity Indicator to be visible with the following code:

```
[UIApplication sharedApplication].networkActivityIndicatorVisible = YES;
```

4. The `webView:didFailLoadWithError:` method.

5. The `openURL` method.

CHAPTER 9 ANSWERS

1. The framework required to use an `MKMapView` is the `MapKit.framework`.

2. The framework used to get the current location of an iOS device is the `CoreLocation.framework`.

3. The `mapView:didUpdateUserLocation:` method of the `MKMapViewDelegate` is called when the user's location is determined.

4. The MKLocalSearchRequest class is used to create the request, while the MKLocalSearch class is used to perform the search and process the results.

5. Local search results are returned using MKMapItem objects.

6. The ^ character is used to denote the beginning of a block.

7. The subclass of MKAnnotation you can use to show a pin on an MKMapView is the MKPointAnnotation class.

8. The property of the MKPinAnnotationView class you can set to animate the pin onto the MKMapView is the animateDrop property.

CHAPTER 10 ANSWERS

1. The three types of NSURLSession tasks are NSURLSessionDataTask, NSURLSessionDownloadTask, and NSURLSessionUploadTask.

2. The name of the technology Apple introduced in iOS 4 to reduce the complexity of threading for developers is Grand Central Dispatch.

3. The class you can use to parse JSON into Objective-C objects is the NSJSONSerialization class and its JSONObjectWithData:options:error: method.

4. The framework required to use the MPMoviePlayerViewController is the MediaPlayer .framework.

CHAPTER 11 ANSWERS

1. The Trailing Space to Container auto layout constraint.

2. The showFromBarButtonItem:animated: method.

3. By implementing the popoverControllerDidDismissPopover: method of the UIPopoverControllerDelegate protocol.

CHAPTER 12 ANSWERS

1. The common name for beta or developer preview builds is an ad hoc build.

2. The difference between a debug build and a release build is that a release build has the debug symbols removed.

3. You need an App ID, a Signing Certificate, and a list of UUIDs the app is permitted to run on.

4. The name of the portal is iTunes Connect.

INDEX

P